GENOCIDE IN CONTEMPORARY CHILDREN'S AND YOUNG ADULT LITERATURE

Children's Literature and Culture
Jack Zipes, *Founding Editor*
Philip Nel, *Series Editor*

For a complete series list, please go to
routledge.com

Reading Victorian Schoolrooms
Childhood and Education in
Nineteenth-Century Fiction
Elizabeth Gargano

Soon Come Home to This Island
West Indians in British Children's Literature
Karen Sands-O'Connor

Boys in Children's Literature and
Popular Culture
Masculinity, Abjection, and the
Fictional Child
Annette Wannamaker

Into the Closet
Cross-dressing and the Gendered Body
in Children's Literature
Victoria Flanagan

Russian Children's Literature and Culture
Edited by Marina Balina and
Larissa Rudova

The Outside Child In and Out of the Book
Christine Wilkie-Stibbs

Representing Africa in Children's Literature
Old and New Ways of Seeing
Vivian Yenika-Agbaw

The Fantasy of Family
Nineteenth-Century Children's Literature
and the Myth of the Domestic Ideal
Liz Thiel

From Nursery Rhymes to Nationhood
Children's Literature and the Construction
of Canadian Identity
Elizabeth A. Galway

The Family in English Children's Literature
Ann Alston

Enterprising Youth
Social Values and Acculturation in Nineteenth-
Century American Children's Literature
Monika Elbert

Constructing Adolescence in
Fantastic Realism
Alison Waller

Crossover Fiction
Global and Historical Perspectives
Sandra L. Beckett

The Crossover Novel
Contemporary Children's Fiction and Its
Adult Readership
Rachel Falconer

Shakespeare in Children's Literature
Gender and Cultural Capital
Erica Hateley

Critical Approaches to Food in
Children's Literature
Edited by Kara K. Keeling and
Scott T. Pollard

Neo-Imperialism in Children's Literature
About Africa
A Study of Contemporary Fiction
Yulisa Amadu Maddy and Donnarae
MacCann

Death, Gender and Sexuality in
Contemporary Adolescent Literature
Kathryn James

Fundamental Concepts of Children's
Literature Research
Literary and Sociological Approaches
Hans-Heino Ewers

Children's Fiction about 9/11
Ethnic, Heroic and National Identities
Jo Lampert

The Place of Lewis Carroll in Children's
Literature
Jan Susina

Power, Voice and Subjectivity in Literature
for Young Readers
Maria Nikolajeva

"Juvenile" Literature and British Society,
1850–1950
The Age of Adolescence
Charles Ferrall and Anna Jackson

Picturing the Wolf in Children's Literature
Debra Mitts-Smith

New Directions in Picturebook Research
Edited by Teresa Colomer, Bettina
Kümmerling-Meibauer, Cecilia Silva-Díaz

The Role of Translators in Children's
Literature
Invisible Storytellers
Gillian Lathey

The Children's Book Business
Lessons from the Long Eighteenth Century
Lissa Paul

Humor in Contemporary Junior Literature
Julie Cross

Innocence, Heterosexuality, and the
Queerness of Children's Literature
Tison Pugh

Reading the Adolescent Romance
*Sweet Valley and the Popular Young Adult
Romance Novel*
Amy S. Pattee

Irish Children's Literature and Culture
New Perspectives on Contemporary Writing
Edited by Valerie Coghlan and
Keith O'Sullivan

Beyond Pippi Longstocking
*Intermedial and International Perspectives
on Astrid Lindgren's Works*
Edited by Bettina Kümmerling-Meibauer
and Astrid Surmatz

Contemporary English-Language
Indian Children's Literature:
*Representations of Nation, Culture,
and the New Indian Girl*
Michelle Superle

Re-visioning Historical Fiction
The Past through Modern Eyes
Kim Wilson

The Myth of Persephone in Girls'
Fantasy Literature
Holly Virginia Blackford

Pinocchio, Puppets and Modernity
The Mechanical Body
Edited by Katia Pizzi

Crossover Picturebooks
A Genre for All Ages
Sandra L. Beckett

Peter Pan's Shadows in the Literary
Imagination
Kirsten Stirling

Landscape in Children's Literature
Jane Suzanne Carroll

Colonial India in Children's Literature
Supriya Goswami

Children's Culture and the Avant-Garde
Painting in Paris, 1890–1915
Marilynn Olson

Textual Transformations in Children's
Literature
Adaptations, Translations, Reconsiderations
Edited by Benjamin Lefebvre

The Nation in Children's Literature
Nations of Childhood
Edited by Kit Kelen and Björn Sundmark

Subjectivity in Asian Children's Literature
and Film
Global Theories and Implications
Edited by John Stephens

Children's Literature, Domestication, and
Social Foundation
Narratives of Civilization and Wilderness
Layla AbdelRahim

Charles Dickens and the Victorian Child
*Romanticizing and Socializing the
Imperfect Child*
Amberyl Malkovich

Second-Generation Memory and
Contemporary Children's Literature
Ghost Images
Anastasia Ulanowicz

Contemporary Dystopian Fiction for
Young Adults
Brave New Teenagers
Edited by Carrie Hintz, Balaka Basu, and
Katherine R. Broad

Jews and Jewishness in British Children's
Literature
Madelyn J. Travis

Genocide in Contemporary Children's and
Young Adult Literature
Cambodia to Darfur
Jane M. Gangi

GENOCIDE IN CONTEMPORARY CHILDREN'S AND YOUNG ADULT LITERATURE

Cambodia to Darfur

JANE M. GANGI

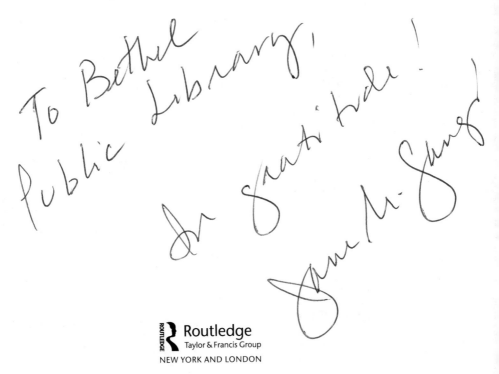

To Bethel Public Library!
In gratitude!
Jane M. Gangi

Routledge
Taylor & Francis Group

NEW YORK AND LONDON

First published 2014
by Routledge
711 Third Avenue, New York, NY 10017

and by Routledge
2 Park Square, Milton Park, Abingdon, Oxon OX14 4RN

Routledge is an imprint of the Taylor & Francis Group, an informa business

Library of Congress Cataloging in Publication Data
Gangi, Jane M.
  Genocide in contemporary children's and young adult literature : Cambodia to Darfur / by Jane M. Gangi.
    pages cm. — (Children's literature and culture)
  Includes bibliographical references and index.
  1. Children's literature—20th century—History and criticism. 2. Children's literature—21st century—History and criticism. 3. Genocide in literature. I. Title.
  PN1009.5.G46G36 2014
  809'.93358—dc23
  2013021974

ISBN13: 978-0-415-69908-2 (hbk)
ISBN13: 978-1-315-88418-9 (ebk)

Typeset in Minion
by IBT Global.

SUSTAINABLE FORESTRY INITIATIVE
Certified Sourcing
www.sfiprogram.org
SFI-01234
SFI label applies to the text stock

Printed and bound in the United States of America by IBT Global.

To those who have died during the genocides of the last forty years, and to their loved ones who remain.

Contents

Figures and Tables

Figures

Tables

Permissions

Chapter One: Cover from *A Song for Cambodia* by Michelle Lord; illustrations by Shino Arihara. New York: Lee & Low Books, 2008. Permission arranged with LEE & LOW BOOKS, INC.

Cover from *Half Spoon of Rice: A Survival Story of the Cambodian Genocide* by Icy Smith; illustrations by Sopaul Nhem. Manhattan Beach, CA: East West Discovery Press, 2010. Photo credit: East West Discovery Press.

Chapter Two: Cover from *The Girl from Chimel* by Rigoberta Menchú, with Dante Liano; illustrations by Domi. Toronto, Canada: Groundwood Books, 2005. Taken from *The Girl from Chimel* by Rigoberta Menchú copyright © 2005 published by Groundwood Books.

Chapter Three: Cover from *My Childhood under Fire: A Sarajevo Diary* by Nadja Halilbegovich. Tonawanda, NY: Kids Can Press, 2006. Material from *My Childhood under Fire* by Nadja Halilbegovich used by permission of Kids Can Press, Ltd., Toronto, Canada. Text © Nadja Halilbegovich.

Cover from *The Music Lesson* by Tammy Ryan. Photo: Mark Garvin. Woodstock, IL: Dramatic Publishing, 2002. Reprinted with permission.

Chapter Four: Cover from *Broken Memory: A Novel of Rwanda* by Élisabeth Combres. Toronto, Canada: Groundwood Books, 2010. Taken from *Broken Memory* by Élisabeth Combres copyright © 2009 published by Groundwood Books.

Cover from *Genocide in Rwanda* by Frank Spalding. New York: Rosen Publishing, 2009. Reprinted with permission.

Cover from *Hutu and Tutsi* by Aimable Twagilimana. New York: Rosen Publishing, 1998. Reprinted with permission.

Chapter Five: Cover from *Darfur: An African Genocide* by John Xavier. New York: Rosen Publishing, 2008. Reprinted with permission.

Cover from *Sudan, Darfur and the Nomadic Conflicts* by Philip Steele. New York: Rosen Publishing, 2013. Reprinted with permission.

Chapter Six: Cover from *Genocide* by Jane Springer. Toronto, Canada: Groundwood Books, 2006. Taken from *Genocide* by Jane Springer copyright © 2006 published by Groundwood Books.

Series Editor's Foreword

The Children's Literature and Culture series is dedicated to promoting original research in children's literature, children's culture, and childhood studies. We use the term "children" in the broadest sense, spanning from earliest childhood up through adolescence. The already capacious term "culture" encompasses media (radio, film, television, video games, blogs, websites, social networking sites), material culture (toys, games, products), acculturation (processes of socialization), and of course literature, including all types of crossover works. Since children's literature is defined by its audience, this series seeks to foster scholarship on the full range of children's literature's many genres and subgenres: fairy tales, folk tales, comics, graphic novels, picture books, novels, poetry, didactic tales, nonsense, fantasy, realism, mystery, horror, fan fiction, and others.

Founded by Jack Zipes in 1994, Routledge's Children's Literature and Culture is the longest-running series devoted to the study of children's literature and culture from a national and international perspective. In 2011, expanding its focus to include childhood studies, the series also seeks to explore the legal, historical, and philosophical conditions of different childhoods. An advocate for scholarship from around the globe, the series recognizes innovation and encourages interdisciplinarity. In Zipes' words, "the goal of the Children's Literature and Culture series is to enhance research in this field and, at the same time, point to new directions that bring together the best scholarly work throughout the world."

Philip Nel

Preface

In 2007, Lindsey Keller and other honors students at Manhattanville College, where I was then teaching, noticed that although there were courses on the Holocaust, there were none on genocides that have occurred since 1945. Lindsey asked the coordinator of the honors program, Dr. Nancy Todd, for such a course. Dr. Todd sent out a call to faculty for proposals. I responded that because I had been studying children's and young adult refugee literature, I could teach part of the course.

I was given the whole course. In "Genocide in Literature and Art" my students and I shared powerful experiences that impacted our lives: Two students subsequently went on to human rights law, another is getting his master's in Africa Studies, and others, although in different fields, continue to bear witness to genocide. Because I considered myself a colearner with the students, at the end of the semester I took the final with them. The exam questions were: What did you learn? How did you learn it? What do you plan to do with what you have learned? A pattern emerged across all of our papers: We all wrote that, knowing what we now knew, we must keep alive the memory of those who suffered and died. It was then I knew I had to write this book.

Meg Wheatley, co-founder and president emeriti of the Berkana Institute, writes that:

> "bearing witness" . . . is not a religious practice. Rather, it's a simple practice of being brave enough to sit with human suffering, to acknowledge it for what it is, to not flee from it. It doesn't make the suffering go away, although it sometimes changes the experience of pain and grief. When I bear witness, I turn toward another and am willing to let their experience enter my heart. I step into the picture by being willing to be open to their experience, to not turn away my gaze. (86)

I was inspired and humbled by the determination and bravery of students in their late teens and early twenties who chose to sit with human suffering, to not avert their gaze; their willingness helped me center my gaze and not flee.

Thus, this work is for scholars of genocide and children's and young adult literature, for teachers, and for those who wish to sit with human suffering through children's and young adult literature written in English on genocides since 1945.

Overview

In the Introduction I explain the challenges of writing about genocide and how I evaluate children's and young adult literature on genocide.

Chapter One describes and evaluates children's and young adult literature of Cambodia; Chapter Two, Guatemala and Kurdish Iraq; Chapter Three, Bosnia-Herzegovina and Kosovo; Chapter Four, written with Isabelle Umugwaneza, Rwanda; Chapter Five, Darfur; and Chapter Six, comprehensive texts on genocide.

In Chapter Seven, I discuss the ways in which I and others have taught genocide; in Chapter Eight, I address problems, issues, and solutions in writing about genocide for children and young adults. I also offer some concluding thoughts on genocide—possible explanations and possible solutions.

There is a comprehensive bibliography at the end of the book.

Works Cited

Wheatley, Meg. *Turning to One Another: Simple Conversations to Restore Hope in the Future.* 2nd ed. San Francisco: Berrett-Koehler, 2009.

Acknowledgments

Students, colleagues, family, friends, authors, publishers, filmmakers, and organizations have contributed to this undertaking, which would have been impossible without them.

As an undergraduate at Colorado College, I saw Sidney Lumet's film *The Pawnbroker*, the first film in English to present a Holocaust victim's perspective. I was not a stranger to the Holocaust. I had read Anne Frank's diary, but the visual images of this film overwhelmed me for months; I wanted, someday, to respond to what I had learned and experienced. I thank Sidney Lumet and also Rod Steiger, who played Sol Nazerman, for provoking in me the first intensely painful experience I had in thinking about the Holocaust. I began to reflect on how to respond. In some way, *The Pawnbroker* led me to study subsequent genocides.

Over the years, as a public school teacher and then professor of literacy and literature in teacher education, I focused on multicultural and international literature when working with students and teachers. In 2000 I read Deborah Ellis's *The Breadwinner*, a story of an eleven-year-old girl growing up in Afghanistan under Taliban rule in the late 1990s. Ellis, a Canadian author who visited refugee camps in Pakistan along the Afghan border, met families who told of young girls who had to cut off their hair and dress up as boys so they could go outside to forage food for their hungry families. Their fathers and brothers were dead, in prison, or conscripted in the Taliban army. Neither their sisters who had reached puberty nor their mothers were allowed outside. I was deeply moved by Ellis's book, which has been translated into dozens of languages and has sold millions of copies. Ellis wrote two more books to complete The Breadwinner Trilogy: *Parvana's Journey* and *Mud City*, and donates all her royalties, which have amounted to millions, to Canadian Women for Women in Afghanistan.

The Breadwinner, like *The Pawnbroker*, provoked me. After reading Ellis's books, while continuing my research on multicultural and international children's and young adult literature, I increased my focus on children's and young adult literature of war. I thank Deborah Ellis for her inspiration and

Patsy Aldana, former publisher of Groundwood Books in Toronto and publisher of Ellis's books, for her willingness to take publishing risks. She has made sure that children scarred by war throughout the world can have images of themselves in books and that more privileged children can have access to their stories.

I am grateful to two organizations: the Children's Literature Association (ChLA) and the International Network of Genocide Scholars (INOGS). Members of those organizations work diligently to expand our understandings of children's and young adult literature and genocide, and there is overlap— ChLA supports scholars working on genocide, and INOGS always has an educational strand. I have been attending ChLA's richly worthwhile conferences since 1999, and thank them for awarding me the Faculty Research Grant that allowed me to travel to Bosnia in the summer of 2011. I especially thank Kenneth Kidd for his support and guidance on how to approach this most difficult topic; both Kenneth and Susan Griffith, also of ChLA, helped me think through the organization and theoretical framework for the Introduction. Kate Capshaw Smith supported me from across our state of Connecticut and came to my rescue with eleventh-hour research.

I have attended all three INOGS conferences: the University of Sheffield in Sheffield, England, in 2009; the University of Sussex in Falmer, England, in 2010; and San Francisco State University, San Francisco, California, in 2012. At each of these conferences I learned from scholars who devote themselves to the study of genocide, and who conduct research beyond my ability to carry out. I thank Nigel Eltringham for encouraging me to write this book, and for his brilliant book on the Rwandan genocide, *Accounting for Horror: Post-Genocide Debates in Rwanda* (2004). My appreciation also goes to Elisabeth Hope Murray for setting up the INOGS Facebook page, which has functioned for me as a free graduate assistant.

My gratitude to former students Lindsey Keller, Declan Galvin, Tina Gallante, Kim O'Toole, Lisa D'Aprile, Megan Ford, Lauren Gagnon, Richard Dunn, Nicole Foti, Kristina Palushajk, Emily Reynes, and Antoinette Marsullo. Without the journey into genocide on which we embarked together in 2007, this book would not have been written. That these young people could willingly study the worst excesses of which humanity is capable has inspired me more than they know.

For critical feedback on the Cambodia chapter, I am grateful to Denise Heywood, about whom more will be said in the chapter on Cambodia. For help with the Rwanda chapter, I thank Yvette Rugasaguhunga and Isabelle Umugwaneza; both are young women from Rwanda, and Isabelle is my co-author for the Rwanda chapter. Isabelle's father, John Nyombayire, and sister, Sandrine Umutoni, also read the Rwanda chapter and I am grateful for their advice. For Guatemala, Abigail Adams offered critical feedback; thanks to John Ryan for making the connection between Abigail and me. For help with the Bosnian section, my appreciation to Merisa Karović, whom I met at the INOGS conference in 2010 and who invited me to Sarajevo in 2011. There I met with Professor Smail Čekić, director of the Institute for Research of Crimes against Humanity and International Law of the Sarajevo University; Muhamed Šestanović, a psychologist who studies the impact of genocide on children; and Zilha Mastalić-Košuta, whose research gives voice to children affected by the genocide in Bosnia. Special recognition to Enis Omerović, who translated the conversation during our 2011 meeting in Sarajevo and in 2012 translated for Professor Smail Čekić prior to the 2012 INOGS conference my paper on Bosnia (which became the basis of the Bosnia chapter in this book); Professor Čekić approved its contents. Enis and I were able to meet again at the INOGS conference in 2012. After the chapter on Bosnia was completed, Enis read the chapter again and helped me understand legal terminology. For his assistance, for our continuing correspondence, and for the enjoyment of his company—I am grateful to call him friend. Anastasia Batzer, who is from Croatia, supplied much help prior to my trip to Bosnia. On Darfur, Hawi Debelo provided insightful comments; Hawi is my Ethiopian daughter and she will have more of an introduction in Chapter Five.

Recognition also goes to Theresa Davis, Interlibrary Loan Librarian at Mount Saint Mary College, and JoAnne Elpern of Western Connecticut State University; both Theresa and JoAnne ordered many, many books for me. Thanks also to the Bethel Public Library librarians in Connecticut; they processed a plethora of books from Connecticut's excellent library system.

I thank my outgoing Chair, Dr. Reva Cowan, for her support and kindness. To my "cell" mates in the Collaborative for Equity in Literacy Learning (CELL) at Mount Saint Mary College (MSMC): Janine Bixler, Rebecca Norman, David Gallagher, and Matt Hollibush, thank you for inviting me into your affinity group, which I have been delighted to join. To my incoming Chair, Dr. Joan Miller, thank you for encouraging me and for carefully reading sections of the book. And Theresa Brundage and Jeanette Grossman, who competently run our offices, thank you for your helpfulness and friendly banter. Lindsay Panko, an undergraduate at MSMC, gave competent, calm, and exceedingly careful assistance in the preparation of the manuscript; my gratitude goes to her. James FitzGerald, a graduating senior at MSMC, prepared the comprehensive bibliography at the end of the book; I am thankful for his work. An MSMC graduate, Sean Winchell, shouldered the difficult work of indexing—much appreciation to him.

My gratitude also to Liz Levine, who acquired the manuscript; credit also to Emily Ross, Acting Commissioning Editor, and Philip Nel, Series Editor, for helpful suggestions and seeing this book to press.

I could not have undertaken this endeavor without my circle of dearly loved and loving friends: Don Durivan, Susan Griffith, Nancy Heilbronner, Sara Ingram, Courtney Ryan Kelly, Mary Ellen Levin, Kelly and Michèle O'Donnell, Mary Ann Reilly, Connie Rockman, Chris Rowe, Laconia Therrio, and Michelle Ule. I am grateful to Cathy Blondel, Mary Korin, and Sue

Roberts, my friends, neighbors, and walking partners, who helped keep me sane. Kelly O'Donnell pointed me to the Aleksandr Solzhenitsyn quote that frames this book. Mary Ellen Levin is not only the salt of the earth but knows my writing voice better than I. She carefully edited, read, and reread each and every chapter, and I am forever indebted to her for staying so close to me during the writing of this book, where we went together to many dark places.

I also could not have undertaken this work without the love and encouragement of my precious family: my children, Devin, Caryn, and Peter; my niece, Sarah, and her beloved Gregg and Aidan; my sister, Susan, and her husband Jim (in whose home I stayed while I finished this book); and my sister-in-law and brother-in-law, Caryn and Dale Hughes. Lynn and Tim Ellis, my cousin and her husband, gave me the quiet I desperately needed for several days for which I am thankful. To my husband, Robyn, thank you for walking with me in difficult territory.

Works Cited

Ellis, Deborah. *The Breadwinner.* Toronto: Groundwood Books, 2000.

———. *Mud City.* Toronto: Groundwood Books, 2003.

———. *Parvana's Journey.* Toronto: Groundwood Books, 2002.

Eltringham, Nigel. *Accounting for Horror: Post-Genocide Debates in Rwanda.* London: Pluto, 2004.

The Pawnbroker. Dir. Sidney Lumet. Perf. Rod Steiger. Landau Company. 1964. Film.

Introduction
Approaching Children's and Young Adult Literature of Genocide

Let the lie come into the world, let the lie even dominate the world—but it will not come through me.

—Aleksandr Solzhenitsyn

People of good will all over the world joined Jews in saying "never again" when the full truth of Adolf Hitler's atrocities became known. Hitler and the Nazis murdered 6 million Jews and more than 700,000 homosexuals, Roma, and individuals with disabilities during World War II and the Holocaust. Yet despite this resolve, since 1945 *génocidaires* have slaughtered at least as many persons as were slaughtered in the Holocaust. Political scientist Brian Grodsky estimates that there have been "twenty-two million non-combatant deaths" since 1945 resulting from genocide and mass murder (4). Genocide scholar Samuel Totten and historian Paul Bartrop observe that "the number of genocidal eruptions has actually *increased* during this time" (xiv–xv; italics in the original).

Journalists, human rights activists, employees of nongovernmental organizations, political scientists, historians, anthropologists, and others have produced scholarship on these post-1945 genocides. Few scholarly studies, however, have been written in the field of children's and young adult literature on genocides beyond the Holocaust. Although the scholarship of children's literature of the Holocaust informs my work, in this book I consider how texts written in English for children and young adults represent genocides that have occurred in Cambodia, Guatemala, Kurdish Iraq, Bosnia-Herzegovina, Kosovo, Rwanda, and Darfur. As well, I discuss comprehensive texts on genocide and teaching genocide.

1

Challenges in Writing about Genocide

As a White middle-class American woman, I am an outsider to the cultures and genocides of which I write. As such, I am likely to miss innuendoes, cultural mores—the tacit knowledge shared by "cultural insiders"—that are difficult for "cultural outsiders" to grasp. As a member of a dominant culture, my perspective is most often seen as the norm; because of this, my voice is heard above those of others with less privilege and authority. In "The Problem of Speaking for Others," philosopher Linda Alcoff writes:

> We should strive to create wherever possible the conditions for dialogue and the practice of speaking with and to rather than speaking for others. If the dangers of speaking for others result in the possibility of misrepresentation, expanding one's own authority and privilege, and a generally imperialist speaking ritual, then speaking with and to can lessen these dangers. (23)

I have sought to speak *with* and *to* rather than *for* others. Where possible, I include in each chapter those from inside the culture who have helped me understand the genocide that occurred in their countries. When that was not feasible, I asked genocide scholars to critique my work.

In addressing seven vastly different countries and cultures—Cambodia, Guatemala, Kurdish Iraq, Bosnia-Herzegovina and Kosovo, Rwanda, and Darfur—I risk inadvertently producing "historical slippages," aspects of the genocides I have not noticed or understood. By speaking with others and by consulting available academic literature on the genocides, I hope to offset slippages. Nonetheless, because I am a fallible human being, scholar, and writer, slippage may occur.

There is also the difficulty more generally of speaking about the unspeakable. As Lydia Kokkola writes in *Representing the Holocaust in Children's Literature* (2003), genocide "is so horrifying that ordinary words do not seem fit tools for the task" (2). So, too, with the genocides since 1945. It is daunting to produce words to describe the most horrible abuses of which human beings are capable and to discuss how those abuses are represented to children and young adults. From the outset, what I speak of the unspeakable is inadequate. As Henry James said about World War I, "'one finds it in the midst of all this as hard to apply one's words as endure one's thoughts. The war has used up words; they have weakened, they have deteriorated'" (qtd. in Krieger, 37). In *Schindler's List* (2004), as Oskar Schindler and Rabbi Itzhak Stern fervently work to save Jews from certain death, they equivocate over the meaning of the words *special* and *preferential*. Stern knows that *special treatment* has come to mean extermination. Schindler asks, "Do we have to invent a whole new language?" Stern replies, "I think so." It is with imperfect words and inadequate language I write of children's and young adult books of genocide. It is also my hope to avoid speaking of those about whom I write as, in Paul Slovic's words, "human beings with the tears dried off."

Evaluating Children's and Young Adult Literature of Genocide

To develop postcolonial theory, literary theorist Edward Said built on philosopher Emmanuel Levinas's concept of "the Other." As genocide scholar Donna-Lee Frieze says of Levinas's theory, "Always capitalized, the Other is not an alien other who disturbs my freedom, or who is an extension of me. Rather, the Other is the one who is treated ethically, who commands my highest respect, and is apprehended in all their Otherness. ... to face the Other is to humanize the Other, and to regard the person as a unique being" (222). But what happens when "the Other" is perceived as alien, as one who disturbs my freedom, as one who does not command my highest respect, who is not apprehended in all their otherness, and whom I do not regard as a unique being? In *Orientalism* (1978) Said explored these questions and conceptualized what transpires when "the Other" is seen as alien, against freedom, not worthy of respect, not unique, but instead "threatening" (23). Although Said was writing about European perceptions of those from the Middle East, the term "the Other" has migrated to describe European perceptions of those who are not of European descent. Postcolonial theory, Clare Bradford explains, is "used by literary critics to refer to the effects of colonization, and to reading strategies capable of interrogating the (often naturalized) manifestations of colonial discourse that appear in texts of all kinds and times" (177).

More than thirty years later, Said's concept of "the Other" continues to provide a constructive theoretical lens through which to analyze literature; "the Other"—and "othering" (reducing a human to an alien) captures the tendency of westerners, and some western writers, to view nonwesterners as backward, degenerate, and unequal—creating an "us versus them" mentality (206). Anthropologist Elizabeth Hallam and language professor Brian Street aptly call this phenomenon the "'West and the rest'" (1) and note that the process is constructed. Hallam and Street cite Johannes Fabian: "'Awkward and faddish as it may sound, othering expresses the insight that the Other is never simply given, never just found or encountered, but made'" (qtd. in Hallam and Street, 1). This is especially true for the books written about the African genocides and Bosnia. Although Bosnia is a part of Europe, because the victims in Bosnia were mostly Muslim, it may be argued that efforts to help end the genocide were slowed by the perception that the approximately 300,000 Muslims slaughtered were part of the rest, not the West. The process of othering, as Black feminist scholar Patricia Hill Collins explains, also includes treating people as things:

Objectification is central to this process of oppositional difference. In either/or dichotomous thinking, one element is objectified as the Other, and is viewed as an object to be manipulated and controlled. Social theorist Dona Richards (1980) suggests that Western thought requires objectification, a process she describes as the 'separation of the "knowing self" from the "known object." (69)

Based on these analyses, in examining the literature of genocide, one of my considerations is how and whether human beings are objectified or "othered."

A second criterion is to examine whose values, symbols, cultures, and truths are being presented. Texts privilege some voices and marginalize others. As Allan Luke and Peter Freebody explain, reading is not only decoding, making meaning, and using texts. From a critical literacy perspective, readers must also be able to "critically analyze and transform texts by acting on knowledge that texts are not ideologically natural or neutral—that they represent particular points of views while silencing others and influence people's ideas" (n. pag.). Literary theorist Roland Barthes, in *Mythologies* (1972), describes the process by which myth turns history into nature—assumptions and defaults come to be seen as natural or normal. Barthes writes, "Myth is a system of communication, that is a message. This allows me to perceive that myth cannot possibly be an object, a concept, or an idea" (109). Myth speaks in one direction, without opportunity for response or critique. The myth of the "backwardness, degeneracy, and inequality" (Said 206) of genocide victims who are nonwesterners seems unquestioned in the writings of some children's and young adult authors. The default to whiteness and Eurocentricity has also achieved mythic proportions in some works for young people. In her book *Racial Innocence: Performing American Childhood from Slavery to Civil Rights* (2011), Robin Bernstein writes,

> Whiteness . . . derives its status as an unmarked category. George Lipsitz notes that "whiteness never has to speak its name, never has to acknowledge its role as an organizing principle in social and cultural relations". . . . This "silence about itself" is for Ann DuCille, "the primary prerogative of whiteness, at once its grand scheme and deep cover." (8–9)

Some of the books written by White authors for young people, especially on the African genocides, do not speak about themselves.

Grounding his work in Paolo Freire's critical pedagogy, Clar Doyle, in his book *Raising Curtains of Education: Drama as a Site for Critical Pedagogy* (1993), on theater, suggests questions that might help readers to take a stance:

- What values and beliefs are assumed and/or promoted?
- What symbols and images are being used for what purpose?
- What cultures are being affirmed or ridiculed? Whose voices are not heard?

- Whose truth is represented? (30)

In evaluating books on genocide, I will add a fifth question to this list:

- How is "the Other" situated?

Third, sourcing, context, and corroboration also guide my evaluation of texts on genocide. Drawing from the methods of historians, Steven Stahl and Cynthia Shanahan write that "'truth' is always an approximation, depending on who is doing the telling, the era in which it is being told, and the context of the event" (96). As I write about books of genocide, I am aware that I have strong views about who was culpable and who was not, and the truth I write is an approximation. In evaluating historical texts, Stahl and Shanahan offer the following guidelines on sourcing, context, and corroboration, all of which inform this work:

Sourcing
1. Who produced this document?
2. What biases or predispositions did the author or authors have?
3. How might these biases have affected the content of the document?
4. What other voices might have been included in this document?

Context
1. When was this document produced?
2. Where was this document produced?
3. What was occurring in the time and place that this document was produced?
4. How might the context have affected this document?

Corroboration
1. What information in this document is similar to that of other documents (either in this set or other documents that you know about)?
2. What information contradicts information in other documents?
3. How might the source or the context explain some of the contradictions?
4. What is *not* said in this document that should be included? How does what is left out relate to the source and context? (110–111; italics in the original)

A fourth factor is to estimate the balance in each work between being informative enough but not traumatizing to children and young adults. Kenneth Kidd draws attention to the great divide the Holocaust became in writing for children; before the Holocaust, writing about trauma was taboo for children's and young adult authors. Kidd asks,

> How to explain this shift away from the idea that young readers should be protected from evil and toward the conviction that they should be exposed to it, perhaps even endangered by it? It's almost as if we now expect

reading about trauma to be traumatic itself—as if we think children can't otherwise comprehend atrocity. (120)

How much grisliness is too much in writing for young people? Authors must weigh the sanitizing of historical events against sustaining the child. Kidd adds, "And the project of children's literature, perhaps more than any other literary project, is in part to make the world a bearable or manageable place, a project not always so easy or even justifiable in the face of such atrocities" (Kidd, "Re: Introduction"). Hamida Bosmajian writes in her book *Sparing the Child: Grief and the Unspeakable in Youth Literature about Nazism and the Holocaust* (2002), "Children's literature, given the nature of the genre, insists by definition on the life-affirming support for the child" (xxi). Referring to Franz Kafka's often quoted contention that "a book must be the axe for the frozen sea inside us" Bosmajian writes,

> Those who speak to children or write books for them about the disaster seek to inform, perhaps to teach, but not to shock so severely that the young reader is lost and alienated. A children's book cannot be an axe to the child reader. At most, therefore, children's literature . . . can offer rudimentary tales about these disasters, first stories of a thousand and one recountings to prevent the reduction of collective memory and keep alive the thought that it was the human being who was traumatized and annihilated at the site of atrocity. . . . Although the representation of this difficult subject must continue to be attempted, its limitations should be fully acknowledged by writers and adult readers. (248)

A book cannot be an axe to the child, but then there is the possibility of presenting a sanitized view. Writing about children's and young adult books of the Holocaust, Naomi Sokoloff asks, "Will an overly simplistic, naïve message emerge? . . . . will there be a grotesque collision of values with narrative results too intense for younger children?" (175). From her book *My Mother's Voice: Children, Literature, and the Holocaust* (2002), Adrienne Kertzer adds, "For if all language is inadequate, as many Holocaust writers say, then ultimately all literature about the Holocaust may be a form of children's literature, trying to describe events with a very limited vocabulary" (39). Using a "very limited vocabulary," writers for young people must navigate this tension between over-simplification and nightmare-inducing intensity.

Conveying genocide requires multiple literary and informational approximations over time—"first stories of a thousand and one recountings." Sensitive teachers, parents, caretakers, and peers need to help gauge what young people can handle and when. My son, Peter, was the kind of child who never had to be told to do his homework. From the minute he entered school, he took full responsibility for himself and his work, wonderfully sparing me from asking that perennial nagging-parent question, "Have you done your homework?" When he was in seventh grade, however, I received a call from one of his teachers that Peter was not doing his homework. I asked what the homework was, and learned he was to read *Night* (1982) by Elie Wiesel. I remembered the ghastly opening scenes of Wiesel's autobiography, and after talking with Peter realized he could not handle it. I asked the teacher if he could substitute another, less graphic, book on the Holocaust—perhaps Lois Lowry's *Number the Stars* (1989). She agreed. Months later, Peter read *Night* on his own, and *Dawn* (1982), Wiesel's sequel, as well.

Peter was twelve. In contrast, while working with Book Clubs in a fifth-grade class, I met José (a pseudonym), a ten-year-old who exclaimed to me how much he loved Immaculée Ilibagiza's book written for adults on the Rwandan genocide, *Left to Tell: Discovering God amidst the Rwandan Holocaust* (2007). I asked him where he had learned about the book. He replied that his older brother, who was in high school, had given it to him. Because the book is hopeful, based on Ilibagiza's devout religious beliefs, perhaps José found enough support.

In evaluating the books, I keep in mind what might be too traumatizing for the child, which will vary from child to child, as these two examples show. I also ask: Does the text sacrifice accuracy to sanitization? Is the message overly simplistic and naïve? How might the book be the first in a thousand and one recountings?

Aesthetics and Literarity

A fifth consideration will be literary quality, a highly subjective notion. For Aristotle in the *Poetics* (1967), as applied to drama, the appraisal of literary quality included plot, character, theme, diction, melody, and spectacle. Of children's and young adult literature of genocide, I note evocative language, compelling plots and characters, and sensory images, although, as Bosmajian observes, "The development of aesthetic sensibilities in such narratives is rarely part of authorial intent" (xix). Nevertheless, I try to evaluate to some extent the aesthetic qualities of the literature of genocide for young people. "Literarity," as Nicholas Harrison says, is part of postcolonial criticism:

> Historicizing literary texts may seem like the bread and butter of post-colonial criticism, but I will be trying to show that this task is more intricate and multi-faceted than postcolonial critics generally allow. When confronting a work of fiction they encounter two demands that can be difficult to reconcile: on the one hand they must give adequate weight to the text in its individuality and "literarity"; on the other, they must apprehend it in the socio-historical context from which it emerged and in relation to which it needs, at some level, to be understood. (1–2)

Joseph Thomas, in Philip Nel and Lissa Paul's *Keywords for Children's Literature* (2011), illuminates "the productive tensions between literature and cultural studies. Any future conversations about aesthetics in children's literature will have to be mindful of such productive tensions" (9). There are some well written texts that I do not recommend from a cultural studies perspective; there are other less well written texts that I recommend because of the sensitivity and insight they provide.

Definitions of Genocide

In addition to postcolonial criticism, critical literacy and pedagogy, historical methods, the scholarship of children's literature about the Holocaust, and aesthetics, a sixth consideration is the definition of genocide and proposed extensions to the original definition. The word *genocide* came about during the mid-twentieth century as the result of the tireless efforts of Raphael Lemkin, a Polish Jew, who lost many family members in the Holocaust. In her Pulitzer Prize-winning *"A Problem from Hell": America and the Age of Genocide* (2002), Samantha Power makes available the background of Lemkin's fervor: While a student of linguistics at the University of Lvov, Lemkin learned of Soghomon Tehlirian's assassination of Mehmed Talaat in 1921 in Germany; Tehlirian was a survivor of the Armenian genocide and Talaat was the Turkish interior minister who oversaw the execution and starvation of nearly 1.5 million Armenians from 1918 until 1921. The German government put Tehlirian on trial, which perplexed Lemkin. He asked one of his professors why the Armenians had not had Talaat arrested, and the professor explained there was no law for it:

> "Consider the case of a farmer who owns a flock of chickens. . . . He kills them and this is his business. If you interfere, you are trespassing."
> "It is a crime for Tehlirian to kill a man, but it is not a crime for his oppressor to kill more than a million men?" Lemkin asked. (qtd. in Power, 17)

From the moment Lemkin learned that state sovereignty suppressed justice, he devoted his life to creating a word for genocide and a law against it.

Because of Lemkin's tireless work, in 1948 the United Nations accepted the definition of the Convention on the Prevention and Punishment of the Crime of Genocide, as stated in Article 2:

> In the present Convention, genocide means any of the following acts committed with intent to destroy, in whole or in part, a national, ethnical, racial or religious group, as such:
>
> A. Causing serious bodily or mental harm to members of the group;
> B. Deliberately inflicting on the group the conditions of life calculated to bring about its physical destruction in whole or in part;
> C. Imposing measures intended to prevent births within the group;

D. Forcibly transferring children of the group to another group (qtd. in Totten and Bartrop, 31)

Lemkin achieved a great victory with this definition.

Although deeply respectful of Lemkin's extraordinary feat, genocide scholars of the twenty-first century find the definition in need of revision. Because it can be difficult to distinguish between atrocities, some propose "crimes against humanity." Given the exceptional effort it took to establish a definition with the United Nations, it is unlikely revisions will be made for several lifetimes; it took the United States forty years to pass the Genocide Convention Implementation Act that President Ronald Reagan signed into law in 1988, thanks in large part to Senator William Proxmire's tenacity in speaking for over twenty years before the Senate to see it passed. Nevertheless, proposed revisions impart important insights for the consideration of books written for children and young adults on genocide. Lemkin most likely would not object; even he expanded on his definition, as in this passage:

> The crime of *genocide* involves a range of actions, including not only deprivation of life and also devices considerably endangering life and health: all these actions are subordinated to the criminal intent to destroy or to cripple permanently a human group. The acts are directed against groups as such, and individuals are selected for destruction only because they belong to these groups. (qtd. in Heidenrich, 3; italics in the original)

Lemkin recognized the staggering loss of cultural and humane contributions when genocide is committed; he wrote:

> Our whole cultural heritage is a product of the contributions of all peoples. We can best understand this if we realize how impoverished our culture would be if the so-called inferior peoples doomed by Germany, such as the Jews, had not been permitted to create the Bible or give birth to an Einstein, a Spinosa; if the Poles had not had the opportunity to give to the world a Copernicus, a Chopin, a Curie, the Czechs a Huss, and a Dvorak; the Greeks a Plato and a Socrates; the Russians, a Tolstoy and a Shostakovich. (qtd. in Totten and Bartrop, 10)

It is possible, had he lived longer, that Lemkin might have broadened his definition.

In his book *Genocide: A Comprehensive Introduction* (2010), Adam Jones provides a table of sixteen post-1948 definitions offered by genocide scholars, some of which I summarize here. I use these expanded definitions in evaluating children's and young adult books of genocide. Peter Drost emphasizes the "'membership of human collectivity'"—a collectivity that becomes a target for slaughter (qtd. in Jones, *Genocide*, 15). In Cambodia, the Khmer Rouge defined human collectivity as intellectuals and city dwellers; in Iraq, the Kurds; in Guatemala, the Maya; in Bosnia-Herzegovina, mostly Muslims; in Rwanda, Tutsis and moderate Hutus; in Darfur, the Zaghawa, Massalit, and Fur people.

But "membership of human collectivity" is not enough for murders to be labeled genocide; there must also be those who can carry it out. As Vahakn Dadrian points out, genocide requires those who have the "'power'" and "'resources'" to kill others, which, although seemingly self-evident, is sometimes left out of books written for children and young adults (qtd. in Jones, *Genocide*, 16). For example, radical Hutus in Rwanda had the power and resources to massacre 800,000 to 1 million Tutsis and moderate Hutus, in large part because the French and Chinese had mightily armed them, whereas their victims were unarmed. The Serbs had access to the full force and weapons of the Yugoslav Army; Bosnian Muslims had no army and few arms. Few books for young people illustrate the importance of power and resources to carry out genocide.

Also not included in some books is the necessary bureaucracy. Irving Louis Horowitz defines genocide as "'destruction of innocent people by a state bureaucratic apparatus'" (qtd. in Jones, *Genocide*, 16). If government-run bureaucracies wish to destroy innocent people, they have the organization and machinery to do so. To create their own bureaucracy of genocide, radical Hutus of Rwanda studied the bureaucratic apparatus of the Nazis; this is important to note because the Rwandan genocide is often presented to young readers as a tribal outburst instead of the carefully orchestrated bureaucratic scheme that it was. Jack Nusan Porter adds to bureaucracy "'ideology and technology'" (qtd. in Jones, *Genocide*, 16). Communism served as the Khmer Rouge's "ends justify the means" philosophy, so butchering those they perceived as capitalistic or intellectual or artistic—90 percent of artists were killed—was, to them, ideologically justified. *Lebensraum* (the justification of taking living space from "the Other" because of their inferiority) and a fascist nationalism fueled the Serbs' belief that they could take what was not theirs and kill and rape those they pleased (but not all Serbs, of course—more in Chapter Three on those who protested). The technologies of the twentieth and twenty-first centuries make genocide easier to carry out—and easier to detect. Satellite photos have documented the Darfur genocide. Whether the knowledge provokes action when detected is another question.

Targeted human collectivity, the power and resources to kill masses of people, access to state-controlled bureaucratic apparatus, ideology and technology—these additional facets extend Lemkin's original definition of genocide. In addition, there is the matter of legitimate warfare: John L. Thompson and Gail A. Quests concentrate on the obliteration of a group "'by purposive actions which fall outside the recognized conventions of legitimate warfare'" (qtd. in Jones, *Genocide*, 17). This perspective is key when looking at books written for children and young adults that label genocide as a civil war. Books about the Rwandan and Bosnian genocides often make this fundamental error: When

800,000 to 1 million Tutsis and moderate Hutus and hundreds of thousands of Bosnian Muslims were unarmed, what occurred cannot be considered a civil war. Attacks on masses of unarmed innocents are beyond the conventions of legitimate warfare. To call a genocide civil war dishonors innocent victims.

Naming and defining can be deadly weapons. I am reminded of poet and activist Audre Lorde's words, "'It is axiomatic that if we do not define ourselves for ourselves, we will be defined by others—for their use and to our detriment'" (qtd. in Hill Collins, 26). In genocide, the perpetrators define who is to be killed and who is to do the killing. Frank Chalk and Kurt Jonassohn note in their definition of genocide that the perpetrators are the ones who circumscribe who will die: "'Genocide is a form of mass killing in which a state or other authority intends to destroy a group, as that group and membership in it are defined by the perpetrator'" (qtd. in Jones, *Genocide*, 17). Exterminated people do not have the privilege of defining themselves. Some of the books for young people on genocide present conflict as a free-for-all in which all sides are at fault when, in fact, most genocides are, as Chalk and Jonassohn discern, one-sided, and as Thompson and Quests note, outside legitimate warfare.

Israel Charny adds to this the observation that genocides are carried out "'under conditions of the essential defencelessness of the victim'" (qtd. in Jones, *Genocide*, 18). In Cambodia, Cambodians were defenseless against the Khmer Rouge; in Kurdish Iraq, Kurds were defenseless against Saddam Hussein's chemical warfare; in Guatemala, Maya Indians were defenseless against a well-armed government; in Bosnia, most Muslims were defenseless in the face of Serbian aggression; in Kosovo, most Albanians were defenseless against Serbian nationalists; in Rwanda, most Tutsis and moderate Hutus had no weapons with which to defend themselves from radical Hutus; and, in Darfur, the Black African Muslims are mostly defenseless from Khartoum's well-armed government and the Janjaweed, an Arab mercenary militia.

Based on these newer sensibilities about the nature of genocide, then, when evaluating children's and young adult literature of genocide, I consider these expanded understandings:

- How are targeted human collectivities represented?
- How are those who have the power and resources to carry out genocide, and those who do not, represented?
- How are state-controlled bureaucracies that make genocide possible represented?
- How are ideologies and technologies used to commit genocide represented?
- How are atrocities that fall outside recognized conventions of legitimate warfare represented?
- How are "sides" represented, and how are those who define who is to be killed represented?
- How are the defenseless represented?

Organization of the Chapters, Including Problematic Books

Although there are many books for children and young adults that are authentic and responsible in their representations of these genocides, there are many that are not. I share high-quality books on the genocides for young adults and point out those that are problematic.

Each chapter presents:

- First, information and context on the genocide
- Second, a description of how I elicited responses from cultural insiders and/or experts to what I write on children's and young adult literature of genocide, an attempt to speak with and to rather than for
- Third, a discussion of "problematic" books
- Fourth, a discussion of recommended books, including those recommended with reservations, as well as some "crossover literature," which Sandra Beckett defines as "literature that crosses from child to adult or adult to child audiences" (58)

Books I consider problematic are those in which the authors, illustrators, and/ or photographers misrepresent what happened through inaccuracies, inauthenticities, or stereotyping, and when they demean those they claim to represent. Books I consider authentic and responsible are those in which authors, illustrators, and photographers aspire to Levinas's treatment of "the Other": They are respectful of and do not dehumanize those about whom they write and they acknowledge the uniqueness of each human being in context. They seek accuracy by including multiple perspectives, and they inform themselves of the genocides about which they write from multiple sources, including cultural insiders when possible.

To help readers find citations and resources for specific genocides, I include a Works Cited section at the end of each chapter; the problematic books are included in the Works Cited. To make my book accessible to teachers as well as academics, the recommended books and recommended with reservations books are in separate sections; hopefully, this departure from standard form will make this book simpler from which to teach. A comprehensive bibliography that contains all references in all chapters is available at the end of the book.

Rationale for Genocides Included

Because I want to draw attention to post-Holocaust genocides, in this book I focus on Cambodia, Guatemala, Kurdish Iraq, Bosnia-Herzegovina and Kosovo, Rwanda, and Darfur. But this is a limited focus—a slippage, perhaps. The range is narrowed because I have access only to books written in English for English-speaking children and young adults primarily in the United

States, Canada, the United Kingdom, Ireland, Australia, New Zealand, and other English-speaking countries. I am also basing my choices on what have been recognized as major genocides—now. In the future, other atrocities may be recognized as such. A. Dirk Moses, for example, in his multivolume work *Genocide* (2010), includes since 1945 the following places as sites of genocide: Chechnya, Bali, Indonesia, Biafra, East Pakistan, Burundi, East Timor, Paraguay, and the Chittagong Hill Tracts of Bangladesh. To this list he adds the Chinese Cultural Revolution. Upon learning my topic, several people have asked if I would include Sri Lanka and Bengal. North Korea should certainly be on this list; this is a government that has starved 40 million of its citizens to death. In the Nanking massacre of 1937, the Japanese executed 150,000 to 300,000 Chinese in less than six weeks; Stalin and his Gulag killed about 20 million Soviet citizens; and the Germans destroyed 64,000 Herrero in Namibia. All of these genocides should be studied; my reason for not including them is that there is limited access to publications written in English for children and young adults on these massacres and that if I attempted to do so, I would not finish this book in my lifetime. The work remains for other scholars of children's and young adult literature.

Works Cited

Alcoff, Linda. "The Problem of Speaking for Others." *Cultural Critique* 20 (1991–1992, Winter): 5–32.

Aristotle. *Poetics*. Ann Arbor, MI: U of Michigan P, 1967.

Barthes, Roland. *Mythologies*. 1957. New York: Hill and Wang, 1972.

Beckett, Sandra L. "Crossover Literature." Nel and Paul, 58–61.

Bernstein, Robin. *Racial Innocence: Performing American Childhood from Slavery to Civil Rights*. New York: New York UP, 2011.

Bosmajian, Hamida. *Sparing the Child: Grief and the Unspeakable in Youth Literature about Nazism and the Holocaust*. New York: Routledge, 2002.

Bradford, Clare. "Postcolonial." Nel and Paul, 177–180.

Doyle, Clar. *Raising Curtains of Education: Drama as a Site for Critical Pedagogy*. Westport, CT: Bergin & Garvey, 1993.

Frieze, Donna-Lee. "The Face of Genocide." Jones, *Evoking*, 222–223.

Grodsky, Brian. "When Two Ambiguities Collide: The Use of Genocide in Self-Determination Drives." *Journal of Genocide Research* 14.1 (2012): 1–27.

Hallam, Elizabeth, and Brian V. Street, eds. "Introduction." *Cultural Encounters: Representing "Otherness."* London: Routledge, 2000.

Harrison, Nicholas. *Postcolonial Criticism: History, Theory and the Work of Fiction*. Cambridge, UK: Polity, 2003.

Heidenrich, John G. *How to Prevent Genocide: A Guide for Policymakers, Scholars, and the Concerned Citizen*. Westport, CT: Praeger, 2001.

Hill Collins, Patricia. *Black Feminist Thought: Knowledge, Consciousness, and the Politics of Empowerment*. New York: Routledge, 2000.

Ilibagiza, Immaculée, with Steve Erwin. *Left to Tell: Discovering God amidst the Rwandan Holocaust*. Carlsbad, CA: Hay, 2006.

Jones, Adam, ed. *Evoking Genocide: Scholars and Activists Describe the Works That Shaped Their Lives*. Toronto: Key, 2009.

———. *Genocide: A Comprehensive Introduction*. 2nd ed. New York: Routledge, 2010.

Kertzer, Adrienne. *My Mother's Voice: Children, Literature, and the Holocaust*. Peterborough, Ontario: Broadview, 2002.

Kidd, Kenneth B. "'A' is for Auschwitz: Psychoanalysis, Trauma Theory, and the 'Children's Literature of Atrocity." *Children's Literature*, 33 (2005): 120–149.

————. "Re: Introduction." Message to Jane M. Gangi. 31 Mar. 2013. E-mail.

Kokkola, Lydia. *Representing the Holocaust in Children's Literature*. New York: Routledge, 2003.

Krieger, Nina. "The Desire to Communicate Something of My Torment." Jones, *Evoking*, 35–42.

Lemkin, Raphael. "Genocide: A Modern Crime." Totten and Bartrop, 6–11.

Lowry, Lois. *Number the Stars*. Boston: Houghton, 1989.

Luke, Allan, and Peter Freebody. "Further Notes on the 4 Resource Model." *Reading Online*, 1999–2000. Web. 31 Mar. 2013. <http://www.readingonline.org/research/lukefreebody.html>

Moses, A. Dirk. *Genocide*. New York: Routledge, 2010.

Nel, Philip, and Lissa Paul, eds. *Keywords for Children's Literature*. New York: New York UP, 2011.

Power, Samantha. *"A Problem from Hell": America and the Age of Genocide*. New York: Basic, 2002.

Said, Edward. *Orientalism*. New York: Vintage, 1978.

Schindler's List. Dir. Steve Spielberg. Perf. Ben Kingsley, Liam Neeson, and Ralph Fiennes. Universal City. 2004. Film.

Slovic, Paul. "The More Who Die, the Less We Care: Psychic Numbing and Genocide." International Network of Genocide Scholars. San Francisco State University, San Francisco. 29 June 2012. Reading.

Sokoloff, Naomi B. "The Holocaust and Literature for Children." *Prooftexts* 25.1–2 (2005): 174–194.

Stahl, Steven A., and Cynthia Shanahan. "Learning to Think Like a Historian: Disciplinary Knowledge through Critical Analysis of Multiple Documents." *Adolescent Literacy Research and Practice*. Eds. Tamara L. Jetton and Janice A. Dole. New York: Guilford, 2004. 94-118.

Thomas, Joseph T. "Aesthetics." Nel and Paul, 5–9.

Totten, Samuel, and Paul Bartrop, eds. *The Genocide Studies Reader*. New York: Routledge, 2009.

Wiesel, Elie. *Dawn*. New York: Bantam, 1982.

————. *Night*. 1982. New York: Hill and Wang, 2006.

Chapter One
Children's and Young Adult Literature of Cambodia

If you had been living in Cambodia during this period, this would be your story too.

—Loung Ung

On April 17, 1975, approximately 2.5 million residents of Cambodia's capital city, Phnom Penh, awakened to find rough young Khmer Rouge soldiers ordering them out of their city. The Americans, the soldiers said, were about to bomb the city; they must evacuate their homes. Doctors, nurses, and their patients were told to abandon the hospitals. The Khmer Rouge shouted through bull-horns that all would be allowed to return in three days. In reality, no one was allowed to return in three days; many never returned at all. During the next four years, millions of Cambodians would die by execution, starvation, and overwork at the hands of the new communist government: Democratic Kampuchea, led by Pol Pot.

The recently formed government considered capitalism unacceptable in any manifestation and cleared out other cities in Cambodia as well. Under the guise of a threat of American bombing of Cambodia's cities, the Khmer Rouge forced families to walk for days on end to country villages; there, peasants would oversee the retraining of these city people in the effort to create a classless society, where all property was shared and all were farmers. Upon arrival in the work camps, children were separated from their parents. Doctors, lawyers, teachers, artists, intellectuals, monks, and anyone wearing glasses faced execution; those who wore glasses were perceived as intellectuals, and intellectuals were useless to the cause of Democratic Kampuchea. All foreigners and journalists were deported. Pol Pot and his party sought to erase history; Year Zero of the new regime began on April 17, 1975. Philip Short, Pol Pot's biographer, writes, "they dreamed dreams, and showed a total disregard for reality" (58). Pol Pot and his compatriots had been educated in France, where they discovered communism and brought to that ideology their own, eventually murderous, interpretation. Short notes,

> Even university-educated Cambodians often found the gulf between western and Asian ways of thinking unbridgeable. As a result, they absorbed European ideas piecemeal rather than as a coherent system of thought. The lack of critical faculties . . . was to be an enduring characteristic of many of Sâr's [Pol Pot's] generation. (58)

No action was too inhumane if it meant achieving their goals. The new government's maxim was "'To keep you is no gain; to lose you is no loss'" (qtd. in Short, 40). Human life—at any age—meant nothing to Pol Pot and the Khmer Rouge. As Barbara Harff writes, the children of "potential political adversaries" were killed (109).

As with all genocides, there are varying estimates of how many died. Yale's Cambodian genocide program estimates that 1.7 million people were killed, almost a quarter of the population. In *Children of Cambodia's Killing Fields* (1997), survivor Dith Pran, whose story was made famous in the film *The Killing Fields* (1984), writes that one third of the population died. All genocides are devastating; the elimination of a quarter to one-third of Cambodia's own peoples makes the Cambodian genocide one of the world's most devastating.

Speaking with and to a Cambodian Scholar

In 2010 I attended the International Network of Genocide Scholars' conference at the University of Sussex in Falmer, England. After the conference, my husband and I spent a few days in Cambridge. As we traveled by train on our way back to London, I noticed a slender, kind-looking woman searching for a seat. With a British accent, she asked if she could sit next to me, and I agreed. She was holding a wildflower in her hand, so I mentioned that we had enjoyed visiting the botanical gardens in Cambridge. She smiled. Nothing more was said for the hour's journey.

As we approached King's Cross, I asked her if she could tell us which way to go to find the train to Heathrow; we had found King's Cross confusing the first time we went through. She said she thought she could and then asked why we had been in England.

I've learned that saying I am studying genocide can shut down a conversation quickly, so I replied, "Attending a conference."

"Where?" she asked.

"At the University of Sussex."

"Oh!" she exclaimed. "I graduated from the University of Sussex. What was the conference?"

When I told her, she immediately told me of having lived in Cambodia, and we agreed that she and I should have been talking the whole time between Cambridge and London. She was Denise Heywood, who had worked as a journalist and photographer in Cambodia for three years in the early 1990s; among her many other books and articles, she had written *Cambodian Dance: Celebration of the Gods* (2008). She lectures widely on Southeast Asia and teaches at the universities of Cambridge and London. At King's Cross we quickly exchanged e-mail addresses, and in 2011 Denise read my paper "Children's and Young Adult Literature of the Cambodian Genocide" that I presented at the Children's Literature Association conference at Hollins University in Virginia and upon which this chapter is based.

Of the paper, Denise wrote:

> It was inspiring and moving to read and such a tremendously important subject. It is so vital for present and future generations of young people to understand what has happened in Cambodia—and elsewhere. I feel on reading it that you have covered it all very carefully, so I have only a few points to make.
>
> You mention that genocide probably killed more than a quarter of the population. Between 1–3 million died out of 7.4 million, although, as you know, precise figures do not exist. While I lived in Cambodia for three years in the 1990s, my experiences there indicated that it was closer to 3 m[illion] than 1 m[illion] since everyone I spoke to had lost entire families. So I myself usually say a third or more of the population died. . . .
>
> I also agree with your important point about contextualisation, accuracy and authenticity. The political complexity of countries emerging from colonisation and then embroiled in civil as well as international wars is challenging for any writer. These are issues hard enough for expert historians to analyse let alone children who must take things more at face value without an ability to understand what lies behind the atrocities they witness and experience. (Heywood, "Re: Cambodian Paper")

I was grateful for her expertise and affirmation of the difficulties of writing about genocide—for adults and for children.

The genocide ended in 1979, when the Vietnamese invaded the country. Since that time, authors, photographers, and illustrators have tried to convey the genocide to children and young adults. I begin with the problematic books on the Cambodian genocide, one of which I recommend with reservations.

Problematic Children's and Young Adult Books about the Cambodian Genocide

The Genocide Was Not a Case of Spontaneous Combustion

Scottish journalist Allan Baillie's seminal work *Little Brother* (1985) was the first children's and young adult novel on the genocide to reach the western world. Baillie had lived and worked in Cambodia before the evacuation of foreigners in 1975. At the genocide's end, Baillie returned to Cambodia, where, in the Khao-I-Dang camp hospital, he met a boy name Vuthy, on whose story *Little Brother* is based. The novel, says Baillie, is about "70% true" (Allan Baillie Homepage): Vuthy fought a Khmer Rouge soldier in the hospital, as does Baillie's protagonist, Vithy; Vuthy escaped alone from the Khmer Rouge and became a hospital orderly after his injuries healed in the camp. Like Vithy, he was a stowaway on a truck out of Phnom Penh, and he paid gold for a bicycle ride out of another town. Baillie based the fictional elements of his novel on his own travels throughout Cambodia before the genocide, including a visit to the historic and magnificent Angkor Wat, through which Vithy passes.

This engaging, well-written novel portrays the desperation of hunger and the constant threat of capture, torture, and death posed by the Khmer Rouge. Vithy is a lovable and believable character, who captures the essence of youthful hope and determination. Particularly captivating is Vithy's construction of his own bicycle from scattered parts he finds in a dump. Predictably, he meets others during his travails—those who help him and those who hurt him—an older woman later steals Vithy's bicycle in her efforts to make it to the Thai border and safety before he does.

Baillie makes a major contribution to children's and young adult literature of genocide. A flaw of the novel is that Baillie does little to contextualize the events that transpired in Cambodia. His author's note states briefly, "Cambodia was a quiet little country lying between Vietnam, Laos and Thailand. It became Kampuchea after the first of two bitter wars and thousands of Cambodians, or Khmers, have since been forced to leave" (2). An uninformed reader might think, from the author's note, that Cambodians were the sole source of their own troubles. Later in the text, this impression continues. Vithy, at a town called Sambor, remembers, "before the Khmer Rouge, before the war, before the generals who threw out the Prince and started everything" (39). And Vithy's older brother, Mang, refers to the Khmer Rouge as merely "a bunch of stupid mountain men" (9).

Left out of the account is the complicity of the French, Americans, Soviets, and Chinese in the genocide. France, which had benefited from almost one hundred years of economic exploitation, did nothing to help its former colony. The United States's war with Vietnam, which spilled over into Cambodia, essentially thrust ordinary Cambodians into the arms of the radical Khmer Rouge. In an illegal 1969 tactic, unauthorized by and unknown to Congress, President Richard Nixon and Secretary of State Henry Kissinger approved bombing inside Cambodia's borders. Cambodian scholar Ben Kiernan observes,

> Pol Pot's revolution would not have won power without U.S. economic and military destabilization of Cambodia, which began in 1966 after the American escalation in next-door Vietnam and peaked in 1969–1973 with the carpet bombing of Cambodia's countryside by American B-52s. This was probably the single most important factor in Pol Pot's rise. (16)

Of his village (Stung Kambot), Thoun Cheng told Kiernan, "'often people were made angry by the bombing and went to join the revolution'" (23). Kiernan writes that the capture of 105 U.S. howitzers also significantly contributed to Pol Pot's supremacy, and China supplied over 13,000 tons of weapons to the Khmer Rouge. Political scientist René Lemarchand points out that "three times as many bombs were dropped on Cambodia between 1969 and 1973 as on Japan during the Second World War, approximately half a million tons," and cites William Shawcross, who "goes so far as to suggest the US bombings 'created' the Khmer Rouge" (151).

Although Baillie's novel is significant, it is critical to inform young readers—whether in the text or in an author's note—that this genocide did not spontaneously combust within the borders of Cambodia. If not implicit in the text, author's notes should contextualize the genocide. In postcolonial criticism, as Steven Lynn says, texts should "help us to understand the complex relationships of a dominant to a dominated culture" (27). The Cambodian situation was complex, and it is likely that had the U.S. not bombed Cambodia, a country with which it was not at war, the genocide would not have occurred. Although I recommend Baillie's fine book, I do so with reservations.

The Problem of Exoticizing "the Other" and Conflating Buddhism with Christianity

Clare Pastore's *Chantrea Conway's Story: A Voyage from Cambodia in 1975* (2001) is part of a series called *Journey to America*. In the novel, Chantrea is the child of a Cambodian mother and an American father, who is away on business when the Khmer Rouge arrive in Phnom Penh. Chantrea, her mother, and grandparents are forced to leave the city; along the way, Chantrea's mother is killed. With her grandparents, Chantrea eventually escapes to a Thai refugee camp. Her American grandparents make it possible for her to come to Ohio, where she is reunited with her father.

Authors do not always have a choice about the covers of their books, but if Pastore did not choose the cover, she should have protested it. The conical hat worn by a girl representing Chantrea was not worn by Cambodians; it is more commonly worn by the Chinese. Postcolonial criticism includes looking at the ways "the Other" is made strange or, in other words, exoticized. To depict Chantrea wearing a non-Cambodian artifact (the conical hat) exoticizes her; this tendency to exoticize "the Other" also occurs, as we will see, on the cover of a children's book about Rwanda.

Pastore's writing is a bit stilted, and she conflates Christianity and Buddhism. In the Thai refugee camp with her grandparents, Chantrea becomes distraught over not having seen her father for six months and disturbed by all the suffering she has witnessed:

> When her work was done, Kosal tried to get her to play, but she refused. How could she play when so many were so sick?
>
> Each afternoon, she sat on the rock near the gate and watched for the truck. Even when the monsoon rains fell on her, she did not move. Finally, Grandmother had had enough.
>
> "You must stop this, Chantrea," she insisted. "It is not good for a young girl to make herself so upset!"
>
> "Others need me, Grandmother," Chantrea said. "I have no right to be happy and healthy. Who am I to be so lucky?"
>
> "Who are you to question why Buddha does what he does?" Grandmother asked. (105)

Buddha never claimed to be divine, and it is unlikely that Cambodians would recognize this Christianized version of him, who has somehow willed genocide and suffering. Short provides insight into the distinctions between the beliefs of the Cambodians and the Vietnamese, distinctions that could have informed Conway's book. Short explains that the Cambodians practiced Theravada Buddhism, which originated in India, and the Vietnamese practiced Confucianism, which originated in China:

> At a personal level, Khmers and Vietnamese might befriend each other; Khmer pupils often remembered their Annamite teachers with affection. But the cultural fracture between the two peoples—between Confucianism and Theravada Buddhism, between the Chinese world and the Indian—was one of mutual incomprehension and distrust, which periodically exploded into racial massacres and pogroms. (25)

It is more likely that the grandmother would have believed in karma. Derek Summerfield writes, "In Cambodia, the local word meaning torture derives from the Buddhist term for karma, an individual's thoughts and actions (often bad) in a prior existence, which affect life in the present. Thus survivors can feel somehow responsible for their suffering" (19). Although her narrative is well-intentioned, Pastore should have made an effort to ensure Cambodian cultural artifacts, such as the conical hat, were authentic, and to develop a more sophisticated understanding of the religious beliefs of the country.

Giving Voice to the Victims of the Cambodian Genocide
while Silencing the Genocide of American Indians

Hundreds of thousands of Cambodians sought refuge in other countries. Nancy Graff focused on one of those families in *Where the River Runs: A Portrait of a Refugee Family* (1993). Richard Howard's accompanying photographs document the lives of three Cambodian boys living with their mother in Boston. Graff opens with:

> In the United States, even today, there are pilgrims. At Thanksgiving, as they are seated around the table, they may not look like the pious, black-frocked Pilgrims who arrived on the *Mayflower* almost four hundred years ago, but they are pilgrims just the same. All of them have come for the same reason that generations of pilgrims came before them: to build a new and better life for themselves. (7)

This trope continues throughout her book. Although I appreciate Graff's efforts to communicate to young readers that Cambodian immigrants are no different from many of the rest of us, of concern is her statement: "All the pilgrims who come leave behind many things that were important to them, but they also bring something of their homelands with them. In the United States, where almost everyone is an immigrant or a refugee or the descendant of one or the other . . . " (8). Prior to the arrival of Europeans, it is estimated that 10 to 12 million American Indians lived in North America; by the beginning of the twentieth century, because of genocide and disease, there were about 1 million. Today, there are approximately 5 million American Indians. In her enthusiasm to legitimize Cambodian refugees, Graff forgets another group that was also the target of genocide. In *Lasting Echoes* (1997), Abenaki author Joseph Bruchac writes that the slaughter of the buffalo was a genocidal act. Because European soldiers could not outfight American Indians, from whom they sought to steal land, the soldiers decided instead to kill their food source—the buffalo—and leave American Indians to starve. General Philip wrote that buffalo hunters:

> *have done more in the last two years to settle the vexed Indian question than the entire regular army has done in the past thirty years. They are destroying the Indians' commissary. . . . For the sake of lasting peace let them kill, skin, and sell until the buffaloes are exterminated. Then your prairies can be covered with speckled cattle and the festive cowboy.* (qtd. in Bruchac, 49; italics in the original)

Bruchac also cites Sir Jeffrey Amherst, who in 1763 wrote: "*Could it not be contrived to send the Small Pox among those disaffected tribes of Indians? . . . You will do well to try to inoculate the Indians by means of blankets, as well as to try every other method that can serve to extirpate this execrable race"* (qtd. in Bruchac, 34; italics in the original). In his novel *Hidden Roots* (2004), Bruchac explores the effect of the Vermont Eugenics Project, carried out in the early part of the twentieth century that sterilized many Abenaki, as well as the disabled and criminals. To ignore purposeful starvation, deliberate attempts to kill with smallpox, and forced sterilization is a serious error and a misrepresentation of United States history.

Graff does provide information about Cambodians' daily lives, their memories of home and the genocide, and their struggles. It is one of the paradoxes surrounding the survivors of genocide that, having gone through so much, they must work harder than most of the rest of us once the genocide has ended. Of Sokha, the mother of the family, Graff writes, "Sokha says that if she had time to think about her life it would exhaust her, but time is a luxury few refugees give themselves" (24). Sometimes, for a person working several jobs while raising children and going to school, there is little occasion for much else. Graff brings in Khmer beliefs that life is like a river, the belief from which she takes her title:

> Sometimes the current is swift, the water treacherous and deep. Then life is hard and difficult to bear. Sometimes the banks are widely set, and the river, clear to the horizon, dances in slow, graceful eddies, a shining symbol of life and hope. . . . Everyone's life follows the river; no one can choose a path different from the channel in which the river runs. (47)

Recommended Literature for Children and Young Adults about the Cambodian Genocide

Picture Books

In 2008, Michelle Lord made publishing history with *A Song for Cambodia*, the first picture book written in English about the Cambodian genocide (Figure 1.1). It is a biography of Arn Chorn-Pond, who now as an adult has returned to Cambodia to save the music that saved him during the genocide. An extensive foreword and afterword contextualizes Arn's story and his current work.

The book opens with imagery of the enchantment and loveliness of the country of Cambodia and its strong family ties:

> In a country of sugar palms, whispering grasses, and bright sunshine there lived a boy named Arn. His home was filled with the sweet sounds of music and laughter. He danced with his eleven brothers and sisters while his grandparents sang songs of long ago. His mother hummed to the little ones while she worked. His father taught the older children operas in the evening. (n. pag.)

Shino Arihara's illustrations capture the beauty of Cambodia's landscape. Lord introduces the "orange-robed" Buddhist monks on the second page and quickly portrays the elimination of religion, philosophy, education, and art as coinciding with the arrival of the Khmer Rouge. Lord acknowledges that the war between Vietnam and the United States "spilled over" into Cambodia, creating fear (n. pag.). When they arrived at his village, the Khmer Rouge took Arn to a children's work camp; Arn never saw his family again. Workers in all work camps throughout Cambodia were abhorrently underfed, as was Arn, who, like many others, resorted to eating insects when he was lucky enough to find them. And there was the silence—talk was forbidden. Even the Khmer Rouge guards tired of it and one day asked for volunteers to learn to play the *khim*. A teacher, who was later executed, taught several boys the instrument, and Arn excelled. For him as for many children of genocide, art made life more endurable. Lord writes, "The gentle sound of the khim was heaven to Arn. When he practiced he thought of a world far from the pain and suffering of the work camp. Songs filled Arn's empty stomach and soothed his broken heart. Hidden feeling flowed through him as the mallets struck various tones on the khim" (n. pag.).

When the Vietnamese invaded Cambodia, Khmer Rouge soldiers sent children to the front to fight, but Arn was able to escape. By following packs of monkeys—he knew whatever they ate or drank would be safe—Arn found his way to a Thai refugee camp. When the camp flooded and Arn was close to drowning, Reverend Peter Pond saved Arn's life and brought him back to America. As a teenager Arn worked to help other teens understand war and made visits back to Cambodia. In 1989 he returned permanently to find a poverty-stricken country with "millions of land mines," as Lord writes in her afterword (n. pag.). Arn has received the Reebok Human Rights Award and the Spirit of Anne Frank Award for his efforts to help survivors. He founded, among other organizations, the Cambodian Living Arts program to support the few artists who were not killed by the Khmer Rouge and to preserve Cambodian music. Arn says, "'the more good things that I do to help and care for others' suffering—not just my own—I know that I will find myself free from my own suffering and from my own horrible past'" (n. pag.). Lord and Arihara's picture book biography is a remarkable contribution to children's literature of the Cambodian genocide, providing young readers with a beautiful mentor in Arn Pond.

Icy Smith's picture book *Half Spoon of Rice: A Survival Story of the Cambodian Genocide* (2010) opens with the evacuation of Phnom Penh (Figure 1.2). Illustrator Sopaul Nhem portrays the confusion and surprise as well as the youthfulness of the Khmer Rouge; most were rural teenagers with little experience of the world. The story is told from the point of view of Nat, a nine-year-old boy, who quickly realizes that the claim that the three-day evacuation is necessary because the Americans were going to bomb the city "is a lie" (9). Days later, as "Millions walk, some without anything but the

Figure 1.1   Book cover from Michelle Lord; illustrations by Shino Arihara: *A Song for Cambodia*. New York: Lee & Low Books, 2008.

clothes on their back," Nat asks, "Dad, I never heard any bombing. Why did we need to leave home?" (13–14). Along the way, Nat meets a girl, Malis, who has become separated from her family; Nat's family takes Malis into theirs until the Khmer Rouge separate them all into different work camps. Although heartbroken to be taken from his family, Nat knows that, to survive, he must say nothing. Smith avoids extreme grisliness by having Nat say, "I see some terrible things, and I do not want to die" (21). Nat tells of what happens to those starving people, including children, who steal food; they are never seen again. Desperate for food one night and willing to risk death to eat, Nat sneaks out to catch a frog; the taste is disgusting but fills him fleetingly, and serendipitously he reunites with Malis, who has also crept out. From then on, the two try to meet regularly, after their guards have fallen asleep. And so it goes, for four years. After the Vietnamese invasion, when the Khmer Rouge have deserted the work camps, Malis and Nat walk to one of Thailand's refugee camps. Providentially, Nat's parents are there, but Malis's parents are not; Nat's parents adopt her.

Smith's Author's Note is extensive. She writes, "More than 2.7 million tons of bombs were dropped on Cambodia by the United States from 1962–1973— far more than the total ordnance released during World War II, including the nuclear bombs dropped on Hiroshima," and, "hundreds of thousands of innocent civilians were killed" (38). She also describes the 4 to 6 million land mines left in the country and includes photographs of some of the 20,000

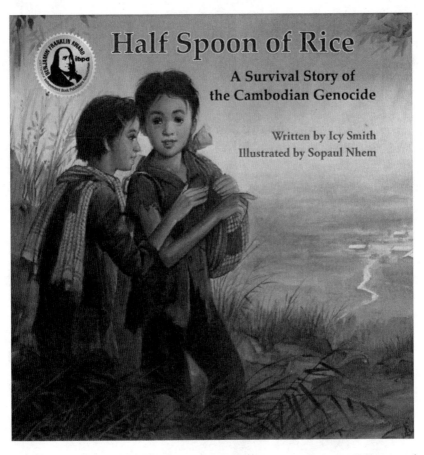

Figure 1.2 Book cover from Icy Smith; illustrations by Sopaul Nhem: *Half Spoon of Rice: A Survival Story of the Cambodian Genocide.* Manhattan Beach, CA: East West Discovery Press, 2010.

killing fields. She closes with "The dark history of the Cambodian genocide is largely untold in schools around the world. This book is intended to help ensure that Cambodia's 'killing fields' will not be forgotten" (41). Her book is a witness to the Cambodian genocide—as Hamida Bosmajian was quoted in my Introduction—"first stories of a thousand and one recountings to prevent the reduction of collective memory" (248).

Novels

In 1979, when Minfong Ho watched with the rest of world the appalling images of what had transpired during the previous four years in Cambodia, she took a leave of absence from Cornell University to return to her country, Thailand, to join relief efforts at the Thai border. In the midst of this sea of suffering, a precious moment occurred for Ho: A little girl created for her a clay marble out of mud. This incident inspired the title of her 1991 novel, *The Clay Marble*, which tells the story of Dara, a twelve-year-old girl, and her family. When her father is murdered, Dara and her family escape to a Thai refugee camp, where she meets Jantu, a new friend, who helps her cope with her losses and whose friendship gives her strength to bear more losses to come.

Ho explains in her preface that part of Cambodia's problems stemmed from other countries' backing of "various political groups," acknowledging that Cambodia's troubles came not solely from within (3). In the text, from Dara's point of view, Ho depicts the gradual intrusion of outside forces on her young life: "At first the war had been distant and mysterious. Tiny silver airplanes, like fishes in the sky, would fly over us before disappearing into the horizon. Then the bombing had come closer, so close that the bombs shook the soil beneath my bare feet" (9), which conveys the encroaching terror from a child's perspective. Because she was there, Ho writes realistically of conditions in refugee camps and creates convincing characters in Dara and Jantu. In her preface Ho writes:

> I remember my first day at the Border. There are no words to describe the intensity of suffering I saw there. The sickness, the starvation, the sheer silence of this vast sea of people overwhelmed me. I wanted to shut my eyes, turn around, and go back home.
>
> Then I felt a small hand on my arm. Looking up at me was a ragged little girl. She held one palm out to offer me a small round ball of mud. I took it, then impulsively bent down and scooped up some mud from a nearby puddle, and rolled my own clay marble. When she saw that I was offering her this marble in exchange for the one she had given me, her face broke out into a beautiful wide smile. (4)

Soon, Ho reports, children crowded around her to show her toys they had made from banana leaves, tin cans, and other materials readily at hand. Ho observes that it is through this creativity and play that people can become victors instead of victims.

Writing in the 1930s, disturbed by the fascism and communism that he saw all around him, Johan Huizinga, in *Homo Ludens: A Study of the Play-Element in Culture* (1955), theorized play as the basis for civilization. Protesting "that economic forces and material interests determine the course of the world," Huizinga argued that "civilization is rooted in noble play and that, if it is to unfold in full dignity and style, it cannot afford to neglect the play-element" (210). In a refugee camp in Thailand, in the middle of human devastation and tragedy, children began to regain their dignity through play. Arn Pond's music, too, indeed all of the arts, are forms of play. Artistic creations can generate civilization in the midst of barbarism.

During the Armenian genocide, Armenian children found comfort in making lace. Of these children, Rose Lane Wilder (Laura Ingalls Wilder's daughter) writes a touching passage. Because of World War I, relief workers could not come to Armenia until 1918, three years after the genocide began. Wilder writes:

> The crochet stitch itself must be nearly as old as fingers, which seem mysteriously impelled to pull a loop through a loop. I say mysteriously, remembering how this impulse baffled the American Near East Relief workers who went into Caucasian Armenia. . . . Every hut in every village was totally destroyed. In the ruins and in the miles of wild grasses the Americans found 25,000 orphaned children hiding, lost, sick, starving and dying. They were three to ten years old and knew nothing but hunger and fear. The Americans gathered them . . . cleaned, deloused, fed, healed and saved most of them alive. But it was impossible to keep bandages on their sores. Untaught, and constantly admonished not to, they couldn't resist pulling ravelings from the gauze and with their tiny fingers looping them into crude Armenian lace. (qtd. in Armenian Relief Cross of Lebanon, 18)

The Armenian culture of creating art through lace making, embroidery, and carpet weaving helped these children find and engender beauty where there was none, as did Cambodian children in their own way. Ho powerfully depicts this noble human impulse, one of the few hopes amidst genocide. This scene in her novel is reminiscent of Ho's experience with the little girl in the refugee camp. Dara and Jantu are playing:

> "But it took you so long to make it," I said.
>
> Idly Jantu scooped up a lump of mud from a puddle by her feet and began to knead it in her hands. "Sure, but the fun is in the making," she said.
>
> She looked down at the lump of mud in her hands with sudden interest. "Have you ever noticed how nice the soil around here is?" she asked.

"Almost like clay." She smoothed the ball with quick fingers, then rolled it between her palms.

When she opened her palm and held it out to me, there was a small brown ball of mud cupped in it. "For you," she announced.

I looked at it. . . . "I don't want it," I said. "It's just a mud ball."

"No, it's not. It's a marble," Jantu said. Her eyes sparkling, she blew on it. "There! Now it's a magic marble."

I took it and held it. Round and cool, it had a nice solid feel to it. I glanced at Jantu. She was smiling. Slowly I smiled back at her.

Maybe, I thought, maybe she did put some magic in the marble. After all, why else would I feel better, just holding it? (43)

It is the magic marble that helps the girls keep their strength during future sorrows and enables them to momentarily forget their troubles whenever they can engage in the "fun" of making: "The toy village became the center of our world, and Jantu and I played with it every day. Each time we would add a few more things—a rice barn, rain barrels, a pigsty—and as Jantu shaped them, we would make up more stories about our new lives after we left the Border" (53). Huizinga writes, "Into an imperfect world and into the confusion of life it [play] brings a temporary, a limited perfection" (10). Jantu and Dara's play brought into their vastly imperfect world a momentary relief.

Toward the end of the novel, Jantu is accidentally shot. As she is dying, she helps Dara understand that she must create her "own magic marble" (135). Through Jantu's play, Dara learns to believe and find strength in herself.

In 2003 Ho published a second novel on the Cambodian genocide, *The Stone Goddess*. This book highlights Cambodian classical dance and one family's participation in it. Denise Heywood explains the significance of Cambodian dance:

In Cambodia, classical dance is the quintessence of the country's identity. An art form that is religious in origin, its traditions hark back more than a thousand years to the great Khmer empire which flourished from the 9th-15th centuries AD. Dancers performed in temples and were the living embodiment of *asparas*, celestial dancers carved on the walls of Angkor Wat. Their role was so revered that the king created the Royal Ballet to act as intermediaries between the monarch and the spiritual realm. . . . With their sacred symbolism, graceful gestures and exquisite costumes, they came to represent the soul of Khmer culture. (10)

Sadly, Pol Pot and the Khmer Rouge destroyed much of this heritage. Although they were initially greeted as heroes who would bring peace to Cambodia, artists soon learned differently. Heywood writes, "Announcements were made that dancers were to register with the new authorities. Ninety percent of the performers and musicians who did so were killed" (78). David Chandler adds, "Of over two hundred trained dancers in 1975, only seventeen survived the 'Pol Pot time'" (190).

Ho's novel is told through the point of view of Nakri whose sister Teeda is known for her accomplishments in Cambodian dance. The opening paragraphs paint vivid images of classical dance:

> We had been dancing for hours, going through the strict steps that we practiced each day in the palace's airy dance pavilion. Fingers flexed far back, wrist circling continuously, back arched, shoulders straight, ankles bent, feet alternately flat on the floor or lifting—every movement had to be controlled, and in perfect unison with other dancers. (1)

Of her sister, Nakri says, "Like a goddess she was, like the asparas of old that we were supposed to be, her gestures so precise and graceful that one flowed naturally into another. It looked so effortless, these subtle dance movements, and yet I knew it took years of disciplined training to do properly" (2). Ho soon introduces the bombing the girls hear, the nightmares the bombs create, and the coming of the Khmer Rouge. Based on numerous accounts, her description accurately portrays their arrival; Nakri says:

> Looking up, I saw dark, disheveled men dressed in black riding on top of the jeeps. Each one held an assault rifle at the ready. One of the men in the first jeep had a bullhorn, and was shouting through it.
> "Surrender your weapons!" His voice boomed out in the early morning quiet. "The war is over! Raise a white flag and lay down your weapons at once!
> ... "Comrades, victory is ours! We are the Angkar. We are the new government of Kampuchea!" (9)

Nakri's family is told the same lie as Nat's in *Half Spoon of Rice*, and they pack to leave.

The Khmer Rouge separate the two sisters, Teeda and Nakri, from their family and send them to a work camp. Teeda knows she may be killed if she reveals that she is a classical dancer, but she cannot resist performing the dances she loves so well. Teeda tells Nakri of a trip she made to Angkor Wat where she encountered the asparas—the dancing goddesses—through a stone goddess there. Under the Khmer Rouge, she would lie awake at night "and go through the whole dance in her mind, visualizing each move she would make from beginning to end. The music too she would try and imagine. In her head, she said, it all came together like a beautiful dream" (66–67). Baillie includes a similar passage in telling about Vithy's arrival at Angkor Wat, where he remembers his mother:

Vithy stopped before a flat stone area in front of the building, and realized with a low thrill that this must be where Mum [note the Scottish version of maternal address] had danced. He could even see the battling elephants on the wall she had talked about. She would glide out of the shadows, glittering in her green and gold costume, and tell ancient tales with her hands and her eyebrows. The other girls would follow her and they all would be the legendary dancing girls of Angkor, the *Aspara*. (66; italics in the original)

Just as Arn Pond played his music and Vithy's mother danced, Teeda dances—if at times only in her mind—to cope. Teeda becomes ill and feverish, and in her weakened state, dances for the last time, when she is discovered by a guard. But it is too late to punish her; Teeda soon dies, leaving Nakri alone.

With the Vietnamese invasion of Cambodia, Nakri and her brother are able to return to Phnom Penh and reunite with some family members. They eventually immigrate to America, where Nakri, in honor of Teeda, does her best to dance. She writes, "And gradually, not that day nor the day after or even the year after, I began to sometimes feel that effortless sweetness that had infused my childhood" (189).

In an essay at the end of the book, Ho contextualizes the genocide: "When I was growing up in Thailand in the 1950s and '60s, neighboring Cambodia was a prosperous and fertile country, ruled by a benign young king" (191). It is important for young readers to know that Cambodia should not be defined by genocide; it was and is a beautiful country that could not control the international forces, which brought about so much tragedy. Ho also discusses "surviving dancers in Cambodia" who work "to revive and preserve Khmer dance" (200). As play functions in *The Clay Marble*, dance functions in *The Stone Goddess*; "in the making," in Jantu's words, is a way forward to the "effortless sweetness" that can, at times, characterize childhood.

The genocide created hundreds of thousands of refugees, some of whom were allowed to immigrate to other countries. In 1980, a Cambodian refugee family worked on Linda Crew's farm in Oregon. Crew became friends with them and conducted research for over a year, including many interviews with Cambodians, before writing her novel *Children of the River* (1991), which was rejected sixteen times before publication. The protagonist, Sundara, is away from home helping an aunt and uncle and is therefore separated from her immediate family when the Khmer Rouge arrive and begin forcing evacuations. Without knowing whether her parents are dead or alive, Sundara immigrates to the U.S. with her aunt and uncle who become her stand-in parents. Crew writes about Sundara's difficulties in traversing two cultures—difficulties that increase when she falls in love with an American boy, Jonathan, of whom her aunt and uncle disapprove. After ongoing ordeals, Sundara is able to declare her love for Jonathan and learns from a newly arrived fellow Cambodian that at least her sister is alive in a refugee camp.

On a personal note, my daughter, Caryn, liked this book so much she voluntarily read it twice in sixth grade; I have also assigned it in children's literature classes and had students tell me it is the best book they have ever read. Crew is to be praised for her diligent research to represent the unique suffering of Cambodian teenagers who had not only to witness genocide but also to adjust to a new culture, and for her engaging style of writing.

Biographies and Autobiographies

Nawuth Keat was nine-years-old when the Khmer Rouge arrived in his village and killed most of his family; although wounded, to stay alive, he pretended he was dead in the ditch where most of his family was murdered. Years later, as a college student who had been very quiet in Martha Kendall's class at San Jose City College in California, he asked, on the last day, if he could tell his story. So moved was the class and Kendall that Kendall offered to transcribe and shape it for the book *Alive in the Killing Fields: Surviving the Khmer Rouge Genocide*, published in 2009.

Nawuth's story is like so many others: forced labor and little food, although he is able to live with a married sister after the deaths of most of his family. "All we had was love for our family, and that's what made us want to survive," writes Nawuth (36). Because his father had been prosperous before the Pol Pot regime, he was a wanted man, who, for a time, survives by hiding out in the jungle. Nawuth is able to join him for a short time, and his father teaches him how to survive: "Besides the monkeys, we lived on crickets, rats, snakes, and frogs. . . . In the jungle I did not spend much time worrying about poisonous snakes. The Khmer Rouge seemed far more dangerous to me" (44). The Khmer Rouge later finds his father and executes him. Nawuth then stays with an older sister, who has little food for her family. Nawuth becomes seriously ill from eating rice chaff: although indigestible, it is all that is available. When the Vietnamese gain control of Battambang, Nawuth and his sister's family leave their work camp, walking at night to get to safety. Upon arrival in Battambang, Nawuth feels free, only to find it immensely difficult to survive. They leave for a Thai refugee camp, from which, like the immigrants in *Children of the River*, Nawuth goes to Oregon. In America, Nawuth eventually marries, and he and his wife open a bagel shop in California; Nawuth also works as a machinist. "I work seven days a week . . . but I have no complaints," he says (125). Access to three meals a day, and other possibilities, are freedom to him. Access to Nawuth's book could help those of us, children and adults, who are not hungry and maltreated, to gain a perspective on what life looks like when one barely managed to stay alive four long years. Nawuth and Kendall's joint venture in *Alive in the Killing Fields* is a most productive one.

Andy Koopmans's biography, *Pol Pot* (2005), is well-researched and relies on recognized Cambodian scholars Ben Kiernan and David Chandler; his

"Works Consulted" is one of the lengthiest in any of the books for children and young adults on Cambodia, and his "For Further Reading" section is helpful for finding resources. Koopmans traveled to Cambodia to write the book, which is both readable and informative. Koopmans makes reference to the outside forces that contributed to the Cambodian genocide, "particularly France, the United States, China, and Vietnam," although he observes that "just as Adolf Hitler was the predominant villain of the Nazi Holocaust, Pol Pot was the predominant villain of the Cambodian genocide and the main architect of his brutal regime" (6). Koopmans explains Pol Pot's elusiveness as a subject of a biography—he often lied, spoke little, and wrote little. As Koopmans notes, "The picture is incomplete, leaving many questions unanswered, and at times the facts seem contradictory. For example, those who knew Saloth Sar/Pol Pot personally often had difficulty reconciling his affable and charming personality with the horrific crimes of his regime" (7).

This is a recurring pattern among *génocidaires*; some are able to magnetize and fascinate. Augustin Bizimungu of Rwanda and Slobodan Milošević of Serbia, among others, were reported to be charismatic. Such knowledge—that one cannot believe all one sees—might become a protective factor for children later in their lives. In *Pol Pot: Anatomy of a Nightmare* (2004), Short writes, "On this point, all testimonies concur. He was a 'self-composed, smooth-featured teacher who was fond of his students, eloquent, unpretentious, honest, humane.' One young man . . . declared after their first meeting: 'I [felt] I could easily become his lifelong friend'" (120).

Koopmans provides what little is known of Pol Pot's early, privileged life—privileges that he later sought to disguise. Although not a particularly good student, Pol Pot received a scholarship to go to Paris, where he became enamored with communist thought, and met friends who would later collaborate to carry out his dreadful regime. Upon his return to Cambodia, Pol Pot became a teacher while secretly working politically against King Sihanouk's government. Soth Polin, later a well-known Khmer novelist, studied French literature with him:

> I still remember [Pol Pot's] style of delivery in French: gentle and musical. He was clearly drawn to French literature in general and poetry in particular: Rimbaud, Verlaine, de Vigny. . . . He spoke in bursts without notes, searching . . . a little but never at a loss, his eyes half-closed, carried away by the lyrical flow of his thoughts. . . . The students were enthralled by this teacher who was so approachable, always dressed in a short-sleeved white shirt and dark blue trousers. (qtd. in Short, 120)

Koopmans highlights the incongruous nature of Pol Pot and includes in his book for young people parts of the above quotation by Soth Polin.

As the American-backed Lon Nol government uprooted the Sihanouk government, U.S. bombings inside Cambodia increased. Koopmans deftly shows young readers the impact of U.S. actions on the rise of Pol Pot and the Communist Party in Cambodia:

> Several events and forces aided the Communists in recruiting. Foremost among these were massive ground operations and aerial bombing campaigns launched by the U.S. government, ostensibly to destroy Vietnamese Communist bases within Cambodia's borders. Ordered by President Richard Nixon and long kept secret from the U.S. public and Congress, these actions killed an estimated *six hundred thousand* Cambodians and created untold numbers of refugees. However, rather than weakening the Communist presence in Cambodia, the destruction drove hundreds of thousands into the CPK/Khmer Rouge. (51; italics added)

With huge infusions of recruits for the Khmer Rouge, in large part thanks to President Nixon, Lon Nol realized by April 1975 that he had to leave the country, making way for the establishment of Pol Pot's government.

Soon thereafter Pol Pot and his Cambodian friends from his Paris days, now called "Angkar," ordered the eight-point policy:

1. Evacuate people from all towns.
2. Abolish markets.
3. Abolish the Lon Nol regime currency and withhold the revolutionary currency that had been printed.
4. Defrock all Buddhist monks and put them to work growing rice.
5. Execute all leaders of the Lon Nol regime, beginning with the top leaders.
6. Establish high-level cooperatives throughout the country with communal eating.
7. Expel the entire Vietnamese population from the country.
8. Dispatch troops to the border, particularly the Vietnamese border. (qtd. in Koopmans, 61)

Koopmans describes how Pol Pot turned a Phnom Penh high school into an execution center called S-21, or Tuol Sleng, to carry out his purification efforts. Koopmans places the Rules of Imprisonment in a table in his biography, including the horrifying rule "While getting lashes or electrification you must not cry at all" (69). The remainder of the book, until the downfall of Pol Pot 3.5 years later, relentlessly portrays Angkar's many cruelties. When the Vietnamese came in 1979, scores of Cambodians considered them liberators from Pol Pot's awful regime.

Koopmans's biography of Pol Pot is an important one. The details and photographs are graphic and might be too much for some young readers. For example, on one two-page spread there are photographs of "the bones and skulls of victims of S-21 [that] are arranged in the geographical shape of Cambodia" (84), and Cambodian boys standing "in front of the hut containing the remains of some of the victims of Pol Pot's campaign of genocide" (85). Behind them are more skulls and bones, and Kenneth Kidd's question arises again about whether reading about trauma becomes traumatic for young readers.

Informational Texts

David Chandler's *The Land and People of Cambodia*, a spinoff for children and young adults of his scholarly *The Tragedy of Cambodian History* (1991) and other books on Cambodia, was published in 1991. He provides a history of the country, includes numerous photographs, and offers a helpful and clear description of the rise and fall of the Khmer Rouge. He points out that in 1970—five years before the beginning of the genocide—Cambodia was a "peaceful, prosperous country" (3). He emphasizes the complicity of other countries: "In 1973, the United States dropped more bombs on Cambodia with which it had never been at war, than it dropped on Japan in 1944–1945" (132). Chandler also shows Cambodia as a site where the hostilities between China and the Soviet Union erupted—the Chinese supporting the Cambodians and the Soviets supporting the Vietnamese.

In a series entitled Genocide in Modern Times, Sean Bergin writes a straightforward account in *The Khmer Rouge and the Cambodian Genocide* (2009), including biographical information on Pol Pot, whom he describes as "seemingly, happy, peaceful, and unremarkable" as a child, an account confirmed by numerous sources (14). In addition to restating what is known about the Khmer Rouge's takeover, Bergin includes two children's stories, collected by Dith Pran. Seath Teng, who was four-years-old in 1975, told Pran,

> The Khmer Rouge soldiers told us not to love our parents or to depend on them because they are not the ones who supported us. They told us to love the new leaders and to work hard so that our country could be prosperous. If we didn't do as they said, we would get a severe beating for punishment. (qtd. in Bergin, 35)

Gen Lee was seven-years-old and remembers:

> All I knew for over three years was that hunger and death were forever present. All I cared about was food, and sometimes I did not want to live. Rations of food were meager. .... It was difficult to work more than ten hours a day on an empty stomach. I ate creatures . . . that I would not have eaten during better times. (qtd. in Bergin, 35)

Bergin's inclusion of the voices of those who were children during Pol Pot's reign strengthens his book. He also reproduces some of Vann Nath's art work; Nath is famous for his paintings of horrendous scenes from Tuol Sleng.

Although authors may not have control over the design of their books, one distraction is the design; photographs are framed by three images of spiked pipes and barbed wire that fade into the photograph. The pipes are curved like canes; I have seen similar images from the Holocaust and question their appropriateness as a design for a book on Cambodia. The Khmer Rouge did not imprison Cambodians in concentration camps; instead, they patrolled open fields at night to keep their fellow citizens from escaping.

Bergin accurately explains the Vietnamese invasion, which ended the genocide and marked the creation of a new government in 1979 called the People's Republic of Kampuchea (PRK). What might be surprising to readers is that, after the genocide, the U.S. backed Pol Pot. Bergin writes,

> Still smarting from its defeat in Vietnam, the United States refused to recognize the PRK and instead supported Pol Pot and his still numerous Khmer Rouge troops, who were mostly exiled in Thailand. It did so despite the stories of Pol Pot's Cambodian genocide, which were finally beginning to be told to the outside world. (43)

From an ethical and moral perspective, it seems in this instance that the United States marginalized the victims of the genocide and gave voice to the *génocidaires*. By including the above passage, Bergin begins to restore voice to the marginalized.

Crossover Literature

Loung Ung's *First They Killed My Father: A Daughter of Cambodia Remembers* (2000) describes her family's evacuation from Phnom Penh. Confused by the upheaval, Ung asks her father what to make of the situation. He replies: "The bombs kill farming families, destroy their land, and drive them out of their homes. Now homeless and hungry, these people come to the city seeking shelter and help. Finding neither, they are angry and take it out on all the officers in the government" (11). Because of the bombing inside Cambodia's borders, Phnom Penh's population had swelled from 1 million to over 2 million by 1975. The Ungs had family who were farmers; when ordered out of the city, they first went to stay with them. But as refugees poured into their family's village, Ung's father thought it time to move on lest he be recognized as a member of Lon Nol's government. He is eventually caught and executed and, at genocide's end, Ung immigrates to California.

Denise Affonço, the daughter of a Vietnamese mother and a French Hindu father, tells her story in *To the End of Hell: One Woman's Struggle to Survive Cambodia's Khmer Rouge* (2005). At the genocide's beginning Affonço was married to a Cambodian. She reflects on the forces outside Cambodia that brought such tragedy to Cambodia:

The Lon Nol years also see Cambodia sucked inexorably into the war in IndoChina. North Vietnamese troops intervene in the country, which is pounded by American air power. . . . It's during this period that the Khmer Rhouge start peddling their nationalist movement in the countryside, rallying the young and mostly illiterate peasantry to their cause and creating an army. (11)

Affonço calls attention to Pol Pot's practice of recruiting the most vulnerable and susceptible young people to carry out his genocidal plans—those who had fewest opportunities. With the Khmer Rouge's arrival, Affonço, like over a million others, is marched to work camps, where she helplessly watches her nine-year-old daughter slowly starve to death. The same fate awaits her two nieces, after the death of their mother. Her desperately hungry eight-year-old nephew is shot for stealing food. Affonço and her son are later granted asylum in France. There, she reflects,

> But for all its ups and downs, our life was a long tranquil river. It could have and should have flowed on like this in the most unremarkable way in the world, in a land where the sun always shone, peacefully and without any worries. How could one have imagined for a moment that, overnight, on 17 April 1975, it would be plunged into horror? (8)

And horror it was. In her foreword, Affonço writes, "I have lived off cockroaches, toads, rats, scorpions, grasshoppers and termites."

Conclusion

The murderous Khmer Rouge perpetrated one of the most deadly genocides ever recorded. Pol Pot and the butcher-comrades whom he met in Paris misled a generation of young, uneducated soldiers, giving them permission to destroy most of a culture thousands of years old. That the story is now being told for people of all ages, Cambodians and others as well, who need to learn the lessons of heartless foreign intervention is an encouraging end to the terrible history of genocide. As more and more survivors reach middle and old age, more stories of the experience of the Cambodian genocide will be told. Perhaps those who listen can help prevent another similar disaster.

Works Cited

Armenian Relief Cross of Lebanon. *Armenian Embroidery.* Beirut: Author, 1999.
Baillie, Allan. "Allan Baillie Homepage." n. d. Web. 5 July 2012. <http://www.allanbaillie.com.au/faq.htm>.
Bosmajian, Hamida. *Sparing the Child: Grief and the Unspeakable in Youth Literature about Nazism and the Holocaust.* New York: Routledge, 2002.

Bruchac, Joseph. *Hidden Roots*. New York: Scholastic, 2004.
———. *Lasting Echoes: An Oral History of Native American People*. New York: Avon, 1997.
Chandler, David P. *The Tragedy of Cambodian History: Politics, War, and Revolution since 1945*. New Haven: Yale UP, 1991.
Crew, Linda. "Linda Crew Website." n. d. Web. 21 Jan. 2013. <http://www.lindacrew.com/children_of_the_river_55440.htm>
Graff, Nancy, and Richard Howard (Photographs). *Where the River Runs: A Portrait of a Refugee Family*. Boston: Little, Brown, 1993.
Harff, Barbara. "The Etiology of Genocides." Totten and Bartrop, 108–120.
Heywood, Denise. *Cambodian Dance: Celebration of the Gods*. Bangkok, Thailand: River Books, 2009.
———. "Re: Cambodian Paper." Message to Jane M. Gangi. 19 June 2011. E-mail.
Huizinga, Johan. *Homo Ludens: A Study of the Play-Element in Culture*. Boston: Beacon, 1955.
Jensen, Steven L. B., ed. *Genocide: Cases, Comparisons and Contemporary Debates*. Trans. Gwynneth Llewellyn. Njalsgade, Denmark: The Danish Center for Holocaust and Genocide Studies, 2003.
Kiernan, Ben. *The Pol Pot Regime: Race, Power, and Genocide in Cambodia under the Khmer Rouge, 1975–1979*. New Haven: Yale UP, 1996.
The Killing Fields. Dir. Roland Joffé. Perf. Haing S. Ngor, John Malkovich, and Julian Sands. Warner Brothers. 1984. Film.
Lemarchand, René. "Comparing the Killing Fields: Rwanda, Cambodia and Bosnia." Jensen, 141–173.
Lynn, Steven. *Texts and Contexts: Writing about Literature with Critical Theory*. 2nd ed. Boston: Longman, 2011.
Pastore, Clare. *A Voyage from Cambodia in 1975*. New York: Berkley Jam, 2001. Journey to America Ser.
Pran, Dith, comp. *Children of Cambodia's Killing Fields*. New Haven: Yale UP, 1997.
Short, Philip. *Pol Pot: Anatomy of a Nightmare*. New York: Holt, 2004.
Summerfield, Derek. "The Social Experience of War and Some Issues for the Humanitarian Field." *Rethinking the Trauma of War*. Eds. Patrick J. Bracken and Celia Petty. London: Free Association/Save the Children, 1998. 9–37.
Totten, Samuel, and Paul Bartrop, eds. *The Genocide Studies Reader*. New York: Routledge, 2009.
Yale University. "Cambodian Genocide Program." 2010. Web. 6 Feb. 2013.

Recommended Children's and Young Adult Literature about the Cambodian Genocide

Bergin, Sean. *The Khmer Rouge and the Cambodian Genocide*. New York: Rosen, 2009.
Chandler, David P. *The Land and People of Cambodia*. New York: HarperCollins, 1991.
Crew, Linda. *Children of the River*. New York: Doubleday, 1991.
Ho, Minfong. *The Clay Marble*. New York: Farrar, 1991.
———. *The Stone Goddess*. New York: Orchard, 2003.
Keat, Nawuth, with Martha E. Kendall. *Alive in the Killing Fields: Surviving the Khmer Rouge Genocide*. Washington, DC: National Geographic, 2009.
Koopmans, Andy. *Pol Pot*. New York: Thomson Gale, 2005.
Lord, Michelle, and Shino Arihara (Illus.). *A Song for Cambodia*. New York: Lee & Low, 2008.
Smith, Icy, and Sopaul Nhem (Illus.). *Half Spoon of Rice: A Survival Story of the Cambodian Genocide*. Manhattan Beach, CA: East West Discovery, 2010.

Recommended with Reservations: Children's and Young Adult Literature about the Cambodian Genocide

Baillie, Allan. *Little Brother*. New York: Viking, 1985.

Recommended Crossover Literature about the Cambodian Genocide

Affonço, Denise. *To the End of Hell: One Woman's Struggle to Survive Cambodia's Khmer Rouge*. London: Reportage, 2005.
Ung, Loung. *First They Killed My Father: A Daughter of Cambodia Remembers*. New York: Harper Perennial, 2000.

Chapter Two
Children's and Young Adult Literature of Guatemala and Kurdish Iraq

Ours is a long history, and the circumstances of our lives have been very sad.
—Santos, Communities of Population in Resistance of the Sierra

Because they both occurred in the 1980s and there are fewer children's and young adult books in English about them than about other genocides, I address the Guatemalan and Iraqi genocides together in this chapter.

Guatemala

Led by President Efrain Ríos Montt, the Guatemalan government in the 1980s used the Guatemalan army to exterminate approximately 200,000 mostly indigenous and noncombatant Maya Indians. Ríos Montt associated the Mayas with guerrilla armies, which had formed in the 1960s and 1970s in protest to the huge economic discrepancies in the country; the guerrilla armies were influenced by similar uprisings in Nicaragua and El Salvador. Romeo Lucas García, who was president of Guatemala from 1978 until 1982, when Ríos Montt staged a coup and overthrew him, had begun a campaign of terror that Ríos Montt intensified. Although the attacks were largely against the Maya, some *ladinos*—those of mixed Spanish and indigenous heritage—were also targeted. After interviewing 11,000 people, the Report of the Commission for Historical Clarification, "Guatemala: Memory of Silence" (1997), estimates "that the number of persons killed or disappeared as a result of the fratricidal confrontation reached a total of over 200,000," and that "[e]ighty-three percent of fully identified victims were Mayan and seventeen percent Ladino" (n. pag.).

Derek Summerfield, a psychiatrist who studies genocide, writes, "Guatemala . . . has long had the most distorted land ownership in Latin America: 75 per cent of all land is owned by 2 per cent of landowners. Landless peasants can thus be kept dependent on seasonal work, under feudal conditions, on the large estates" (11–12). These disparities especially affected children. Maya anthropologist Victor Montejo observes, "By the mid-1970s 75% of Guatemalan children, most of them Mayas, were malnourished" (40). It is not surprising that guerilla armies would materialize in dissent over poverty and lack of opportunity, by which the Guatemalan government was unfazed.

Ríos Montt and his government responded savagely to the guerrilla armies, killing approximately 200,000 innocent men, women, and children. During her fieldwork in Guatemala in the 1990s, anthropologist Victoria Sanford met Don Pablo, a Maya, who asked her, "How could they say these were guerrilleros? How can an infant of six months or a child of five, six, or seven years be a guerrillero? How can a pregnant woman carrying her basket to market be a guerrillero?" (47). A scorched-earth policy was employed, increasing the hunger and suffering of blameless people. The Guatemalan government tried to keep the genocide under the radar of international attention. They would burn villages, forcing the Maya into the jungle, assess international attention, then burn and kill more. Those fortunate enough to escape execution were forced to flee to the rainforest, where they faced wretchedness. Doña Claudia told Sanford of the "coldness of the mountains":

> I was always only wet, very wet. I slept in the same wet clothes without drying them. I slept in wet clothes in the rain. I was always crying in the mountains, crying for the massacre in my village, my house that had been burned, my animals that had been killed. We were all crying there in the mountain without food. (183)

Summerfield helps us understand how, for the Maya, it was a double genocide. The Maya felt, Summerfield says,

> that their collective body had been wounded, one which included the ants, trees, earth, domestic animals and human beings gathered across generations. Mayan origin myths are linked to land and maize. To them the burning of crops by the army was not just an attack on their physical resources, but on the symbol which most fully represented the Mayan collective identity, the people of maize. . . . When they talked about "sadness" they meant something experienced not just by humans but also by these other interconnected elements which had been violated. (17)

Although all genocides are catastrophic, this genocide was catastrophic in its own way. From the Maya's perspective, the genocide included the genocide of the land, and of their spirituality. Displacing them removed them from their spiritual connections to their land, which was deeply disorienting. Gradually some of them developed Communities of Population in Resistance, declared civilian organizations, that have worked together collectively to rebuild in new communities.

Interestingly, some of the Guatemalan army had no idea why they were participating in the extermination of the Mayas. In the documentary *When the Mountains Tremble* (1983), a soldier is asked why he is involved and he responds, "I don't know." Montejo writes of conscription into the Guatemalan army:

Once shanghaied into military service, the young men were brutally indoctrinated into ranks. They were promised that they would become real men with the power to order others, but first they must suffer through three months of savage basic training. Spanish speaking was obligatory, and Spanish lessons were compulsory for most Maya men enrolled in the army. To persist in speaking a Maya language was to invite a beating. (63)

Jesuit priest and anthropologist Ricardo Falla speaks of the systemic racism against the Maya people, an instilled racism we will see again in the Rwandan and Darfur genocides. He writes,

I believe that the army in the field and in Guatemala City was influenced by this stereotype to massacre the indigenous communities. The stereotype contains three salient aspects: (1) that the Indian is a vile and despicable being, whose life is worth less than a normal person's and whom one can therefore exterminate without scruples to save the country from a great evil such as communism; (2) that Indians lie and are by nature treacherous, so that even if an Indian is not lying the *ladino* suspects that he is deceiving him and thinks he does not need to prove it, even if the Indian's life is in the balance; and (3) that Indians are like children—easy prey to the deceit of others. (185)

Dehumanization of the "the Other" is a pattern in genocides; here the Maya are "vile and despicable" and "like children." We will see that the Armenians were cast as microbes, the Jews as maggots and fungus, and the Tutsis as cockroaches. And, as we saw in the Cambodian genocide, other countries influenced the outbreak of genocide. Francisco Goldman writes of United States complicity:

Those U.S. administrations told the world that the Guatemalan Army was fighting for democratic freedoms, but the Guatemalan Army was never fighting for anything but power. In the name of anti-Communism, the United States empowered the Guatemalan Army, helped it grow rich and above the law, and looked the other way when faced with any evidence of the true nature of its Frankenstein monster. . . . The Guatemalan Army never fought for democracy; they fought to preserve and strengthen their murderous military mafia's hold on real power. Their reign was one of terror and brutality. (93–94)

United States President Ronald Reagan called Ríos Montt, who is currently on trial in Guatemala for genocide, "a great democrat" (qtd. in Moller, 206).

Speaking with and to a Guatemalan Scholar

John Ryan, a former student, made the connection between Abigail Adams and me. Abigail is an anthropology professor at Central Connecticut State University in New Britain, Connecticut, and had made numerous trips to Guatemala. Abigail pointed me to the Report of the Commission for Historical Clarification (1997), which informs much of this chapter, as do many of Abigail's insights. She also helped me distinguish between *Maya* and *Mayan*; the former refers to the people, the latter to the language. Readers will note that authors who write about Guatemala use the terms interchangeably.

I was unable to speak with a Kurd or a Kurdish Iraqi scholar in researching this book, and so consulted available academic literature.

Problematic Children's and Young Adult Books about the Guatemalan Genocide

Although Charles Shields's *Guatemala* (2003) is meant to be an informational text on aspects of Guatemala—such as geography, weather, and economic outlook—his handling of the genocide in the early 1980s is brief and not named as such. His six-page chapter on the history of Guatemala, entitled "A National Identity Marred by Conflict," starts with the "great ancient civilization" of the Maya in the past (17), the Spanish conquest, and political unrest since. Of the 1980s, he writes, "On July 18, 1982, General Rios Montt, the president of Guatemala, was quoted in the *New York Times* as telling an audience of native Guatemalans, 'If you are with us we'll feed you; if not, we'll kill you.' Under Rios Montt and others, thousands died at the hands of secret death squads" (21). Hundreds of thousands is a more accurate estimation, and the death squads were not "secret." The Guatemalan army was clearly identified in the attacks; they wanted to be. Their planes, helicopters, and uniforms were meant to intimidate the indigenous Maya people and prevent them from joining the guerrillas. Montejo writes,

> In the towns where the army established bases at the end of 1981, horrible events began to occur. Helicopters would arrive with gagged men transported in bags, brought in from distant communities to be tortured and

executed inside the military barracks. Local townspeople could hear the screaming of men being tortured late at night. The nocturnal screams and the almost constant noise of submachine gun fire instilled panic among the local people. Skulls and dismembered parts of human bodies were found on the outskirts of towns, and dogs and buzzards fought over the carrion. (48)

Falla quotes a Maya witness's gruesome story:

"Delicious chicken," the soldiers, killers of people, say. And they grab another and another, and another . . . and they go killing them and throwing them into the pit.

The soldiers grab firewood, because there is chopped firewood right there. They dump the people into the pit, and throw more and more firewood over them. They pour gasoline over the firewood. They drench the firewood with gasoline. Then they stand back and light a match and throw it in. When it reaches the firewood, it explodes like a bomb. Bang . . . a huge fire. (1)

There was nothing surreptitious about the Guatemalan army's carrying out of the genocide; they wanted as many Maya to view their unspeakable cruelty as possible in order to intimidate and terrorize them. One informant told Sanford during her fieldwork in Guatemala in the 1990s: "What I want to tell you, Victoria, is that it is the impunity of the act. Those men didn't even wear masks to cover their faces" (35).

Shields does mention Rigoberta Menchú's publication of *I, Rigoberta Menchú: An Indian Woman in Guatemala* (1983) as awakening college students in the United States to the Maya's plight, and their pressuring the U.S. government to cut off military aid to Guatemala, which is one positive aspect of his book.

In *Guatemala* (1999), Anita Dalal, like Clare Pastore in *Chantrea's Journey*, discussed in Chapter One, exoticizes "the Other." Early in her book, she writes, "Half of the people who live in Guatemala today are Indians. Their ancestors ruled Guatemala a thousand years ago. The Mayan Indians worshipped many different gods and even offered human sacrifices to them at special fiestas" (6). Although this may be true in some instances, if Dalal brings up human sacrifice, she should also bring up the government's slaughter of 200,000 Maya in the early 1980s. Such an omission neutralizes the Guatemalan government while making strange the Maya. Because the book is about fiestas, Dalal provides information on celebrations, festivals, arts, and crafts. In a section called "Patron Saints," Dalal writes,

Guatemala has lots of fiestas every year to celebrate patron saints. Most villages have their own patron saint. On that saint's special day the schools close and no one goes to work.

> Life in the villages is simple but hard. People weave their own clothes and grow their own food. Their saint helps them and deserved a party. (22)

Life in the villages has been anything but simple for the last five decades; they have experienced conflagration and their food sources have been destroyed. Dalal's romanticization of Maya life, whether she intends it or not, is a way of denying genocide.

Although Sean Sheehan and Magdalene Koh's *Guatemala* (1998) is well-designed and contains stunning photographs of this beautiful country, their treatment of the genocide is almost nonexistent. In a chapter called "History," they cover the history of Maya immigration to Guatemala in 1500 B.C., the Maya Golden Age, and the Spanish conquest. The authors spend eight pages on Guatemala's history up to the 1970s. Of the 1970s, they write, "Some 25,000 Guatemalans were killed during the Romeo Lucas García presidency that began in 1978" (27). Of the 1980s, which are arguably the most devastating in Guatemala's history, there is no mention; the authors skip immediately to the 1990s. That Ríos Montt overthrew Lucas García in 1982, and scaled up the attacks, is not discussed. In addition to at least alluding to the horrible tragedy that overtook the country in the 1980s, they might also have explained who they meant by "25,000 Guatemalans." Lucas García targeted anyone who might oppose the government, mostly indigenous people. They might also have mentioned the United States's complicity in the genocide. The Report of the Commission for Historical Clarification says that United States "military assistance was directed towards reinforcing the national intelligence apparatus and for training the officer corps in counterinsurgency techniques, key factors that had significant bearing on human rights violations" (n. pag.).

They are right to include the U.S.-backed overthrow of President Jacobo Árbenz in 1954. Árbenz was trying to address the huge inequities that existed in Guatemala—that were set up by forces outside its borders, including the Spanish *encomienda* system and the United Fruit Company in the United States, which owned over 40 percent of Guatemalan land. But they miss the opportunity to discuss the genocide. They write,

> Things did not improve following the U.S.-sponsored military coup in 1954. Successive military governments treated the Indians in much the same way the Spanish had. Indigenous people were the chief victims of the military's systematic abuse of human rights in recent decades, partly because they were the ones that various guerrilla movements turned to for support. Many Guatemalans hoped that the 1996 Peace Accords would lead to significant improvements for the Indians and their culture. (64)

Although Sheehan and Koh acknowledge human rights abuses, to skip from 1954 to the 1990s with no description of the atrocities of the 1980s avoids the most turbulent era in Guatemalan history.

In a later chapter in a sidebar headed "Refugees," they tell of the "widespread persecution against Indians [that] led to thousands fleeing Guatemala for safer havens in Mexico and other countries" in the 1980s (67). Again, there is no mention of the 200,000 slaughtered. In a chapter called "Lifestyle," they get closer to naming what happened in Guatemala, but not close enough:

> Guatemala has one of the poorest human rights records in all Latin America. Between the 1960s and the 1990s about 80,000 Guatemalans are estimated to have died at the hands of the paramilitary death squads. Armed guerrillas fighting to overthrow the government represent only a fraction of this figure. Most of the victims were innocent civilians, largely Indians, whose villages were attacked because they allegedly were used as hiding places for guerillas. (75)

Although they are correct that "most of the victims were innocent civilians," their estimate of 80,000 is a small fraction of the 200,000 who died. Like Dalal, in a later chapter on religion, they introduce human sacrifice: "Slaves and prisoners were common sacrificial victims" (85). Yet they fail to mention that the Guatemalan army and Ríos Montt sacrificed 200,000 Maya Indians in the 1980s, and that most of the world turned a blind eye to the genocide. To introduce human sacrifice while suppressing genocide is a form of exoticizing "the Other."

Ben Mikaelsen's novel *Tree Girl* (2004) was favorably reviewed, as most books for children and young adults on genocide are, by *School Library Journal, Booklist, Kirkus,* and *Teacher Magazine.* The book jacket states, "This novel is based on a true story told to the author one night by the real Tree Girl in a secure safe house in Guatemala." Although that may be true, there are questionable aspects to *Tree Girl.*

The protagonist, Gabriela, is a Maya, cheerfully living in her village with her family. The western individualism of the passage below does not ring true to the collective and communal consciousness of the Maya. Gabriela's parents choose her to be the one to go to school instead of her brother; her mother explains:

> It's because you think differently than the other children, Gabi. You look up at the sky when the other children stare at the ground. Why do you think you love to climb trees? You see the beauty the other children are blind to. You ask questions the other children in the cantón never think to ask. (13)

This passage seems to reflect American exceptionalism more than Maya culture and beliefs. Mikaelsen persists in calling *ladinos* Latinos; the difference is that *Latinos* refers to those people who live in or who have immigrated from the Caribbean, and Central and South America to other parts of the world; *ladinos,* Abigail Adams explained, are Guatemalans of mixed Maya and Spanish blood who have deliberately renounced their Maya ancestry.

Another troublesome aspect of Mikaelsen's book is the rape Tree Girl (Gabriella) watches. It is the most gruesome I have ever read in *any* book—for young people or adults. As Kenneth Kidd wonders: Should reading about trauma be traumatic for the young reader?

Recommended with Reservations: Children's and Young Adult Literature about the Guatemalan Genocide

The purpose of Anita Croy's informational text *Guatemala* (2009) is to give young readers a sense of the country as a whole; it is not focused specifically on the genocide. Plants, animal and fish life, weather, and geography are more emphasized than people, as would be expected in a National Geographic book. Late in the book, Croy discusses "Coups and Conflicts," explaining that the United States feared that President Jacobo Árbenz, who was elected in 1951, would turn Guatemala into a communist country and therefore had him removed. Armed rebel forces who agreed with Árbenz's policies of land redistribution fought back, but the U.S. supported the government troops. Lasting peace did not come to the area until 1996 (35). A sidebar mentions Rigoberta Menchú's *I, Rigoberta Menchú: An Indian Woman in Guatemala.* There is no mention of the genocide Menchú was protesting.

In another sidebar, "A Crusading Bishop," Croy tells of the heroic Monsignor Juan José Conedera, of whom she writes:

> In 1999, the bishop released a report that showed that most of the 200,000 deaths of the civil war were caused by government troops. Two days after the report appeared, Gerardi Conedera was murdered. His killing became a turning point in the ongoing struggle between the people and Guatemala's military. In 2001, three army officers were convicted of the archbishop's murder. (56)

What is not reflected in Croy's text is that Gerardi Conedera was an outspoken advocate for the Maya. There is no reference to genocide. The Report of the Commission for Historical Clarification acknowledges the Catholic Church's shift after the Second Vatican Council to:

> Prioritizing its work with excluded, poor and under-privileged sectors and promoting the construction of a more just and equitable society. These doctrinal and pastoral changes clashed with counterinsurgency strategy, which considered Catholics to be allies of the guerillas and therefore part of the internal enemy. . . . A large number of catechists, lay activists, priests, and missionaries were victims of violence and gave their lives as testimony to the cruelty of armed confrontation. (n. pag.)

Croy's glossary defines *civil war* but not *genocide* (60)—further evidence of Croy's misrepresentation of tragic events. In a civil war, all sides would have access to weapons, and the Maya did not. Croy is truthful in some details but silent on details that are important to the Maya people, and the liberation theologians of the Catholic Church who helped them.

Michael Dahl's purpose in *Guatemala* (1998), like Croy's in her book, is to provide information about the country. Dahl acknowledges the role of indigenous people:

> Long ago, Mayan people built stone cities and temples. Today, the remains of these cities and temples still stand. . . .
>
> Mayan people make up 53 percent of Guatemala's population. . . . In the 1500s, Spanish explorers came to Guatemala from Spain. They fought the Mayan people and took over Guatemala. (9)

It is the silences that are of concern here. Dahl refers to Spanish colonization but not to the attacks on the Maya people by their own government in the 1980s. The slaughter of 200,000 Maya should not have been omitted from Dahl's text.

Marlene Targ Brill and Harry R. Targ's *Guatemala* (1993) has much to recommend it—many colorful pictures and a clean, simple design. Objectionable is their version of Spanish colonization:

> Guatemala's story reveals a tale of conflict. The story tells how two cultures in one country clash. One Guatemalan culture includes the descendants of pre-Columbian Maya Indians. These people treasure their old ways. They live in villages known for multicolored costumes, crafts, and marketplaces.
>
> Another main cultural group traveled from Spain to what became Guatemala more than four and one-half centuries ago. Through the years they tried to impose their Spanish ways of living on the people they called Indians. (7)

Here *travel* is a euphemism for invasion and massacre; Spaniards did not simply "travel" to Guatemala, and "try" to influence the Maya. After the Spanish conquest of the Aztecs in Mexico, Pedro de Alvarado led conquistadors to Guatemala in the sixteenth century and, in their search for gold, killed tens of thousands of indigenous people. When the Spaniards did not find gold in Guatemala, they took valuable land instead, land that remains in the hands of the wealthy few today.

Brill and Targ do include peaceful protests, which other informational texts on the Guatemalan genocide do not. They write: "Many peaceful demonstrations ended in violence against protestors. On January 31, 1980, a group called Campesino Unity Committee (CUC) occupied the Spanish Embassy.

They protested military activities in the Highlands. The Guatemalan military burned thirty-nine protestors alive in the embassy" (59).

Better than other texts, Brill and Targ pinpoint the dreadful dilemma the Maya faced: "Ríos Montt introduced policies forcing villagers to serve as local soldiers. As such the villagers had to fight against their neighbors who might be guerrillas. If they fought, the guerrillas would kill them. If they refused, they or their families would be killed by the army" (59). Abigail calls this a "brilliant poisonous strategy": they were called civilian self-defense patrols, euphemistically named "volunteers." For the Maya men conscripted into these patrols, it was a no-win situation. Whichever stance they chose, they would be forced into labor, die, or have to flee the country. Brill and Targ, however, underestimate the number of those who died: "Human rights groups estimated that more than 150,000 Indians and ladinos were murdered or kidnapped, and hundreds of villages and homes were destroyed. *Le Monde*, a French newspaper, claimed that the military committed 15 killings for every one committed by the rebels" (60). The figure of 150,000 is too low, but the inclusion of *Le Monde's* estimations is useful in understanding how the Guatemalan army made the Maya pay for guerrilla activity in which many Maya did not participate.

Recommended Children's and Young Adult Literature about the Guatemalan Genocide

Autobiography

Nobel Prize winner Rigoberta Menchú provides a delightful picture of her world prior to the genocide in *The Girl from Chimel* (2005). She begins with her grandparents' love affair and her grandfather's founding of the village of Chimel. He was an enchanting storyteller, and Menchú retells several of her grandfather's stories. Striking is his response to his grandchildren's question of why humans have different skin colors. He said, "Because Ajaw, our Maker and Creator, made some people out of white corn and other out of black corn. He made still others out of red corn and he made us out of yellow corn and that's why our skin is yellow. Ajaw wanted us to be as different as the colors of the field" (16). The Maya did not recognize a hierarchy of ethnicities, as their European conquerors did.

Menchú tells of her mother's care for all of nature, her knowledge of its healing powers for her family's aches or illnesses, and of her family's keeping bees for honey. The sensuous beauty of Chimel is apparent throughout the book—plums, blackberries, bird song, and orchids (Figure 2.1).

Informational Texts

Brent Ashabranner's *Children of the Maya: A Guatemalan Indian Odyssey* (1986), with photographs by Paul Conklin, was one of the first books written

Figure 2.1 Book cover from Rigoberta Menchú, with Dante Liano; illustrations by Domi: *The Girl from Chimel.* Toronto, Canada: Groundwood, 2005.

for children and young adults on genocide of the Maya. Ashabranner focuses on those Maya who fled to refugee camps in Mexico, some 150,000, and who then made their way from the Mexican refugee camps to Indiantown, Florida, known for its seasonal influx of migrant workers. The Report of the Commission for Historical Clarification estimates the number of displaced persons from "500,000 to a million and a half people in the most intense period from 1981 to 1983" and confirms Ashabranner's estimate that "150,000 people sought safety in Mexico" (n. pag.). Ashabranner writes, "The year-round residents of Indiantown had seen every kind of misfortune, every kind of misery that people of the road can bring—or so they thought. In late 1982 and early 1983 they discovered that they were wrong" (4). These were the years the Maya came to Indiantown. Ashabranner says,

> They came by ones and twos, by single families, a few times in small groups. Some came as part of migrant crews, but most simply appeared on their own. No matter how they came, their condition was the same. They had no money, no clothes except the tattered ones they wore, no idea of how to function in an American setting of gas stoves, electricity, laundromats, hot and cold running water, bathtubs and showers, flush toilets, supermarkets. (4)

They were led, perhaps, to Indiantown because of the promise of migrant work, and once a few Maya families became established in Indiantown, Maya friends and family also made their way there.

Ashabranner explains the genocide:

> Between 1980 and 1984 the national army of Guatemala carried out a campaign of terror and dislocation against the Mayan Indians who live in the central and western highlands of that country. By its own count, the army destroyed 440 villages and damaged many others. . . . The Guatemalan government ordered or agreed to the army's campaign against the Mayan Indians because the mountainous areas where they live were becoming a stronghold of guerilla rebels. (15)

The number of guerillas, Ashabranner indicates, was not more than four to six thousand; the Guatemalan government's actions were unjustified. *Any* actions against civilians are unjustified. He comments, "The violence against its own people by the Guatemalan army has gone largely unnoticed in the United States because of our preoccupation with El Salvador and Nicaragua" (19). Here he is mistaken; the U.S. actively supported Ríos Montt's murderous regime in the name of stamping out communism, and recent declassified documents establish that President Ronald Reagan undoubtedly knew about the violence against the Maya. The United Fruit Company also had large land holdings in Guatemala, and lobbied the U.S. government not to interfere with Ríos Montt's pro-U.S. policies.

Ashabranner's next chapter is told in the words of Juan Salazar, who with his sons left the village of Tres Valles and fled to Mexico in 1981 to avoid being killed by the Guatemalan army. His wife insisted that the three of them leave separately, as their chances of survival would be better that way. He and his family were eventually reunited in Indiantown. In the following chapters, other Guatemalans tell their stories in their own words. Luis Garcia's father was accused of working with the guerrillas and brutally killed. Garcia says,

> They beat him and then shot him and cut off his head. They killed his friend, too, and threw them both in a ditch.
>
> The next day we found my father and carried him home. We washed him and put him in a coffin. I remember that his head did not fit very well with his body. It is something I wish I could forget, but I can't. (40)

The guerrillas threatened to kill Garcia if he didn't join them, so his mother told him he must go to Mexico. He was only fifteen and had never been on his own. An aunt and uncle in Indiantown were eventually able to offer him a home.

Ashabranner includes children's illustrations of their villages and homes before and after army attacks. In one drawing, before the violence, a quetzal bird is pictured. This bird is known for its glistening and colorful beauty and is Guatemala's national bird. In the after-violence drawings, helicopters and planes are raining bullets down on praying victims. One boy writes, "They just do it. . . . I don't know why" (79). Ashabranner's closing paragraph describes the Maya's respect for twenty-one Roman Catholic priests who were martyred in the violence in Central America.

Marion Morrison's *Guatemala* (2005) is a comprehensive text on all facets of the country. More than other informational books, Morrison helps young readers understand the influence of Spanish colonization:

> Guatemala was a Spanish colony for about 300 years. Unlike Mexico and Peru, it did not have vast gold and other riches. Instead, land was the most prized possession. After seizing the Maya's land, the Spanish soon set up the *encomienda* system in Guatemala. Under this system, a few leading Spaniards were given vast estates, and the Maya were forced to work the land. Indians who refused to work the land were killed. The *encomienda* system virtually enslaved the Maya. (47; italics in the original)

Morrison explains that Carlos V, a Spanish King, tried to reduce the negative effects of *encomienda* in 1542. The establishment of this exploitative system five hundred years ago still impacts the poverty of the Maya. This was one of the findings of the Report of the Commission for Historical Clarification; it concludes that:

> the structure and nature of economic, cultural and social relations in Guatemala are marked by profound exclusion, antagonism and conflict—a

reflection of its colonial history. The proclamation of independence in 1821, an event prompted by the country's elite, saw the creation of an authoritarian State which excluded the majority of the population, was racist in its precepts and practices, and served to protect the economic interests of the privileged minority. (n. pag.)

Morrison's estimate of the number killed during Ríos Montt's reign is low (30,000), but in her chapter called "Governing Guatemala" she describes President Álvaro Arzú, who helped reach the Peace Accords in 1996. She writes that "Investigations revealed that 90 percent of human rights abuses during the war had been committed by the army and other government forces. Of the 200,000 who died during the conflict, 80 percent were unarmed Maya men, women, and children" (59). One of the extensions of the definition of genocide in my Introduction is Frank Chalk and Kurt Jonassohn's notion of "one-sided mass killing"; when 80 percent of those killed were unarmed, genocide has occurred.

In his book *Guatemala* (2004), Roger Dendiger begins with a photo of Lake Atitlán and a quotation from Aldous Huxley, who called Guatemala "'the most beautiful place in the world'" (qtd. in Dendiger, 8). Dendiger then describes the landscape, crops, and so on. His reference to the genocide is succinct but fitting:

> Rios Montt's brief presidency was the bloodiest period of the 36-year civil war. Estimates are that nearly 200,000 mostly unarmed indigenous civilians were killed. Although leftist rebels and right-wing death squads also were responsible for assassinations, disappearances, and torture of non-combatants, the majority of human rights violations were carried out by the Guatemalan military. (72)

The book is well-written, with an easy-to-follow design. The inclusion of photographs verifies Huxley's claim that Guatemala is "the most beautiful place in the world."

Crossover Literature

Rigoberta Menchú's *I, Rigoberta Menchú: An Indian Woman in Guatemala*, for which Menchú won the Nobel Peace Prize in 1992, is a highly controversial and misunderstood book. The controversy centers on David Stoll's *Rigoberta Menchú and the Story of All Poor Guatemalans* (1999). Based on his own fieldwork and other sources, Stoll accused Menchú of fabricating certain parts of her story, such as witnessing her brother being burned alive. Menchú was not present when her brother died by gunshot, but she is correct that many Maya were burned alive. Part of the controversy may stem from cultural distinctions regarding what constitutes valid research. Menchú employed *testimonio*, a qualitative research method in which the speaker (Menchú narrated her story to an anthropologist) speaks not only for herself but for her community. Yoly Zentella explains,

> Testimonio is a class specific oral tradition focusing on the *"I"* through which the narrator links the personal to the group experience. It is a Latin American genre with roots in the Maya culture used to make known the urgent political and social situations of the voiceless, poor disenfranchised, and the shunned indigenous, through the words of a narrator from the same group. (321; italics in the original)

Stoll rejects Menchú's *testimonio* and therefore also a generative research method. Zentella continues:

> Taking the inconsistencies of memory and the impact of trauma aside, what needs to be remembered here is that Rigoberta's motivation was to tell her story to the world of the injustices and atrocities leveled on indigenas and to gain international support for their cause. She was not dictating an academic treatise or giving legal testimony—she was *telling* her interpretation of various incidents in her life and generalizing: retracing, re-tracking, correcting, omitting, generalizing, thinking aloud. Coming from the phenomenological perspective she implies truthfulness and expects acknowledgement of the greater issues by the reader . . . . if Rigoberta's narrative, born out of turbulence in Guatemala, is riddled with discrepancies, they are nevertheless portrayals of holocaust[s], screaming for the world to know and to learn from these horrors. (326; italics in original)

In phenomenological research, the goal is to identify the essence of experience, despite "discrepancies." Menchú's autobiography captures the essence of Maya experience.

Her first chapter, "The Family," opens with:

> My name is Rigoberta Menchú. I am twenty-three years old. This is my testimony. I didn't learn it from a book and I didn't learn it alone. I'd like to stress that it's not only *my* life, it's also the testimony of my people. It's hard for me to remember everything that's happened to me in my life since there have been many very bad times but, yes, moments of joy as well. The important thing is that what has happened to me has happened to many other people too: My story is the story of all poor Guatemalans. My personal experience is the reality of a whole people. (1)

Chapters that follow give information on Maya birth ceremonies, which includes the Maya's belief that the child's "protective spirit . . . will go with him" (18).

Although her childhood in her village was an agreeable one, Menchú gradually becomes aware of the injustices in Guatemala. She works as a maid for a time for very little pay, and learns of racist attitudes against the Maya. She writes,

> But we realized in Guatemala there was something superior and something inferior and that *we* were the inferior. The *ladinos* behave like a superior race. Apparently there was a time when the *ladinos* used to think we weren't people at all, but a sort of animal. All this became clear to me. (123; italics in the original)

One night soldiers come to her village, helping themselves to the food in the Maya's gardens. Menchú becomes an activist, working to try to make her village secure from harm, and then other villages as well. Rape is constant; the soldiers frequently impregnate Maya women. One woman told Menchú, "I hate this child inside me. I don't know what to do with it. This child is not mine" (143). Menchú says, "She was very distressed and cried all the time" (143). Because her life is in danger, Menchú escapes to Mexico. Her new goal is to convey the plight of the Maya to the world, which she does through her autobiography. Although she may have exaggerated parts of her personal story, she did not exaggerate what happened to the Maya.

Jonathan Moller's sensitive photographs of the Guatemalan genocide make *Our Culture Is Our Resistance: Repression, Refuge, and Healing in Guatemala* (2004) an accessible text for young adults. Moller is an artist and human rights activist who combined his passion for both during his work in Guatemala from 1993 to 2001. Many of the photographs published in his book are available on his website (http://www.jonathanmoller.org/portfolio1.htm). In 1993, he hiked for two days from Chajul to Cabá, where he lived with a family with four children in a one-room house. He helped to rebuild homes and photographed exhumations of those killed during the 1980s genocide. After Ríos Montt was overthrown, the killings subsided somewhat, but Moller writes that during his time in Guatemala in the 1990s, "Not a day went by that we didn't hear machine-gun fire or mortar and bomb explosions in the jungle" (13).

In addition to photographs, Moller includes the voices of Maya, whose surnames are not included, probably for safety reasons. Manuel writes,

> One by one we left our homes. We left our corn behind in the villages, we left our beans and our animals. No one had the delusion that "I am going to come back and get my things," because we knew clearly that the army had already destroyed them, that we didn't have anything left.
>
> We ended up in the forest, where we ate wild greens we'd never seen before. We had to eat those things out of sheer hunger; hunger is a powerful force. The children whined and cried. The life we led was horrendous. We had to eat roots and fruits off the trees, and many people died from eating unfamiliar foods. (29)

The book may be intolerable for some young people: Moller's photos of the exhumations are extremely graphic, as are many of the passages, such as this description by Noemi:

> Those poor women were crying as they carried their water jugs. Even so, some of the soldiers followed them and raped them when they went to get water. When they went to get water!
> And finally when the soldiers left town, they killed the women. They stuck them in a hole, lit a fire there among there among the garbage, and burned them. Those five women never left that place. (145)

Moller has through his photographs and inclusion of the voices of the Maya combined artistry and activism that bears witness to the genocide in Guatemala.

Iraq

In 1980, President Saddam Hussein declared war on Iran; he wanted Iran's valuable oil fields near the Iraqi border and feared the forces of Ayatollah Ruhollah Khomeini, who had recently overthrown the government of Shah Mohammad Reza Pahlavi. The new government in Iran was a Shi'a Muslim government, and Hussein was a Sunni, like the minority population in Iraq. Iran's new power, Hussein suspected, might incite Shi'as in Iraq to turn against the Sunnis.

Because Hussein's government had never treated them well, some Kurds sided with Iran in the war. In a genocidal scheme called *Anfal*, Hussein retaliated by ordering the Iraqi militia to gas the Kurds; thus more than 180,000 noncombatant Kurds were killed by the end of 1988. In *Iraq's Crime of Genocide: The Anfal Campaign against the Kurds* (1995), Human Rights Watch/Middle East (HRW/ME) writes, "Kurdish rebels had spoken of 4,000 destroyed villages and an estimated 182,000 disappeared persons in 1988 alone" (xv). HRW/ME researchers interviewed 350 people over six months in the Kurdish region of Iraq during the early 1990s to write their report on the genocide. Forensic specialists examined numerous grave sites and HRW/ME accumulated 4 million documents in their research. Of course oil was involved: "[V]ast oil reserves were discovered in the twentieth century on the fringes of their [the Kurds'] ancestral lands" (HRW/ME, 18).

The genocide was about more than oil and retaliation, though; the Kurds had long wanted their own homeland and had been promised it in 1920, in the Treaty of Sèvres, which was never ratified. Although the 1923 Treaty of Lausanne granted homelands to other ethnic groups, the Kurds were left out. Kurds represent close to 20 percent of Iraq's population, about 4 million. Summerfield writes, "The Kurds—comprising 26 million in Turkey, Iraq, Iran, Syria, Armenia and Azerbaijan—are the largest ethnic group in the world without a nation state" (15).

Ironically, the Kurds were, like Hussein, mostly Sunni, but not Arabs. HRW/ME explains, "The Kurds are indisputably a distinct ethnic group, separate from the majority Arab population of Iraq, and they were targeted during the Anfal as Kurds. (Anthropologically, they are an Indo-European people, speaking a language that is related to Persian)" (xvi). Shi'a Muslims are those who believe that after the Prophet Muhammad's death, his son-in-law should have become the leader of Islam; Sunni Muslims are those who believe that after the Prophet Muhammad's death, a devoted follower should have become the leader of Islam.

Although he shared the Sunni religion of the Kurds, Hussein handed them over to his cousin Ali Hassan al-Majid to exterminate.

Problematic Children's and Young Adult Books about the Iraq Genocide

The informational text *Iraq* (2004), by Susan M. Hassig and Laith Muhmood Al Adely, opens with a profile of Iraq's geography. Their sanitized treatment of the marsh Arabs foretells their sanitized treatment of the Kurds: "Near the city of Basra, where the marshy lake Hawr al-Hammar lies south of the Euphrates, many winding waterways form marshlands where Arabs have for a long time lived in reed houses. These marshlands, the largest in the Middle East, shrank drastically in the 1990s" (8). An action requires an actor: Hussein deliberately drained the marshlands so as to drive the marsh Arabs from their homes.

The Kurds are introduced on the next page as living in the northeastern mountains of Iraq: "The Kurds live in the valleys and foothills of the Zagros Mountains where they cultivate the land. The region has some of Iraq's richest oil fields. However, being so remote, the mountains are also a haven for rebels and criminals" (9). From this passage, young readers might equate Kurds with criminals.

The Iraq-Iran war is explained in a sidebar. After Ayatollah Khomeini came to power in 1979, Hussein worried that "Iran would agitate a rebellion among the Shi'a majority in Iraq," and so declared war on Iran, a war that lasted eight years (23). The Kurds, who were the genocidal victims in this war, are not mentioned. Hassig and Al Adely write, "In 1986 the Iraqis used chemical weapons in the war, with devastating results. With increased military aid from the West Iraq gained the upper hand. The Iranians, realizing that the tide of war was turning against them, agreed to a ceasefire in August 1988" (23). As with the marsh Arabs, an action requires an actor; Hussein used chemical weapons against the Kurds. In an informational text on Iraq, such an omission misleads young readers. In a later chapter entitled "Government," the authors describe the sanctions and inspections other countries imposed on Iran, because they suspected:

Saddam Hussein was manufacturing . . . weapons of mass destruction.

These weapons were believed to include a variety of poisons that could be spread through air or water. Although weapons of this sort had been internationally outlawed since World War I, Iraq was known to have used them against Iran and even against its own citizens, the Kurdish people of northern Iraq. (27)

To their credit, the authors acknowledge the heinous crime against the Kurds, but it seems odd that the information is not given earlier. The authors treat the marsh Arabs similarly; young readers must wait thirty-six pages to learn that the attack on the marsh Arabs was deliberate: "After the first Gulf War, Hussein built large dams and canals in the marshlands, which drained large sections of the marshes and left the land parched. Hussein also launched a brutal campaign to drive political opponents out of the marshlands" (44). To make the draining of the marshlands seem like a neutral act in the early pages gives a false impression.

In a chapter called "Iraqis," Hassig and Al Adely describe Arabs, Bedouins, and the Kurds. Although they do not call it *genocide*, they provide more details on Hussein and the Iraqi army's assault on the Kurds, who had formed guerrilla groups in hopes of founding their own independent state in the 1980s: "In 1988 Saddam Hussein retaliated. Iraqi troops flew over Kurdish regions and dumped poisonous gas on some settlements. In just one offensive, over 5,000 Kurds were killed" (55). In contrast, authorities on the Kurdish genocide estimate that 180,000 Kurds were killed. The time line at the end of the book starts at 9000 B.C. and ends at 2003; the Kurdish genocide of the 1980s is not included, a profound omission.

Simon Ponsford's informational text *Iraq* (2008) is thirty-two pages long; it includes maps, photographs, and sidebars. The opening section is "Geography" and the next section is "A Short History," which includes Iraq's origins in Mesopotamia and Islamic influence beginning in 762 A.D. It is a country that has repeatedly been invaded; Mongols, Persians, Turks, and the British have all wanted Iraq's access to the Persian Gulf for economic gain. British colonization began in 1914 and ended in 1932; the British installed a "pro-British king" (7). This, of course, led to "coup after coup" and such turmoil may have paved the way for the tyrant Hussein, who was in power from 1979 to 2003.

Although Ponsford's history is precise and clear, his handling of the Kurdish genocide in Iraq underestimates the number of lives lost. He writes, "In 1988, Hussein led a notorious ethnic-cleansing campaign against the Kurds. He accused the Kurds of helping Iran during the Iran-Iraq War. As a result, Iraqi troops destroyed hundreds of villages and used chemical weapons to kill Kurds, most infamously in the town of Halabjah" (10). In a sidebar called "Know Your Facts," Ponsford continues:

The name of a northern Kurdish town, Halabjah, symbolizes Saddam Hussein's vicious crackdown on the Kurds. During the Iran-Iraq War in the 1980s, some Kurdish fighters helped Iran. Hussein was outraged at what he saw as gross disloyalty to the nation of Iraq, so in 1988, he ordered his soldiers to kill hundreds of ordinary Kurds in Halabjah. They released a colorless poison gas into the air, which caused a horribly painful death. (10)

This description does not begin to capture the enormity of the 180,000 noncombatants killed. Because it is couched under "Know Your Facts," this error is particularly disturbing.

To his credit, Ponsford reveals the complicity of other nations in the Kurdish genocide. He writes, "Hussein used much of Iraq's oil wealth to buy weapons from other countries, including France, Britain, the former Soviet Union, and the U.S. He also bought technology to make chemical weapons, which he later used against his own people" (13). Young people who read this passage might begin to question their own governments' decisions in making possible the arming of Hussein. Ponsford's "Timeline + Basic Facts" at the end of his book does not include the Kurdish genocide of the 1980s; in fact, the Kurds are not mentioned at all.

Recommended Children's and Young Adult Literature about the Kurdish-Iraq Genocide

Informational Texts

The cover, front and back, of Ann Carey Sabbah's book, *Kurds* (2000), features a magnificent photograph of the mountainous area of Iraq inhabited by the Kurds. The blues and greens of the land are in contrast to the war-torn, dry, desert images most of us see on television and other media sources about Iraq. One pattern that emerges in the study of genocide is that victims understandably always love their homeland; the Kurds are no exception. HRW/ME paints an enticing picture:

It is a land of spring flowers and waving fields of wheat, of rushing streams and sudden perilous gorges, of hidden caves and barren rock. Above all, Kurdistan is a land where the rhythm of life is defined by the relation between the people and the mountains. One range after another, the peaks stretch in all directions as far as the eye can travel, the highest of them capped year-round by snow. (17)

The photograph on the cover of Sabbah's book and the photographs within capture the essence of the passage above. Sabbah opens with a chapter called "Who Are the Kurds?":

The Kurds are a group of people who live mainly in a mountainous region of the **Middle East**. This region was once known as Kurdistan. In the first part of the 20th century, a treaty divided Kurdistan, and although the Kurds wanted a country of their own, they became residents of Iraq, Iran, Syria, and Turkey. (5; emphasis in the original)

Although Sabbah could have made more clear that the Kurds had been promised a country of their own and that the promise had been broken, it is useful for young readers to know that the Kurds are a people without a homeland.

The next chapter is called "History of the Kurdish People"; Sabbah writes, "The Kurds probably descended from Indo-European tribes that migrated to the Kurdistan region around 4,000 years ago" (11). This is beneficial to realize; not all inhabitants of the Middle East are Arabs, although most are Muslims, including the Kurds. She observes that during the Crusades, "Muslim Kurds and Arabs united to fight the Christian crusaders" (11) and that the Iraqis who carried out the genocide were once allies of those they killed. Sabbah explains the genocide: "The government of Iraq did not want the Kurds to join their enemy's army, so they attacked several Kurdish villages with poisonous gas. . . . Estimates suggest that 100,000 Kurds have been killed in Iraq since the mid-1970s" (20). Although Sabbah's estimate is low, she is more accurate than other informational texts on the Kurdish-Iraq genocide. And she includes international response, which is missing from other texts. She writes, "Unfortunately nations around the world virtually ignored what had happened. Some were even partially to blame. The United States and other western nations had supplied Iraq with the chemicals used to make the bombs, and Turkey helped deliver them to Iraqi government officials" (18).

John King's *Iraq: Then and Now* (2006) is mostly about the United States-led invasion of Iraq in 2003. He does, nevertheless, include a summary of Iraq's history. King's treatment of the Kurds in Iraq is brief but correct. In the context of his description of the Iraq-Iran war of the 1980s, King writes, "Saddam Hussein also attacked the Kurdish people inside Iraq, some of whom supported Iran" (22), and "In March 1988 Saddam Hussein ordered a chemical attack on Kurds in the northern Iraqi town of Halabja, killing 5,000 people. The United States expressed horror at the act at the time but soon began to support Saddam Hussein once more" (23). Like other recommended texts on the Kurdish genocide, King includes U.S. complicity; the U.S. and other western countries sided with Iraq in the Iraq-Iran War of the 1980s. In a sidebar entitled "Saddam's Murderous Regime," he writes, "Roughly 180,000 Kurds died in 1988 when they were suspected of cooperating with Iran" (33). King's estimation is consistent with researchers' estimates of the number of those who died.

Heather Wagner's *The Kurds* (2003) is a meticulous treatment of the Kurds' history and life in Turkey, Iraq, and Iran. She opens her chapter on the Kurds in Iraq with:

On April 15, 1987, the war between Iran and Iraq that had polarized much of the Middle East entered a new phase. On that date, a formation of Iraqi planes targeted 13 towns and villages, dropping lethal loads of mustard gas on the helpless population below. By the end of the month, some 30 towns had been similarly targeted, and by the middle of the year, Iraqi planes were dropping chemical weapons on their targets on a daily basis.

These chemical weapons produced horrifying numbers of casualties during their use from 1987 to 1988. But the casualties were not Iranians. The population that Saddam Hussein had targeted, the citizens upon whom his chemical weapons were dropping, were his own people. Or, more specifically, they were Kurds. (69)

Besides those killed, Wagner points out that "more than one-and-a half million Kurds" were displaced (71). Her account of the historical events that led up to the genocide is thorough, including the broken promises to the Kurds that they could have a nation of their own. Wagner brings in the world's indifference to the genocide:

The pleas of the Kurds—to the United Nations, to other world leaders—were largely ignored. The promises the Kurdish forces had received, particularly for American assistance, were empty. The U.S. was more interested in taking advantage of the Iran/Iraq conflict to thwart the influence of the Soviet Union in the region. (91)

Keith Trego is the cover and series designer and has done excellent work with Wagner's text. The background of the title page reflects Islamic geometric designs, and the initial letter at the beginning of each chapter is in the style of the rubrications that originated with Muslims. There are many photographs, which are also framed with geometric designs. Of the books I have read for children and young adults on genocide, *The Kurds* is the best designed.

Conclusion

The 1980s were a terrible time of suffering for the Maya of Guatemala and the Kurds in Iraq. That their plight was ignored by the international community makes the atrocities committed by the Guatemalan and Iraqi governments doubly atrocious. Books for children and young adults that romanticize, minimize, and omit the genocides of the Maya and the Kurds are better left unwritten.

Works Cited

Dalal, Anita. *Guatemala*. Danbury, CT: Grolier, 1999. Fiesta Ser.
Falla, Ricardo. *Massacres in the Jungle: Ixcán, Guatemala, 1975–1982*. Boulder, CO: Westview, 1994.

Goldman, Francisco. "Footprints in History: A Documentary of Remembrance." Moller, 93–95.

Hassig, Susan M., and Laith Muhmood Al Adely. *Iraq*. New York: Cavendish, 2004. Cultures of the World Ser.

Human Rights Watch/Middle East. *Iraq's Crime of Genocide: The Anfal Campaign against the Kurds*. New Haven: Yale UP, 1995.

Mikaelsen, Ben. *Tree Girl*. New York: HarperCollins, 2004.

Moller, Jonathan (Photographer). *Our Culture Is Our Resistance: Repression, Refuge, and Healing in Guatemala*. New York: powerHouse, 2004.

Montejo, Victor. *Voices from Exile: Violence and Survival in Modern Maya History*. Norman: U of Oklahoma P, 1999.

Ponsford, Simon. *Iraq*. North Mankato, MN: Smart Apple, 2008. Countries in the News Ser.

Report of the Commission for Historical Clarification. "Guatemala: Memory of Silence." 5 Feb. 1997. Web. 30 Mar. 2013. <http://shr.aaas.org/guatemala/ceh/report/english/toc.html>

Sanford, Victoria. *Buried Secrets: Truth and Human Rights in Guatemala*. New York: Macmillan, 2003.

Sheehan, Sean, and Magdalene Koh. *Guatemala*. New York: Cavendish, 1998. Cultures of the World Ser.

Shields, Charles J. *Guatemala*. Philadelphia: Mason Crest, 2003. Discovering Central America Ser.

Stoll, David. *Rigoberta Menchú and the Story of All Poor Guatemalans*. Boulder: Westview, 1999.

Summerfield, Derek. "The Social Experience of War and Some Issues for the Humanitarian Field." *Rethinking the Trauma of War*. Eds. Patrick J. Bracken and Celia Petty. London: Free Association /Save the Children, 1998. 9–37.

When the Mountains Tremble. Dir. Thomas Sigel Newton and Pamela Yates. Perf. Rigoberta Menchú. Skylight Pictures. 1983. Film.

Zentella, Yoly. "Review Essay: Speaking from the I: Testimonio, Credibility and Indigena Rights." *Journal of Third World Studies* 28.1 (2011): 321–328.

Recommended Children's and Young Adult Literature about the Guatemalan Genocide

Ashabranner, Brent, and Paul Conklin (Photographer). *Children of the Maya: A Guatemalan Indian Odyssey*. New York: Dodd, 1986.

Dendiger, Roger E. *Guatemala*. Philadelphia: Chelsea, 2004. Modern World Nations Ser.

Menchú, Rigoberta, with Dante Liano, and Domi (Illus.). *The Girl from Chimel*. Trans. David Unger. Toronto: Groundwood, 2005.

Morrison, Marion. *Guatemala*. New York: Scholastic, 2005. Enchantment of the World Ser.

Recommended with Reservations: Children's and Young Adult Literature about the Guatemalan Genocide

Brill, Marlene Targ, and Harry R. Targ. *Guatemala*. Chicago: Children's Book, 1993. Enchantment of the World Ser.

Croy, Anita. *Guatemala*. Washington, DC: National Geographic, 2009. Countries of the World Ser.

Dahl, Michael. *Guatemala*. Mankato, MN: Bridgestone, 1998. Countries of the World Ser.

Recommended Crossover Literature about the Guatemalan Genocide

Menchú, Rigoberta. *I, Rigoberta Menchú: An Indian Woman in Guatemala*. Trans. Ann Wright. London: Verso, 1984.

Moller, Jonathan (Photographer). *Our Culture Is Our Resistance: Repression, Refuge, and Healing in Guatemala*. New York: powerHouse, 2004.

Recommended Children's and Young Adult
Literature about the Kurdish-Iraq Genocide

King, John. *Iraq: Then and Now.* Chicago: Raintree, 2006. The Middle East Ser.
Sabbah, Ann Carey. *Kurds.* Mankato, MN: Smart Apple, 2000.
Wagner, Heather Lehr. *The Kurds.* Philadelphia: Chelsea, 2003. Creation of the Modern Middle
    East Ser.

Chapter Three
Children's and Young Adult Literature of Bosnia-Herzegovina and Kosovo

I often ask myself why I stayed alive when thousands of children were brutally killed. There is no answer. I know that nothing can bring them back, but only forgetting would make them truly dead. They will live in my heart and in the following pages as long as I live and share their stories.

—Nadja Halilbegovich

In April 1992, full-scale war came to Bosnia-Herzegovina. Led by Serbian President Slobodan Milošević and Bosnian Serb leader Radovan Karadzic, Serbian nationalists slaughtered approximately 300,000 Bosnian Muslims, including thousands of children, in three years. Ratko Mladic, a Bosnian Serb, ordered in July of 1995 the execution of 8,000 Muslim men and boys in the United Nations-designated safe haven area of Srebrenica. Serbian nationalists killed 10,000 Albanians in 1999 in the province of Kosovo, which was 90 percent Albanian. In Bosnia-Herzegovina and Kosovo, most of those slaughtered were unarmed. Rape, seemingly always a part of war, was especially prevalent in the Balkans. Sabina Subašić Galaijatović estimates there were 20,000 rapes, including those of young girls, which is consistent with government reports. About 3 million persons were displaced (Ramet 300).

As in most wars, there were atrocities on all sides. In this war, the aggression against Bosnia-Herzegovina and the atrocities against Bosnian Muslims came mostly from the Serbian nationalists and criminals released from prison. This is not to say all Serbs supported the assault on Bosnian Muslims; many protested and others actively protected those under attack. In *Surviving the Bosnian Genocide: The Women of Srebrenica Speak* (2011), Dutch historian Selma Leydesdorff, who interviewed sixty Muslim women of Srebrenica, writes,

Evil became so commonplace that the perpetrator thought nothing of it. The lust for murder was so strong that resistance seemed futile, yet a few did resist. There is the story of the man who let an old acquaintance escape, thus putting himself in danger. At the beginning of the war, there were many stories of Serb neighbors who shared food supplies, helped with an escape, or even hid friends, despite the danger. (12)

Speaking with and to Bosnians and Bosnian Scholars

At the International Network of Genocide Scholars' conference in 2010, I attended sessions led by genocide scholars from Sarajevo. Merisa Karović and I discussed her work; she, Smail Čekić, Muhamed Šestanović, and Zilha Mastalić-Košuta were completing *Zločini nad djecome Sarajeva u opsadi* (*Crimes against Children in the Siege of Sarajevo*) (2010), an 867-page book documenting the fate of every child killed during the siege of Sarajevo. Merisa invited me to Sarajevo, and with the help of a Children's Literature Association Faculty Research grant, I went to Bosnia in the summer of 2011. The name *Bosnia* typically refers to the central and northern parts of the country, while *Herzegovina* refers to the southern part; Bosnia and Herzegovina are usually shortened to *Bosnia*, which I do here as well.

Flying from the north across Croatia into Bosnia, the folds and dips of the green Dinaric mountains and hills lead a windy path down into Sarajevo. A low-flying pilot would be much challenged to navigate the dramatic shifts, made all the more challenging by the distractions of the sheer beauty and majesty of the landscape and the small, colorful towns nestled in almost inaccessible places. I could see why the Illyrians, Romans, Ottomans, Austro-Hungarians, and, in the 1990s, Serbian nationalists wanted to invade Bosnia, a stunningly picturesque country.

Sarajevo, built on both sides of the Miljacka River, is also surrounded by magnificent mountains. The architecture reflects past invasions: In the old city, mosques, synagogues, Eastern Orthodox churches, and Roman Catholic churches stand side by side. Sadly, many of the buildings are pockmarked, evidence of the shelling from the longest siege in history, the Serbian siege of Sarajevo, 1992–1995. The Jews, it should be noted, did not invade Bosnia; Sephardic Jews came there peacefully when Spain evicted them from the Iberian peninsula in the fifteenth century.

Prior to my arrival in Sarajevo, I sent ten books about the Bosnian genocide written for young people to the Institut za istraživanje zločina protiv čovječnosti i međunarodnog prava (Institute for Research of Crimes against Humanity and International Law) at the University of Sarajevo and brought seven more with me; those with whom I met gave me at least as many academic books to bring home. Smail Čekić, the director of the Institute, was my host; also present were Zilha Mastalić-Košuta, whose specialty is the study of children affected by the genocide; Muhamed Šestanović, a psychologist; and Enis Omerović, whose field is international law and who kindly translated for me.

Professor Čekić began our discussion of the damage done to children during the siege of Sarajevo, the longest siege in history, saying that it had "a very hard impact on the mental integrity of children." Professor Šestanović added that the incidence of posttraumatic stress disorder was 350 times higher during the war than in peacetime. Sarajevans fought against what they knew would be adverse effects on children by organizing schools in basements—Serbian snipers targeted school buildings—and educational and art activities, which are reflected in the autobiographies of children who grew up in Sarajevo from 1992 to 1995; the children write about their efforts to continue their learning and to create art. Zilha described children organizing themselves to do creative work in music, TV shows, radio, plays, and journals—whatever they could do to lift their morale.

Čekić discussed the history of the Balkans and the profound shift that occurred in the 1980s, when Serbian nationalists advanced the idea of a Great Serbian state, which would mean taking land from Bosnia and other Balkan countries. Bosnia, he said, had "no military units." It was clear from our discussion that, as stated in my Introduction in the extensions to the definition of genocide, Bosnian Muslims, who call themselves Bosniaks, were subject to a one-sided form of mass killing and were defenseless. The extraordinarily high rate of rape surely fell out of the recognized conventions of warfare, another of the extensions of the definition of genocide as described in my Introduction.

Since the genocide in the 1990s, at least thirty books for young people in a variety of genres have been published. Although most of these publications are accurate, authentic, and have at least some literary quality, a few of the texts are problematic. Some of the issues are:

- Presenting the genocide, because of long-standing ethnic rivalries, as inevitable, which oversimplifies and underestimates the role Slobodan Milošević played in manipulating the media, provoking violence, and recruiting thugs from Belgrade's underworld to carry out his genocidal plans.
- Underestimating the role of Serbian nationalism. Although there were Serbs who protested Milošević's tyranny, there was also a strong belief among Serbs that they, echoing a half century later the Nazi notion of *lebensraum*, had the right to take land from Slovenia, Croatia, Bosnia, and Kosovo, and to force inhabitants of those countries to leave their homes.
- Ignoring the ethnic tolerance that had long prevailed in Bosnia and especially Sarajevo—a tolerance travelers had documented for centuries.
- Treating the genocide in Bosnia as a civil war, which it was not, because Bosniaks were, for the most part, unarmed, and because Bosnia became a sovereign and international independent state on April 6, 1992.
- Ignoring the crime of aggression, which, as Enis explains, is "when one state attacks another state"; "the armed attack of the Yugoslav People's

Army, which . . . commenced on the territory of Bosnia." (Omerović, "My Comments and Suggestions")

Authors of some of the books also cast southern Slavs, in Edward Said's conception, as "the Other"—more violent, more uncontrollable than "civilized" northern Europeans and North Americans, despite the ugly, violent histories of these latter groups that include the Holocaust, the genocide of American Indians, the Middle Passage, and enslavement of Africans.

It should be noted that the Muslims, Croats, and Serbs are all considered "South Slavs." They are descended from the Slavs who migrated from the north (Poland and Russia) to the Balkan countries centuries ago. Under Rome's influence, some became Roman Catholics—mostly Croats. Under Ottoman influence, some became Muslims—mostly Bosnians. Some became Eastern Orthodox— mostly Serbs. But their common ancestral roots are in northern Slavic areas, and they lived side by side in the republics that made up the former Yugoslavia.

Problematic Children's and Young Adult Books about the Bosnia and Kosovo Genocides

The Genocide Was Not a Case of Spontaneous Combustion and Was Not Inevitable; Slobodan Milošević's Role Cannot Be Underestimated

As with Cambodia, the Bosnian genocide was not unavoidable and did not automatically explode. Several books for young readers contribute to the notion that the genocide was inevitable and a fuse ready to ignite.

JoAnn Milivojevic's *Bosnia and Herzegovina* (2004) is an informational text for young readers. The book contains photographs of this beautiful country, is well designed, and is reliable in some places; however, she misrepresents the conflict and ignores Milošević's central role in setting the genocide in motion. She writes,

> When Bosnia declared independence and the European Community recognized it as such in March 1992, Serbs, Croats, and Bosnian Muslims went to war.
>
> For three years the groups fought over Bosnia. War destroyed many of the buildings, homes, mosques, and churches of Bosnia. Croat and Serbian military groups within Bosnia sided with their nations, while the Muslims were divided between the two. At times, Croats and Serbs worked together to rid Bosnia of Muslims; at other times, Serbs and Muslims worked together to push Croats out. The Serbs had the power of the Yugoslav army behind them—at one time, the Serbs occupied nearly 70 percent of Bosnia.
>
> The war was tragic for everyone in Bosnia. The country was heavily bombed. The horrors that were committed against civilians led to

criminal indictments. The United Nations charged military leaders with crimes against humanity. More than 250,000 people had died and 1.8 million were displaced. (50–51)

To correct one inaccuracy, Bosnia declared independence in April, not in March; far more important, Milivojevic's use of the passive voice could mislead young readers into thinking it was a Balkan free-for-all when it was not. Bosniaks had no bombs and few arms; the Serbs, for the most part, were the ones who bombed and shelled. In 1991 the United Nations imposed an arms embargo on the entire region, which essentially ensured the victory of Serbia. The International Criminal Tribunal for the former Yugoslavia has, so far, indicted "forty-six Serbs, eight Bosnian Croats, and three Bosnian Muslims" (Reger 71).

The most aggressive Serb of all was the president of Serbia, Slobodan Milošević. Warren Zimmerman, U.S. ambassador to Yugoslavia during the time of the war, wrote: "'I have no doubt that if Milosevic's parents had committed suicide before his birth rather than after, I would not be writing a cable about the death of Yugoslavia. Milosevic, more than anyone else, is its gravedigger'" (qtd. in Power, 268). Louis Sell, a Milošević biographer, agrees:

> The Yugoslavia that Milosevic destroyed was not inevitably doomed to disappear. Despite its deepening problems, Yugoslavia in the mid-1980s was a functioning multiethnic society. Few Yugoslavs either wanted or expected the country to disintegrate until shortly before the end. (33)

Milošević maliciously drew from the "Serbian criminal underworld . . . the roughest elements . . . motivated as much by the thrill of violence and the prospect of loot as by attachment to the Serbian cause" (Sell 325). Like Pol Pot and his small circle of butchers, Milošević had his own small circle of butchers. Political scientist René Lemarchand writes, "The chief planner and orchestrator was President Milosevic himself, assisted by a handful of cronies among high-ranking officers of the federal army and the Ministry of the Interior" (163). And, as in Cambodia, artists and intellectuals were the first to be killed. Samantha Power—who was a journalist in Bosnia during the time of the genocide—writes: "Bosnian Serb soldiers and militiamen had compiled lists of leading Muslim and Croat intellectuals, musicians, and professionals"; after the dissolution of the former Yugoslavia, "they began to round up non-Serbs, savagely beating them, and often executing them. Bosnian Serb units destroyed most cultural and religious sites in order to erase any memory of a Muslim or Croat in what they would call 'Republika Srpska'" (249).

Milošević deliberately manipulated what he knew the world's perception would be—that the conflict in Bosnia was inevitable because of ancient ethnic hatreds and that the problems arose from within its borders. Noel Malcolm explains this was:

the myth which was carefully propagated by those who caused the conflict, who wanted the world to believe that what they and their gunmen were doing was done not by them, but by impersonal and inevitable historical forces beyond anyone's control. (xix)

The Milošević-controlled media in Belgrade promulgated a steady stream of propaganda to fellow Serbs and to the Western world. The Yugoslav Army conducted a study in 1991 to predict what the West's response to the invasion of Bosnia would be. Milan Radković reported that:

> there was little reason to expect international armed intervention in Yugoslavia. That conclusion was based on the recognition that the EC countries, throughout the Western European Union, could not engage in meaningful military operations without U.S. support, which, because the United States was not significantly involved, was lacking. (qtd. in Ramet, 245)

Although Milivojevic recognizes that the Serbs had access to the full force of the Yugoslav army, she does little to help young readers understand the defenselessness of those who were unarmed. As mentioned in my Introduction, Jack Nusan Porter adds to the definition of genocide "ideology and technology"; Serbian nationalists had the fascist ideology as well as the technology to carry out genocide.

John Isaac and Keith Greenberg's *Bosnia: Civil War in Europe* (1997) is also an informational text. Isaac was a United Nations photographer in Bosnia, which lends him a questionable credibility; he shared with Greenberg in the writing of the text. Both mislead young readers. In a very short book, Isaac chooses to quote President William Clinton, who said in a speech on Bosnia: "One thing I am convinced of is that there is a global hunger among young people for their parents to put down the madness of war" (26). It was hardly possible for unarmed Bosnian Muslims to put down the madness of war; those living in Sarajevo did not choose to have Serb snipers perched on their hills and mountains pounding them with shells day after day and night after night for 3.5 years. Sarajevan writer and resident Dzevad Karahasan says, "They shot at us with their heaviest artillery shells. During the first few months of war, they usually opened fire at night, so that we were dazed all day long with sleepiness and fatigue" (25). Sleeplessness added to the torturous conditions.

Bosnian Muslims did not choose to have their wives and daughters raped. Power writes of "a nine-year-old Muslim girl who had been raped by Serb militiamen and left lying in a pool of blood for two days while her parents watched, from behind a fence, as she died" (265). No parent chooses this; no parent ever chooses this. "Serbs," writes Peter Maass, "carried out 90 percent of the acts of ethnic cleansing in Bosnia"; the guilt cannot be evenly divided (32–33).

Greenberg explains to child readers, "The term 'ethnic cleansing' made head-lines during the Bosnian war. The process meant that one group was driven from an area, while a rival group moved in. The new rulers said the region was 'cleansed' of the old residents" (10). This explanation suggests that ethnic cleansing was occurring equally on all sides, akin to making a claim that Jews ethnically cleansed Nazis during World War II. Greenberg later acknowledges that the Serbs were the first to create concentration camps since World War II. And, as Enis notes, "the title of their book is factually wrong. There was no civil war in Bosnia" (Omerović, "My Comments and Suggestions").

Similarly, Eric Black opens his informational text *Bosnia: Fractured Region* (1999) with,

> From 1992 to 1995, Bosnia . . . was engulfed by a war that claimed the lives of more than 250,000 people. The conflict forced more than two million people from their homes. Atrocities—including mass murder and rape—were committed on a scale not seen in Europe since World War II. (10)

The use of the passive voice could confuse young readers, who must wait twenty pages to read: "Bosnian Serb forces used murder, rape, and terror to drive Bosnian Croats and people of mixed heritage out of the town to make these areas ethnically uniform" (20). If children are old enough to read about "mass murder and rape" on the first page, they are old enough to also read on the first page that, instigated by Slobodan Milošević and his thugs, the situation in Bosnia was, for the most part, what Frank Chalk and Kurt Jonassohn, cited in my Introduction, call a "one-sided mass killing." Authors of children's and young adult literature on genocide do not serve their readers well by pro-moting stereotypes and avoiding the truth.

Bosnia Had a History of Tolerance

Bosnia, Sarajevo especially, had long been recognized as a model of multi-cultural tolerance. Malcolm, in his *Bosnia: A Short History* (1994), tells of an American who visited Sarajevo in the 1920s. The American wrote:

> Here one sees the Bosnian peasant of Orthodox faith drop his contribu-tion into the cup of a blind Mussulman who squats, playing his *goussle*, at the entrance of a mosque. Glancing at the peaceful little stalls where Christians, Mussulmans and Jews mingle in business, while each goes his own way to cathedral, mosque or synagogue, I wondered if tolerance is not . . . the greatest virtue. (qtd. in Malcolm, 168; italics in the original)

During the 1930s, journalist John Bibbons observed "'the oddest thing of all . . . seemed to me the way in which they all fitted in so perfectly happily with each other'" (qtd. in Malcolm, 168). Malcolm provides similar accounts from both French and Turkish travelers to Sarajevo in the seventeenth century. Marriage between Serbs, Croats, and Bosniaks was common; in the 1990s, close to one third of the population intermarried. In her fieldwork in Srebrenica, Leydesdorff encountered similar views and writes, "The aggression was in sharp contrast to the years of peaceful coexistence that preceded it" (21). A Muslim woman, Fikreta, told Leydesdorff, "'You knew from the names; if you said a name, then you knew if they were Serb or Bosniak. Usually you knew, but nobody cared. It was just—warm and sociable'" (qtd. in Leydesdorff, 36). A resident of Srebrenica, Hatidža Mehmedović, said, "'We had a healthy environment, very healthy. But it couldn't stay that way, someone had to destroy Yugoslavia and bring us this poverty, make us poor, so that now we get crumbs and wait for packages'" (qtd. in Leydesdorff, 40–41).

In his informational text *War in Yugoslavia: The Breakup of a Nation* (1993), Edward Ricciuti ignores Bosnia's past. He opens with "During the summer of 1991, deep-seated ethnic hatreds erupted into a brutal and widespread war" (5), and later, "ethnic hatreds had brewed for many years. When they finally exploded, they exploded with great force and brutality" (6). Ricciuti continues the trope: "They are not new enemies. Their animosity is rooted deep in the past" (6), and they have "historically been enemies, or have at least intensely disliked each other" (6). These statements do not recognize their shared northern Slavic heritage. His assertion that "[r]eligious and ethnic differences combined with a history of oppression created enemies for generations" (13) belies the mutual harmony that had existed before Milošević and his nationalist followers appeared. Yet after titillating his readers with inflammatory and ignorant language—with such words as "exploded" and "brutal"—he later says, "[a]lthough there were tensions, many Yugoslavians of different ethnic groups lived side by side without trouble for many years. Often they were good neighbors" (8). Ricciuti should have started here. Far better, then, had he explained that, after World War II, Yugoslavia was cobbled together—consisting of Slovenia, Croatia, Bosnia and Herzegovina, Serbia, Macedonia, and Montenegro—and held collectively by Marshall Tito until his death in 1980. After Tito's death, Milošević made power grabs and ruthlessly destroyed political opponents, including Ivan Stambolić, his own mentor. Slovenia, in 1991, was the first to declare its independence from Yugoslavia; the Serbs briefly fought the Slovenes but were defeated. The same year Croatia declared its independence; the war there was worse there than in Slovenia, with Serbs pounding the ancient city of Dubrovnik, which Lord Byron had called the "pearl of the Adriatic." Bosniaks did not know what to do; Bosniak President Alija Izetbegović appealed to international leaders, and with their blessing declared independence. Having lost Slovenia and Croatia, Milošević savagely responded. Ricciuti would have done better to recognize the source of the aggression and the ideological—not religious—motive.

Greenberg also disregards the religious tolerance that had long prevailed in Bosnia and oversimplifies his message to young readers, "Because of this one issue, individuals with so much in common have grown to hate each other" (13). Another informational text is Douglas Phillips's *Bosnia and Herzegovina* (2004). He naïvely asks and answers, "Why . . . the tragic divisions? Religious differences and extreme nationalism offer the most apparent answers to this question" (9). The information here is partly right ("extreme nationalism"), and partly wrong ("religious differences"). Here, he is mostly wrong: "Leaders of Croats, Serbs, and Bosniaks had cruelly constructed towering walls of nationalism" (97). With no weapons and no army, Bosniaks could hardly construct towering walls of any kind.

In his book *Sarajevo, Exodus of a City* (1993), Karahasan explains Serbian writers' and intellectuals' role in the growth of extreme Serbian nationalism. Traditional sayings of Muhammad, writes Karahasan, express:

> that it is a fundamental sin to say that there is no God, and that a man who utters that statement is capable of doing anything. The same rule applies: after having committed a fundamental sin, this literature behaves as if it is allowed to do anything. And so it calls upon people to burn children to death (Djura Jaksić); it creates a mother who offers to a revolution that had already taken three of her sons as many more sons as it might need (Skender Kulenović); it calls for a final showdown with people of a different faith, or explains that all evil that befalls a collective comes from another collective (Slobodan Selenić). (83–84)

Karahasan demonstrates that these Serb authors, and others, used literature for the "production of evil" (84). Karahasan adds Dobrica Ćosić to this list of extremists, and political scientist Sabrina Ramet agrees, saying that Ćosić's *Vreme smrti* (*A Time of Death*) was one of two novels that, more than any other "defined the new mood of Serbia in the 1980s, a mood that was increasingly self-absorbed, self-righteous, and self-pitying" (199). Ćosić wrote:

> Brave men will fight for love but, driven by hatred, all men will fight. In times of storms and tempests which pull up a nation's roots and destroy a man inside his own skin, hatred is the force which gathers and unites all energies, the force of great evil. . . . With hatred there's nothing a man dare not do, no limit to his endurance. (qtd. in Ramet, 200)

Čekić also calls Ćosić "deeply affiliated with the project of the destruction of Yugoslavia" (*Aggression* 223).

By these observations on the role of Serbian literature in shaping Serbian nationalism during the 1980s, I am reminded of Terry Eagleton's challenge, in *Literary Theory: An Introduction* (1983), to those prone to believe (as I once was and occasionally still am) that literature in and of itself is a good thing. He writes:

[W]hy read literature? The answer, in a nutshell, was that it made you a better person. . . . When the Allied troops moved into the concentration camps . . . to arrest commandants who had whiled away their leisure hours with a volume of Goethe, it appeared that someone had some explaining to do. (35)

Nor did Serbian novelists make Serbian nationalists better people. Instead, writers advanced Milošević's agenda, and those who write about the genocide need to understand the context of Serbia in the 1980s.

Phillips does not use the word *genocide*, which evades the issue. In describing the future of Bosnia, he patronizes Bosniaks, saying, "This means that to get a good job a Bosnian . . . would need to get along with others from different religious and cultural backgrounds" (97). This condescending statement disregards that Bosniaks have had a long history of getting along with others from different religious and cultural backgrounds.

What Happened in Bosnia Was Not a Civil War

Another problem with some of the informational texts is the authors calling what happened in Bosnia a civil war. It was not a civil war; Bosniaks had few arms and no army. The fighting they did was, for the most part, to defend themselves against Serbian and, in the Mostar area, Croatian aggressors. Mostar is close to the Adriatic; Bosnia has twelve miles of the very valuable coastline—very valuable because of its appeal to people all over the world, especially Europeans, as a vacation destination. Bosniaks had to defend the mere twelve miles of spectacular coastline that they had.

The United Nations arms embargo of 1991 did not affect the Serbs, who had the entire Yugoslav army and its materiel at their disposal. In Sarajevo, Karahasan writes,

The citizens . . . met the attack on the city entirely unprepared because they did not believe that an army that has constantly been telling them it is theirs (the people's) will turn against them; although there were those who knew that after that army's attack on Croatia there would be an attack on Bosnia. But even these people met the terror without sandbags piled up in front of basement windows, because it was extremely dangerous to make visible war preparations. (28)

The embargo enabled Serbia's agenda, helping it to succeed (Ramet 245).

In *Bosnia-Herzegovina in Pictures* (2007), part of the Visual Geography Series, Mary Englar writes, "The worst of the violence came in Bosnia, where ethnic Serbs, Bosniaks (Bosnian Muslims), and ethnic Croats battled for power. News reports exposed 'ethnic cleansing' and mass graves. Photos showed gaunt war prisoners behind barbed wire fences" (4). An action requires an actor—it was Serb nationalists who surrounded Sarajevo and Serb nationalists who placed prisoners behind barbed wire. Better that Englar start her book thirty pages later:

> The Bosnian Serbs took over any land they claimed as Serb homeland. Groups of Serb soldiers forced Bosniaks and Croats from the villages and countryside in the areas the Serbs wanted. In just one month, more than 275,000 people had to flee their homes. The Serbs also set siege to Sarajevo. For the next four years, Serb mortars placed on the hills around the city continually bombarded Sarajevo. . . . By the summer of 1992, Bosnian Serb forces controlled almost two-thirds of Bosnia. (34)

Enis writes,

> Slobodan Milosevic was a formal leader and President of Serbia, which belonged to a different state during the aggression against Bosnia. Furthermore, legally, there is an issue when using the term ethnic cleansing as this is not a legal term but a term with the aim to describe the situation on the ground. Instead, I prefer to use crimes against humanity, genocide or even war crimes to ethnic cleansing. (Omerović, "My Comments and Suggestions")

Recommended with Reservations: Children's and Young Adult Literature about the Bosnia and Genocide

Jacqueline Ching's informational text, *Genocide and the Bosnian War* (2009), rightly portrays the tolerance that had long prevailed in Bosnia: "Towns in Bosnia were typically mixed communities. Bosnian Serbs, Bosnian Croats, and Bosnian Muslims were friends and neighbors. They even intermarried" (10). Karahasan confirms both the friendliness and intermarriage; upon hearing of Cyrus Vance's proposal to partition Sarajevo, Karahasan asked,

> How could you possibly divide that? . . . If Sarajevo were to be divided, I could not have a bath because the tub would remain in the Serb province of my wife; my Serb wife could not wash her face, though, because the washbasin would remain in my province. The same goes for nine out of ten apartments in our building. I am afraid that could be complicated even for such an able divider as Mr. Cyrus Vance. (47)

Ching also includes the infamous event that occurred on April 6, 1992: Serb snipers stood atop the Holiday Inn in downtown Sarajevo and fired on a "crowd of peaceful demonstrators" (27). Ching judiciously points out that the crowd included Bosnian Serbs; there were Serbs who protested Milošević's brutal policies both in Bosnia and in Belgrade. In 1992, Ramet writes, "30,000 Serbs staged an opposition in Belgrade, demanding Milošević's resignation" (201), and the Serbian Academy of Arts and Sciences supported this demand.

Because the book was published in 2009, Ching is able to include more recent information, such as the Mothers of Srebrenica lawsuit against the United Nations and the Netherlands for failing to stop the massacre in 1995 in Srebrenica, a supposed safe haven. She also mentions that the Serbian government "offered a $1.4 million reward" for Mladic (48); Mladic was apprehended in 2011. The reward shows a good-faith effort of the new government in Serbia to punish those most responsible for the genocide.

Questionable is Ching's assertion that:

> At least fifteen million Native Americans died during the European colonization of the Americas (1500s–1900). An estimated sixty million Africans died during the African slave trade (1600s–1900s). Some seventy million died in China under Mao Tse-tung's leadership. All of these events involved barbaric acts, but none of them is usually described as genocide. (6)

American Indians do indeed refer to the arrival of the Europeans and their subsequent efforts to destroy indigenous peoples as "genocide," and many African Americans describe the Middle Passage as genocide; googling *African Holocaust* results in 116,000 hits. Ching might better have kept her focus on Bosnia.

David Flint's *Bosnia: Can There Ever Be Peace?* (1996), an informational text with a newspaper format, acknowledges the Serbian aggression during the siege of Sarajevo, the centrality of Milošević's role in Yugoslavia's collapse, that the Serbs controlled the Yugoslavian army, and that Bosniaks did not have the arms with which to fight. Flint's position on whether the genocide was inevitable—I believe it was not—is ambiguous. He writes, "Conflict is not new to the peoples of Bosnia. The crisis in the 1990s stems from rivalries and loyalties that are centuries old. Differences in religion and of historical circumstances combine to create a region where war has been all too common" (9). It is doubtful that war has been less common in Europe, the Americas, or almost any other region compared with the Balkans. As Peter Maass writes, "there is no difference in the cruelty sweepstakes; it is a dead heat" (50). Later in the text, Flint more truthfully writes, "Although there were tensions, the different peoples of Bosnia coexisted peacefully. Muslim families enjoyed good relations with their Serb and Croat neighbors" (19).

Flint's title, *Bosnia: Can There Ever Be Peace?* as well as an ending sentence, "UN expert and local commanders doubt they will achieve a lasting peace settlement in Bosnia in the near future," are also problematic (31). Why Flint or United Nations experts would doubt that there could ever be peace in Bosnia is like wondering if there can be peace almost anywhere. And in hindsight—the book was published in 1996—Flint was too pessimistic. Although there are still tensions in Bosnia—as there are in nations all over the world—Bosnians try to remain confident about their future. The young man who ran our hotel in Sarajevo told us of his recent pleasant vacation in Belgrade. As a Muslim he felt welcome in Belgrade and plans to go back. Flint might have ended his book on a more hopeful note.

In her book *Teenage Refugees from Bosnia-Herzegovina Speak Out* (1997), Valerie Tekavec gives voice to those who are often not heard: young people from the region. To write her book, she interviewed those who immigrated to North America during the war, and she makes the effort to include Croats, Bosniaks, and Serbs. Reflected is the tolerance that had mostly prevailed in Bosnia until Milošević and his henchmen set their genocidal agenda. Enisa, a Bosniak who moved to New York City, says movingly and metaphorically of her country, "But I had my America there. I was so happy . . . I never even knew if some of my friends were Serbs or Croats" (13). Lamija is a political refugee now living in Idaho. Because her father is "a major political figure" in Bosnia for Muslims, Lamija's parents thought she would be safer out of the country. Lamija writes:

> I like the United States pretty much. It was kind of hard at the beginning, all the new people and everything. But now I have some pretty good friends, and that makes me feel better.
>
> Sometimes people here can be annoying because they don't even know where Bosnia is. Or they ask me stupid questions like, "Do you have candy in Bosnia? Do you have houses?" Most American teenagers don't understand that we had absolutely the same life they do. (41)

Lamija's feelings show the provincialism of the West and the assumptions that are often made about "the Other." Ljubica, a Serbian teen who moved to Virginia, writes of his culture and religion:

> My people have a lot to offer me. We have a very rich culture. We're very intelligent people. And we're very good-hearted, even though we're getting this bad rap right now. We have children, we love our children. We go to church, we listen to music. We are people, but we're being portrayed as animals. (23)

It has to be acknowledged that many Serbians did not support the Serbian nationalists, as Ljubica notes. Of concern is Tekavec's introduction. She writes,

> The tactics used by Croats, Muslims, and Serbs were horrific in their cruelty and disregard for human life. Prisoners were put in concentration camps. Some were starved, tortured, raped, and executed. Muslims, Croats, and Serbs alike experienced these atrocities. (12)

No doubt some Croats and Muslims committed atrocities; it was, however, the Serbs who committed at least 90 percent of the atrocities, and it was the Serbs who set up the first concentration camps in Europe since World War II.

A picture book I recommend with reservations is Jane Cutler and Greg Couch's *The Cello of Mr. O* (1999). The book seems to be about the Serbian nationalist siege of Sarajevo and may be based on the true story of Vedran Smailovic, a cellist who, after Serbs shelled and killed twenty-two people standing in a bread line in Sarajevo, openly played his cello outside for twenty-two days in honor of the victims.

The Balkan conflict is not named but implied. Children who must stay inside because of the siege annoy a musician, Mr. O, who lives in the apartment building. All wait for the arrival of the relief truck on Wednesdays, which is hit one day by a rocket, killing dozens, and making an already hard life more difficult. The following Wednesday Mr. O takes his cello and plays at four o'clock, and every day at four o'clock after that. One day Mr. O leaves his cello for a moment because of a cramp. While he leans against a wall, shaking out his leg, his cello is struck. The following day, Mr. O takes his chair out— and plays the harmonica.

Although this is a touching story, it lacks context. If it is about Sarajevo, the author and illustrator should have been true to the setting. The story also lacks specificity; for example, the book jacket reads, "Bombs have devastated the neighborhood." As stated before, actions require actors and, in this case, it was Serbian nationalists and criminal thugs from the Belgrade underground who put Sarajevo under siege. At least an author's note would have been helpful.

Anita Ganeri's *Why We Left: I Remember Bosnia* (1995) is an informational text geared for the second- or third-grade level. Ganeri focuses on Samira, who from her photograph, seems to be about eight-years-old. Refreshingly, Samira appears on the first page and says:

> Hello! My name is Samira, and I am a Muslim from Bosnia. I came here just a few months ago with my family to escape from the war that is destroying our country.
>
> Before the war, our way of life in Bosnia was like life here. We, as Muslims, were used to living in peace with Serb and Croat neighbors. But now all that has changed. . . . Come with me and I'll tell you about Bosnia. I'll tell how it was before the war and what it's like now. (n. pag.)

The book is thirty-two pages long, with large print on one quarter of the pages and striking photographs that vary between three-quarter-page spreads, maps, and set-off boxes. The photographs are worth the price of the book, as they convey the attraction of this dramatically beautiful country's architecture and landscape. There are sixteen topics, including "Bosnia Today," which describes the peace that existed before the war. The second topic is "Country and Landscape," with a photograph of the magnificent

Mostar bridge, destroyed in the war (and later rebuilt). "Climate" includes a photograph of snow-covered mountains, as picturesque as any in the United States. (While in Bosnia I felt as though I were in Yosemite National Park much of the time.) "The Muslims" explains the Arabic origins of the faith and how it came to Bosnia during the Ottoman Empire; Ganeri includes that Bosniak women had more freedom than Muslim women in other countries. "The Serbs and the Croats" explains the Slavic ancestry ("Poland and Russia") of most Bosnians (13). "Beliefs," "Our Way of Life," "Living in the City," "Village Life," "Work and School," and "Sports and Leisure" help young readers see that, prior to the war, Samira and most Bosnians lived normal lives—including, among other things, delicious food, beautiful carpets, and free schools.

Ganeri is certainly making an attempt to speak *with* and *to* rather than *for*. Nevertheless, Ganeri's explanation on the first page, albeit in smaller print than Samira's words, is erroneous; about Serbs, Croats, and Muslims she writes: "All want to seize as much land as possible," thus ignoring the Serbian nationalist quest for *lebensraum* (n. pag.). In concluding the book, Samira writes that, after Bosnia declared independence in 1992, her country "has become a battlefield for a war among the Serbs, Croats, and Muslims. The quarreling groups are fighting each other over land. Thousands of people on all sides are being wounded and killed" (26), thus perpetuating the myth of a deadly Balkan brawl. It would be better for children to realize that some adults are dangerous, as was Milošević, who died in prison while on trial at the International Criminal Tribunal for the former Yugoslavia. A military commander once said that in war, the side that wins is the side that creates the best deception; Milošević was notoriously charming and won much by creating the best deception. Public officials—and the world—were vulnerable, falling for his deceptions. Ambassador Zimmerman wrote, "'Many is the U.S. senator or Congressman who has reeled out of his office exclaiming, 'Why he's not nearly as bad as I expected!'" (qtd. in Power, 260). Milošević was actually far worse than their expectations.

Instead of fanning flames of ethnic hatred and leaving out the malevolent force that was Milošević, James Reger, author of *The Rebuilding of Bosnia* (1997), touchingly opens his book with quotations from love letters of two Sarajevans—one a young Serbian Orthodox man, the other a young Bosnian Muslim woman. The young man, who had been drafted into the Serbian army, wrote, "'My love, you are the only happiness I have.'" The young woman replied that soon they would be together again, "'and then absolutely nothing will separate us'" (6). Tragically, when they tried to escape Sarajevo together, they were killed and died in each other's arms. At our meeting at the University of Sarajevo in July of 2011, Professor Čekić told a similar story of two friends, a Bosniak and a Serb. A grenade killed the Serbian girl; the young Bosniak risked his life to help her as she lay dying. Then a second grenade killed him.

Reger includes vital information that problematic informational texts leave out, but sensitive teachers and caring adults will have to decide how much young readers can handle. Reger graphically describes Serbian concentration camps: "one witness observed, '300 Muslims had been imprisoned in an ore loader inside a cage roughly 700 square feet. The cages were stacked four high and separated by grates. There were no toilets and the prisoners had to live in their own filth, which dripped through the grates'" (24–25) and:

> A 1993 report by the U.S. government to the United Nations cited, among other offenses, slit throats, suffocations, beatings, genital mutilations, rapes, dismemberment of heads, hands, and feet, cigarette burns, electric shocks, shootings, eyes gouged out, knifings, and prisoners being forced to run barefoot over broken glass and to drink caustic materials. (25)

This may cross the line discussed in my Introduction. We might ask, with Kenneth Kidd, when does reading about trauma become traumatic itself for young readers?

Reger describes the admirable city Sarajevo was, "a sophisticated city with cosmopolitan ways and it had long since proven that many diverse cultures, races, and religions could peacefully and prosperously coexist" (26), and mentions the fact that a quarter to a third of Bosnians intermarried. He acknowledges the crucial factor that the Bosnian military was "weak" (7).

Reger shows Croatia's president, Franjo Tudjman, and Bosnia's president, Alija Izetbegović, as multifaceted human beings with both positive and negative qualities. Of Slobodan Milošević, Reger rightly says he was "ultimately most responsible for the war in Bosnia and its most egregious trampling of human rights" (34). He cites Zimmerman on Milošević: "'He is a man of extraordinary coldness. I never saw him moved by an individual case of human suffering nor did I ever hear him say a charitable word about any human being, not even a Serb'" (qtd. in Reger, 34).

Reger includes the horrific massacre in Srebrenica, ordered by Bosnian Serb Ratko Mladic, Milošević's crony. According to Reger, tribunal documents report that:

> After Srebrenica fell, a truly terrible massacre of the Muslim population appears to have taken place. The evidence describes scenes of unimaginable savagery: thousands of men executed and buried in mass graves, hundreds of men buried alive, men and women mutilated and slaughtered, children killed before their mothers' eyes, a grandfather forced to eat the liver of his own grandson. (76)

Once again, readers will have to decide whether Reger's book is too distressing for young people.

Recommended Children's and Young Adult Literature
about the Bosnian and Kosovo Genocides

Picture Books

Although not without controversy, Elizabeth Wellburn and Deryk Houston's *Echoes from the Square* (1998) contains a more responsible representation of cellist Vedran Smailovic than *The Cello of Mr. O*. World-renowned cellist Yo-Yo Ma introduces the book, which tells the story of Smailovic through the eyes of a boy, Alen. In the opening pages, Alen rides his bike through his favorite square in Sarajevo. Mirroring the love of music among many Sarajevans, Alen plays the violin. After the siege begins he must practice in the basement. To help his family survive, Alen stands outside in line for water; Wellburn's writing captures the terror Alen feels about being a possible target for snipers. After the mortar killing of the twenty-two people in the bread line, Alen hears music and sees the cellist playing in a place of certain danger. Wellburn writes, "Day after day, the man is in the square and his music soars above the broken cobblestones, touching the people who gather to listen" (16). In this passage she captures both the sadness of brokenness and the momentary flight from horror with music. Alen's family asks Smailovic to join them for a meal; during it he explains that he has been playing pieces by Albinoni, whose compositions were performed in buildings that had been destroyed during the siege.

Although the author reached out to Smailovic before writing her book, Smailovic has protested that no one should "steal" his name or profit from the genocide (qtd. in Houston, 2012, n. pag.). But Smailovic, Houston reports, has met with those who have offended him, stated his grievances, and resolved the conflict by shaking hands.

Novels

Dutch author Els De Groen, in *No Roof in Bosnia* (1997), tells the story of a Muslim girl in hiding, Aida, who, because she is desperately hungry, risks her life to steal apples from an orchard. Antonia, the owner of the orchard, jeopardizes her own safety by taking Aida in. Aida soon learns that she is not the only teenager Antonia is protecting; there are four others. Although a bit contrived—the teens are Serb, Croat, Muslim, and Roma—De Groen has written an absorbing book about how the youngsters depend upon one another to survive as they seek a safe haven area with the United Nations. There is an element of romance as well, reminding readers that even in war, teenagers everywhere have the same interests. Antonia becomes a spokesperson for the harmony that had long prevailed, especially in Sarajevo. She says to Aida, "In Sarajevo, everyone has a mind of his own, too, but they don't fight about it. That would be pointless, with all those religions and nationalities"

(16–17). Together, the teens make their way to Dubrovnik, Croatia, but not without heartbreak.

To write his novel, Arthur Dorros, a well-established writer for young people in the United States, traveled to Bosnia to conduct research. *Under the Sun: A Novel Based on True Stories of Survival during War* (2006) is about Ehmet, the son of a Muslim father and Croatian mother. Increasing violence in Sarajevo leads Ehmet's father to send his wife and son to relatives in Croatia. But even the countryside is unsafe; when Ehmet's mother is raped, she spirals downward emotionally and physically and eventually dies. For his young readers, Dorros wisely leaves out grisly details of her rape; the scene is implied rather than vividly portrayed. By doing so, Dorros supports young readers—Hamida Bosmajian's "first stories of a thousand and one recountings," as mentioned in my Introduction. After his mother's death, Ehmet travels 400 miles on foot to reach the Children's Home in Croatia, a real place where Muslim, Jewish, Serbian, and Croatian children live peaceably. Dorros has made a sensitive and well researched contribution to the literature on the Bosnian genocide.

Another excellent novel is Gaye Hiçyilmaz's *Smiling for Strangers* (1998). Hiçyilmaz is a British author who lived in Turkey for many years and writes with an understanding of the politics of the region. Her character Nina is a girl who lives with her grandfather in his country home, where they had hoped to escape the violence in Sarajevo. After their home is attacked, Nina's grandfather urges her to leave Bosnia for England, giving her only a picture of a man she has never met and knows practically nothing about except that he was once a friend of her deceased mother.

Along the way she learns lessons for survival, including how to present oneself when one is starving and destitute. When she saw the possibility of desperately needed aid,

> She crawled backward into the protection of the forest and quickly changed into her one clean shirt. . . . By the stream she could quench her thirst and wash her face and hands. She could even brush her teeth. It was one of the lessons she had learned during the war: to be helped, you had to look worth helping. If your need is too great, people cannot bear it and they turn away from you. (51)

Aided by the United Nations, Nina arrives safely in England and learns that the man whose picture she holds onto is of her father, with whom she starts a new relationship and with whom she lives. Hiçyilmaz is a fine author who has written an engaging story.

To write her two novels on the Serbian occupation of Kosovo in 1999, Alice Mead traveled to Kosovo several times, motivated by her interest in the Kosovo refugees she had met in her home state of Maine. Having lost Slovenia, Croatia, and Bosnia by that time, Milošević was determined not to lose Kosovo as well, and Mead empathized with the suffering of the Albanians, who made up 90 percent of the population in Kosovo. In *Adem's Cross* (1996), Adem witnesses his family being torn apart—Serbs murder his sister, and Adem feels responsible because he had not stopped her from performing publicly what he knew would seem to the Serbs a seditious poem. The Serbs also brutalize his father. Besides providing a glimpse into the hardships of family life on all fronts, Adem also grasps the impossibility of the situation for Albanians as a group:

> The Serbs wanted to take over Kosovo. Only 20 percent of the Albanians could stay. But we were now nearly 90 percent of the population. Where could two million of us go? We had no cars, no money, no passport visas, and the United Nations refugee camps were far away in Croatia and Germany. . . .
> Here, the rocks and the trees were ours. The mines and the vineyards. The cornfields and the little red foxes that ran under the stars. We lived here. That was the problem. And the Serbs said we were different from them. That was worse. They called us animals. But no animals I'd ever seen would hurt one another the way people did. (60)

As noted in my Introduction, Bosmajian observes that the development of aesthetic sensibilities is rarely the purpose of books on war and genocide. In this passage, Mead's evocative writing is well crafted, while simultaneously helping young readers understand the hard truth that Albanians in Kosovo simply had no place else to go. As Mead explains in her introduction to *Girl of Kosovo* (2001), for Albanians "it was home—and one of the poorest, most undeveloped regions in Europe" (vii).

In *Girl of Kosovo* Mead provides an extensive introduction, explaining the history of Yugoslavia, including the Serbian perspective on Kosovo: it "was the historic cradle of their culture" (vii), thus highlighting the claims both groups had to the land. Based on the true story of a child Mead met in Kosovo, the novel opens with the words of Zana, an eleven-year-old Albanian girl: "I loved our village life. I loved our farm and the apple orchard. I had my friends at school, and at home I did chores—helping with the cow, fetching water, bringing in firewood" (3). Readers soon learn that Zana's best friend, Lena, is a Serb, and that Zana's uncle Vizar, a member of the guerrilla Kosovo Liberation Army (KLA), objects to their friendship. As tensions between the KLA and the Serbian police grow, so do violent attacks. Zana watches her brothers and father die in a Serb attack, and she herself is badly wounded: "My leg collapsed. My boot was gone, and so was the bottom half of my sweatpants. My foot hung dangling from my leg. My other leg gave way and I lay on the ground, screaming" (31).

Because the hospital in Kosovo is unable to care for her, Zana is sent to Belgrade in Serbia. The Serbian doctor who operates on her has a seven-year-old daughter, who upon hearing Zana's story, sends chocolate to Zana in the Belgrade hospital. Mead shows that some Serbs were kind and compassionate to Albanians.

Throughout the story, Zana repeatedly remembers her father's wise words—wise for anyone who suffers injustice: "'Don't let them fill your heart with hate'" (61). When she is sent back to her village, where her life has become very limited because of the injuries to her leg, Zana struggles with sadness. Lena encourages her, and both girls are determined to stay friends in spite of all that has happened and continues to happen. The North Atlantic Treaty Organization (NATO) and the UN Security Council order Milošević and his troops out of Kosovo; when Milošević defies the order, NATO begins bombing Serb troops in Kosovo. In the midst of this Zana's leg becomes infected, and it is Lena's Serbian father who takes her to the hospital. After the NATO victory, it is Lena's family who must leave for safety in Montenegro.

As Mead was moved by the plight of Kosovo-Albanian refugees she knew in Maine, so, too, was Katherine Paterson, who has won numerous awards for her lifelong career as a children's author, moved by the refugees she knew from her church in Vermont. In *The Day of the Pelican* (2009), Paterson narrates a story through the eyes of Meli Lleshi and her family, who left Kosovo for a refugee camp in Macedonia, then immigrated to Vermont, sponsored by a church. Before leaving Kosovo, Meli learns that her brother Mehmet has joined the KLA, which Serbs considered a terrorist organization; the KLA takes care of Mehmet after he is badly beaten by Serbian troops. Mehmet's involvement in the KLA makes it too dangerous for the Lleshi family to stay, so they face a difficult journey to Macedonia, where Mehmet calls living in a refugee camp "like being chickens sentenced to jail" (81). In the refugee camp, they hear on the radio of the NATO bombing and its inevitable deadly miscalculations (euphemistically known as "collateral damage"); a group of refugees was mistaken for Serbian soldiers and killed. Meli's father says, "War is madness. . . . It is the innocent who always suffer the most" (84). Meli's father is undoubtedly right. Deborah Ellis opens her book *Three Wishes: Palestinian and Israeli Children Speak* (2004) with: "In World War I, 15 percent of all casualties were civilians. In World War II, 50 percent of all casualties were civilians. In 2004, 90 percent of the casualties in war are civilians" (5). And more than half of those casualties are children.

Shortly after the Lleshis' arrival in Vermont came 9/11: The World Trade Center twin towers fell at the hands of suicidal terrorists. Because they are Muslim, albeit secular, both Meli and Mehmet are bullied at their school in Vermont, with American children taunting them and calling them terrorists. Meli thinks, "War, like a tiger prowling in the shadows, had followed their scent, and now it had them in its sight and was ready to pounce" (131). Paterson's use of figurative language crystallizes Meli's plight. The situation at school is resolved when sensitive coaches visit the Lleshi home to apologize and to intervene on behalf of Meli and Mehmet.

Poetry

In *Something about America* (2005) Maria Testa, a well-known poet from Maine, creates a poetic narrative to convey the true story of a burn victim whose family had to immigrate to America for the medical care she needed. She has adjusted to American life but her parents have not, in part because of the prejudice against Muslims, which wears them down. When her family learns of racism against Somalis in Lewiston, Maine, her father organizes a protest. The protagonist learns that, for its flaws, at least in America protests can be organized.

A Play

Tammy Ryan is a Pittsburgh playwright; she based her play *The Music Lesson* (2002) on a true story. Ivan, a violinist, and Irena, a pianist, are refugees from Sarajevo now living in Pittsburgh. In Sarajevo they tutored musical prodigies,

Figure 3.1 Book cover from Tammy Ryan; photograph by Mark Garvin: *The Music Lesson*. Woodstock, IL: Dramatic Publishing, 2002.

and Irena is haunted by Maja, her most brilliant student, who was killed during the siege. In America, both Ivan and Irena must find work where they can, and they now tutor less committed students than those they knew in Sarajevo. The play focuses on the relationship between Irena and Kat, a self-centered and exasperating American teen. Through flashbacks to Sarajevo, Irena is portrayed as struggling with the loss of Maja and her present burden of tutoring Kat. In time, Kat learns Irena and Maja's story and undergoes a change for the better. Intermittent excerpts from classical music enrich the play; it is a poignant and aesthetically engaging work. Among other awards, Ryan won the American Alliance for Theatre and Education Distinguished Play Award in 2004 for *The Music Lesson* (Figure 3.1).

Autobiographies

When the siege of Sarajevo began, Nadja Halilbegovich was twelve-years-old and kept a diary. In a unique multigenre format, *My Childhood under Fire: A Sarajevo Diary* (2006), Nadja revisits her childhood diary, juxtaposing her entries from the 1990s with her current adult perspectives. Before the war, her life in Sarajevo was a delightful one, and she reminds readers that the Winter Olympics were held there in 1984. Her world turned upside down on April 6, 1992, when Serbian snipers opened fire on a multiethnic group of protestors from atop the Holiday Inn in downtown Sarajevo. Three weeks later, to survive this new turmoil in her life, Nadja began her journal: "Instantly this diary became a friend who listened to all that I desperately needed to share. It was my only place of peace amid the chaos" (9). She initiates a radio show where she and other children can share their poetry, and an adult friend offers Nadja and her friends knitting and sewing lessons; together they make "stuffed toys" (17). Calling themselves the "Tenants of the Basement," they exhibit their drawings and crafts, sending handmade invitations to other tenants in their apartment building, and she continues her singing and playing of the guitar, remnants of happier times before the war. In 1995, she wrote, "Today's young Bosnians don't allow their different faiths to come between them. We know that we can and must live together. The aggressor obviously cannot grasp this" (96). Thus Nadja confirms what many observers have said about the peace and tolerance that existed in Sarajevo before the war.

More than other writers, Nadja explores what happens to adults in time of war. She writes of her parents "feeling hopeless and discouraged" (91). "War," she says, "turned us all into frightened children" (91). While working in refugees camps in Pakistan along the Afghanistan border with Afghans who had fled the brutal Taliban regime, Ellis, in her book *Women of the Afghan War* (2000) notes similarities: Some adults are so stressed that children must, at times, become the caregivers. As early as 1992, Nadja notes the lack of response from the rest of the world; in October, "No one in the world seems willing to save the people of Bosnia from extermination" (21), and in November: "They say that thirty thousand children have been killed in my country. Yet the world remains silent" (32). She records Sarajevans' view that Sarajevo had become "'the world's largest death camp'" (23). On July 14, 1995, she and her family learn of the massacre in Srebrenica. She writes,

There has been a loathsome crime—genocide against the civilians of Srebrenica. Tens of thousands of civilians experienced their worst nightmare as the aggressor took over the city. The UN watched and did nothing:

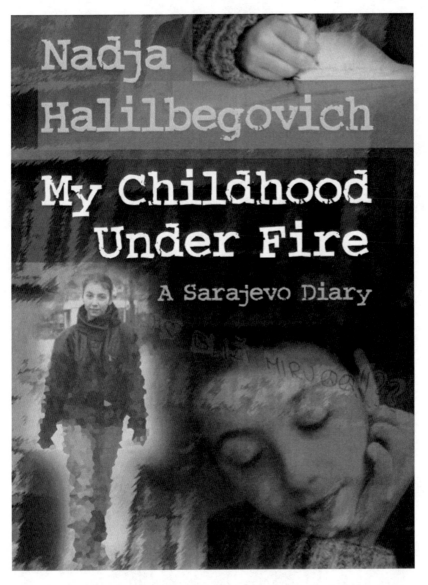

Figure 3.2 Book cover from Nadja Halilbegovich: *My Childhood under Fire: A Sarajevo Diary*. Tonawanda, NY: Kids Can Press, 2006.

the rest of the world closed its eyes. . . . On TV they showed a little girl who had been raped and an eighty-year-old woman who was beaten and forced to march for hours in the burning sun. (100)

Like so many other children who tired of basement living, Nadja begs her mother to let her go outside. Worn down, her mother reluctantly agrees. Once outside Nadja is immediately hit by shrapnel. At the hospital she sees children in similar circumstances undergoing the extraction of shrapnel without anesthesia. Because of her wound, the Women of Bosnia and Project Shelter grant her passage to the United States to live with an American family, but she and her mother must leave Sarajevo illegally through a wretched underground tunnel. Safe from sniper fire, they hitchhike to Croatia; from there Nadja flies alone to America. Her book is well-crafted and honors those to whom it is dedicated: "To all innocent victims of war—especially children" (Figure 3.2).

Like Nadja, Zlata Filipović also kept a diary during the siege, published as *Zlata's Diary: A Child's Life in Sarajevo* (1994), where she details her day-to-day living, including not only the boredom and extreme hardship but also her childlike pleasures in weddings, food, and other small surprises that brighten her long and difficult days. Also like Nadja, she too was involved in writing, singing, and other activities, which she kept up as best she could throughout the siege. As for other Sarajevan children, much of her time was spent in a basement and she witnessed the deaths of friends. Before the war Zlata did not know or care who among her friends were Croat, Muslim, or Serb. Her autobiography contains many photographs of better days, including a trip to Dubrovnik, Croatia, with her family. There are also reproductions of her actual diary, ornamented with Zlata's drawings.

The book has been an international bestseller, translated into dozens of languages. There has been some controversy over *Zlata's Diary*, first published by UNICEF in Croatia in 1993 and picked up by Viking Penguin in 1994. David Rieff states that certain political commentary had apparently been added in the Viking Penguin edition: "[I]n a significant number of these entries, material included in the Viking Penguin edition is simply absent, both from the first English translation and from Zlata's handwritten original" (33). Rieff also finds the comparison between Anne Frank and Zlata Filipović overdrawn and questions the book's almost instant celebrity status. Why, he asks, were adult books on Bosnia not given similar attention? "What is needed," wrote Rieff in 1994 (before the war was over), "to make the Bosnian case . . . is an adult viewpoint, and that is the one thing Zlata, in any language . . . cannot provide" (34). Rightly, Rieff wonders why the world was so ready to embrace a publisher-declared Bosnian Anne Frank but not attend to the voices of adults pleading for help from inside Bosnia. Now an adult, Zlata in 2006 published *Stolen Voices: Young People's Diaries, from World War I to Iraq* with coauthor Melanie Challenger. Apparently her childhood experiences have given shape to her career as an adult, writing about children who suffer from war.

Informational Texts

Julia Waterlow's *A Family from Bosnia* (1997) focuses on the Bucalovic family. The introductory pages include a map of the region and a photograph of the family sitting outside their badly damaged apartment building with all their belongings, a statement of how little they have. Photographs and text convey the Serbian siege of Sarajevo and the difficulties the family faced in surviving. The point size of the font is large—it could easily be read by third to fifth graders— and the text gives enough information without traumatizing the reader.

Diane Yancey's *Life in War-Torn Bosnia* (1996) is a frank and hard-hitting account of the Bosnian genocide for young adults. Particularly noteworthy is her inclusion of an excerpt from Anna Cataldi's *Letters from Sarajevo*, which describes the Jewish response to Bosnian Muslims' troubles. Jewish members of the American Joint Distribution Committee arrived in Sarajevo to help. They asked two questions: "'What do you need?' and 'How many are you?'" They explained, "'As Jews we feel a duty to help others, because so many people helped us after the war'" (qtd. in Yancey, 77). Despite the dreadful circumstances, some gleams of humanity emerged through Jewish compassion for the Muslims of Bosnia.

Michael Schuman's *Bosnia and Herzegovina* (2004) is also a credible account. He calls the country "a true mosaic of cultures," acknowledging the tolerance that existed in pre-Milošević Bosnia (v). Schuman writes, "Much of its demise began with the actions of the president of the Serbs, Slobodan Milošević ... who had seized control of the office in 1989" (38). Although Bosnians had a four-year wait for the world's help, an unsteady peace came in 1995. Then, Milošević moved on to other territory—Kosovo.

In *Kosovo: The Splintering of Yugoslavia* (2000), Tricia Andryszewski begins with a history of the region, including NATO intervention in Bosnia and the Dayton Peace Accords of 1995. In Dayton, Andryszewski writes, all "promised to work together to find a peaceful solution to the Serb-Albanian conflict in Kosovo. But no deadlines were set, and no talks were scheduled" (25). Milošević was, once again, given the world's permission to plunder and kill as he pleased.

Like Slovenia, Croatia, and Bosnia, Kosovo wanted independence from Serbia. In March 1999, Milošević launched an all-out attack on the Albanians of Kosovo. NATO responded quickly, bombing "air defenses and communications equipment" (Andryszewski 37) but making it clear that they would not send ground troops into the area. With that knowledge, Serb troops stepped up the war, evicting hundreds of thousands of Albanians from their homes. Andryszewski summarizes, "As in Bosnia, the paramilitaries included gangs of tough and scary criminals set loose to terrorize the targets of ethnic cleansing" (38). As in Cambodia and Bosnia, "journalists, teachers, doctors, and other community leaders" were immediately executed. As in Darfur, aid workers were targeted as well; forcing the world's nongovernmental organizations to pull out for fear of the safety of their employees is an effective strategy to remove international intervention.

Andryszewski includes aerial photographs taken by NATO of mass graves inside the country. As NATO increased its involvement, Milošević was eventually backed into a corner, and Serbia's ally Russia brokered an agreement to withdraw Serbian troops from Kosovo in June 1999.

Andryszewski incorporates the voices of Kosovo-Albanians throughout her impassioned book. The introduction shares the voices of eleven people, for example, "The police came to my house and told us we had to leave. I asked what do we do, and the police told me and my family to go or be shot. . . . People are killed. Everything is burned. We have nothing" (4). Andryszewski's book is an informative and notable one on the Kosovo genocide.

In *One Boy from Kosovo* (2000), Trish Marx explores what happens to one Albanian family forced to flee to a refugee camp in Macedonia. Marx and photographer Cindy Karp found a family and their twelve-year-old Kosovar boy, Edi, who were willing to tell their story to the world. Except for Serbian rules that kept his parents from earning full pay and employment, Edi's childhood was a pleasant one. When Serbs began ethnic cleansing in March of 1999, "[a]lmost one million Kosovars were forced to leave their country, shoved on crowded train cars and in the backs of trucks" (Marx 7). A tumultuous journey to the Brazda refugee camp followed for Edi and his family; there, they joined thousands of others living in a tent city. Edi described what life was like in a refugee camp:

> There was a line for everything: using the wood-and-canvas toilets set on the edge of the camp; taking a shower in a canvas shower stall, with water that had been warmed by the sun; and filling the plastic jugs with water from the row of metal spigots that supplied the whole camp. Brazda was intended to house twenty thousand people, but there were close to thirty thousand people living there. It seemed to Edi that he was either standing in a line, with nothing to do but wait, or sitting in his tent, with nothing to do but wait. (13)

Edi became a volunteer at the children's center in the camp, encouraging younger children to read, write, and draw about their experiences. Like Nadja Halilbegovich and Zlata Filipović, Edi kept a journal of his experiences. After the June 1999 peace agreement, Edi and his family were able to return home to Kosovo.

Crossover Literature

A Bosnian Serb, Savo Heleta grew up in the Muslim-dominated city of Goražde where, prior to the war, one's ethnicity and religion were not barriers to friendships. When Serbs surrounded Goražde, matters quickly spiraled downward.

Heleta's father was a journalist and his mother an administrator; neither believed that the war would ever become as terrible as it did, nor did they believe that their Muslims friends would betray them. Because the Heletas were Serbs, they quickly became suspects and were arrested by Muslim police and held in a detention center for four months. The family was later helped and hidden by Muslim friends, but a Muslim almost killed Heleta's father. In his autobiography, *Not My Turn to Die: Memoirs of a Broken Childhood in Bosnia* (2008), Heleta tells his family's story of mistreatment, hunger, and finally swimming across a cold river to safety. Later, when he encounters the man who almost killed his father, Heleta wants revenge, but his father stops him. Now committed to conflict resolution and reconstruction, he inspiringly writes:

> For a long time after the war, I considered reconciliation as a weakness. I saw revenge as the only way, the "manly" way to move on with my life. But with the help of my family, and after my life changed for the better and I got exposed to education and traveled all over the world, I realized that was wrong. I realized that only brave and strong people can put years of suffering behind them, reconcile with the past, and move on with life. I wanted to be one of them. (225)

Conclusion

A spectacularly gorgeous country is Bosnia, with strengths in its history that, with a different cast of characters in power in Serbia, could have prevented genocide. Yes, there had been violence in Bosnia's past—but no more than in France, Germany, Italy, or any other European or American countries. Sarajevo, in particular, had been a model of multicultural tolerance from which the rest of the world could learn. The tragic destruction of human life, museums, libraries, mosques, and historic marketplaces, like the Bascarsija, did not have to happen. The ruthless cruelty could have been recognized and stopped.

Today, Bosnia is poor; annual per capita income is about $3,000, and unemployment is high. Leydesdorff found in her study that the women of Srebrenica are "still frozen in the trauma" (48). Čekić describes the

> increased mortality … particularly in younger and relatively young people, stemming from non-characteristic causes of death (cancerous diseases, heart and brain attacks, increased suicidal and psychical illness rates, PTSD and the enormous growth of sociopathologic phenomena and problems which destroy the natural social tissue of the Bosnian society which, up to the aggression, was quite healthy. (*Research* 185)

Bosnia will find its health again; it was there once. Zilha, Enis, Merisa, and other young people with their vision and energy, are leading the way.

Works Cited

Black, Eric. *Bosnia: Fractured Region*. Minneapolis, MN: Lerner, 1999. World in Conflict Ser.

Čekić, Smail. *The Aggression against the Republic of Bosnia and Herzegovina: Planning, Preparation, Execution*. Trans. Branka Ramadanović. Sarajevo, Bosnia: Institute for the Research of Crimes against Humanity and International Law, U of Sarajevo, 2005.

———. *Research of Genocide Victims, with a Special Emphasis on Bosnia and Herzegovina: Problems and Issues in Scientific Theory, Methods and Methodology*. Trans. Branka Ramadanović and Samir Kulaglić. Sarajevo, Bosnia: Institute for the Research of Crimes against Humanity and International Law, U of Sarajevo, 2009.

Čekić, Smail, Muhamed Šestanović, Merisa Karović, and Zilha Mastalić-Košuta. *Zločini nad djecome Sarajeva u opsadi (Crimes against Children in the Siege of Sarajevo)*. Sarajevo, Bosnia: Institute for the Research of Crimes against Humanity and International Law, U of Sarajevo, 2010.

Eagleton, Terry. *Literary Theory: An Introduction*. Minneapolis, MN: U of Minnesota P, 1983.

Ellis, Deborah. *Three Wishes: Palestinian and Israeli Children Speak*. Toronto: Groundwood, 2004.

———. *Women of the Afghan War*. Westport, CT: Praeger, 2000.

Englar, Mary. *Bosnia-Herzegovina in Pictures*. Minneapolis, MN: Twenty-First Century, 2007. Visual Geography Ser.

Galaijatović, Sabina Subašić. "Sexual Abuse of Women in Bosnia and Herzegovina—An Instrument of the Crime of Genocide." International Network of Genocide Scholars. U of Sussex, Brighton, England. 29 June 2010. Reading.

Houston, Deryk. "Vedran Smailović—'The Cellist of Sarajevo.'" *The Economic Voice*. 7 Feb. 2013. Web. 10 Feb. 2013.

Isaac, John (Photographer), and Keith Greenberg. *Bosnia: Civil War in Europe*. Woodbridge, CT: Blackbirch, 1997. Children in Crisis Ser.

Jensen, Steven L. B., ed. *Genocide: Cases, Comparisons and Contemporary Debates*. Trans. Gwynneth Llewellyn. Njalsgade, Denmark: The Danish Center for Holocaust and Genocide Studies, 2003.

Karahasan, Dzevad. *Sarajevo, Exodus of a City*. Trans. Slobodan Drakulić. New York: Kodansha, 1993.

Lemarchand, René. "Comparing the Killing Fields: Rwanda, Cambodia and Bosnia." Jensen, 141–173.

Leydesdorff, Selma. *Surviving the Bosnian Genocide: The Women of Srebrenica Speak*. Trans. Kay Richardson. Bloomington: Indiana UP, 2011.

Maass, Peter. *Love Thy Neighbor: A Story of War*. New York: Knopf, 1996.

Malcolm, Noel. *Bosnia: A Short History*. New York: New York UP, 1994.

Milivojevic, JoAnn. *Bosnia and Herzegovina*. New York: Children's, 2004. Enchantment of the World Ser.

Omerović, Enis. "My Comments and Suggestions." Message to Jane M. Gangi. 12 Mar. 2013. E-mail.

Phillips, Douglas A. *Bosnia and Herzegovina*. Philadelphia: Chelsea, 2004. Modern World Nation Ser.

Power, Samantha. *"A Problem from Hell": America and the Age of Genocide*. New York: Basic, 2002.

Ramet, Sabrina Petra. *Balkan Babel: The Disintegration of Yugoslavia from the Death of Tito to Ethnic War*. 2nd ed. New York: Westview, 1996.

Reger, James P. *The Rebuilding of Bosnia*. San Diego, CA: Lucent, 1997. World in Conflict Ser.

Ricciuti, Edward R. *War in Yugoslavia: The Breakup of a Nation*. Brookfield, CT: Millbrook, 1993.

Rieff, David. "Youth and Consequences." *New Republic* 28 Mar. 1994: 31–34.

Sell, Louis. *Slobodan Milosevic and the Destruction of Yugoslavia*. Durham, NC: Duke UP, 2002.

Recommended Children's and Young Adults Literature about the Bosnian and Kosovo Genocides

Andryszewski, Tricia. *Kosovo: The Splintering of Yugoslavia*. Brookfield, CT: Millbrook, 2000.

De Groen, Els. *No Roof in Bosnia*. Trans. Patricia Compton. Barnstaple, Devon, UK: Spindlewood, 1997.

Dorros, Arthur. *Under the Sun: A Novel Based on True Stories of Survival during War.* New York: Amulet, 2006.
Filipović, Zlata. *Zlata's Diary: A Child's Life in Sarajevo.* New York: Scholastic, 1994.
Filipović, Zlata, and Melanie Challenger, eds. *Stolen Voices: Young People's Diaries, from World War I to Iraq.* New York: Penguin, 2006.
Halilbegovich, Nadja. *My Childhood under Fire: A Sarajevo Diary.* Tonawanda, NY: Kids Can, 2006.
Hiçyilmaz, Gaye. *Smiling for Strangers.* New York: Farrar, 1998.
Marx, Trish, and Cindy Karp (Photographer). *One Boy from Kosovo.* New York: HarperCollins, 2000.
Mead, Alice. *Adem's Cross.* New York: Farrar, 1996.
———. *Girl of Kosovo.* New York: Farrar, 2001.
Paterson, Katherine. *The Day of the Pelican.* Boston: Houghton, 2009.
Ryan, Tammy. *The Music Lesson.* Woodstock, IL: Dramatic, 2002.
Schuman, Michael A. *Bosnia and Herzegovina.* New York: Facts on File, 2004.
Testa, Maria. *Something about America.* Cambridge, MA: Candlewick, 2005.
Waterlow, Julia. *A Family from Bosnia.* East Sussex, UK: Wayland, 1997.
Wellburn, Elizabeth, and Deryk Houston (Illus.). *Echoes from the Square.* Oakville, Ontario: Rubicon, 1998.
Yancey, Diane. *Life in War-Torn Bosnia.* San Diego, CA: Lucent, 1996.

Recommended with Reservations: Children's and Young Adult Literature about the Bosnian and Kosovo Genocides

Ching, Jacqueline. *Genocide and the Bosnian War.* New York: Rosen, 2009.
Cutler, Jane, and Greg Couch (Illus.). *The Cello of Mr. O.* New York: Dutton, 1999.
Flint, David. *Bosnia: Can There Ever Be Peace?* Austin, TX: Raintree Steck-Vaughn, 1996.
Ganeri, Anita. *Why We Left: I Remember Bosnia.* Austin, TX: Raintree Steck-Vaughn, 1995.
Reger, James P. *The Rebuilding of Bosnia.* San Diego, CA: Lucent, 1997. World in Conflict Ser.
Tekavec, Valerie. *Teenage Refugees from Bosnia-Herzegovina Speak Out.* New York: Rosen, 1997.

Recommended Crossover Literature about the Bosnian Genocide

Heleta, Savo. *Not My Turn to Die: Memoirs of a Broken Childhood in Bosnia.* New York: Amacom, 2008.

Chapter Four
Children's and Young Adult Literature of Rwanda

written with Isabelle Umugwaneza

They are the living-dead who, rightly, feel that they have been abandoned by their fellow-citizens and the world.

—A Kigali teacher

On April 6, 1994, radical Hutus from the north of Rwanda began the world's swiftest genocide, one that killed close to a million Tutsis and moderate Hutus in 100 days. Of those who survived, 8 in 10 children witnessed the murder of family members and hundreds of thousands of children were orphaned. In addition, 250,000 women and girls were raped.

The reasons for the catastrophe are complex and include agendas from outside Rwanda's borders. Prior to the arrival of Europeans in Rwanda, Hutus, Tutsis, and Twa lived in Rwanda in relative peace; this is not to say that there was no conflict, but nothing on the scale of that after contact with Europeans. Tutsis were primarily the ruling class, and Hutus, who outnumbered Tutsis, were farmers. Before European influence the roles were flexible; Tutsis could become Hutus, and Hutus could become Tutsis. For instance, if a Hutu gained ownership of enough cows, he could become Tutsi, and if a Tutsi became a farmer, he could become Hutu. They also intermarried, making the distinctions more difficult to detect. The Twa were about 1 percent of the population and, as hunter-gatherers known for their pottery, kept to themselves.

In 1885 at the Conference of Berlin—without a single African present—Europe divided Africa, and Rwanda was given to Germany. Germany did not take much interest in Rwanda and, after World War I, part of Germany's concession was to hand over Rwanda to Belgium. Informed by the eugenics movement, Belgians introduced racist theories into Rwandan culture, where previously none had existed, by favoring the taller, lighter-skinned Tutsis over the Hutus.

In the 1940s and 1950s, Tutsis pushed back against their Belgian conquerors, and, in anger, the Belgians switched sides, and promoted Hutus. Power struggles ensued, with many Tutsis fleeing the country over the following decades because of discrimination and sporadic killings of Tutsis in the countryside, notably in 1959, 1961, 1973, and in the early 1990s. Uganda, especially, was a place of refuge, and was the country from which the Rwandan Patriotic Front (RPF) created a platform; the RPF was composed mostly of Tutsis (grown children of many of those who had fled in the 1960s and 1970s) and some Hutus. The RPF launched an invasion into northern Rwanda in 1990. Although the RPF was armed, its influence was limited to the north.

Speaking with and to Rwandans

Isabelle Umugwaneza was twenty-one years-old when we met in 2010, and was an International Management major at Manhattanville College, where I was then teaching. She has since graduated and now works in Hong Kong. We ate lunch together about once a week throughout the semester to discuss books written in English for children and young adults on the Rwandan genocide. Our conversations continue via e-mail, and Isabelle's insights enrich this chapter.

Isabelle was not in Rwanda at the time of the genocide. Because of quotas that prevented them from continuing their studies in Rwanda, her parents moved to Burundi and then to Congo, where Isabelle was born. Her family moved back to Rwanda after the genocide in 1994. She grew up acutely aware of the disaster and notes that, for young Rwandans, knowing that the world did nothing is almost as hard as knowing about the genocide itself. But it is a double-edged sword: Young Rwandans, says Isabelle, now know that they must rely on themselves; she says she is proud of her generation because they have decided to build their own future.

Another young woman from Rwanda, Yvette Rugasaguhunga, graduated from the college several years before; she and I exchanged e-mails and have met on several occasions. Yvette is a survivor who was fourteen-years-old during the genocide and who witnessed the brutal murder of family members. Yvette's responses to several books about the genocide are included here.

In reviewing children's and young adult literature written in English on the Rwandan genocide, Isabelle, Yvette, and I found that five misconceptions emerged in problematic texts:

- That it was a civil war
- That European racist theories and colonization had no effect worth mentioning

- That it was a spontaneous tribal outburst
- That nongovernmental organizations (NGOs) were helpful and readily provided protection and relief workers
- That Rwandans have largely recovered from the genocide

We also saw the role that propaganda played in the media as well as some authors' propensities to exoticize "the Other." We first discuss those books containing misconceptions and inaccuracies, written by authors who seem to have done little to inform themselves about the genocide before misrepresenting it to young readers. Then, we share those books that we think represent the genocide well to young readers.

Problematic Children's and Young Adult Books about the Rwandan Genocide

The Rwandan Genocide Was Not a Civil War

A civil war implies that both sides are armed and that both sides have an organized militia, which was not the case in Rwanda. Although the Tutsi-led RPF was armed and had a stronghold in northwestern Rwanda, Tutsis and moderate Hutus in the central and southern parts of the country—like the close to 7 million Jews, Roma, homosexuals, and disabled people of the Holocaust—were defenseless. As mentioned in my Introduction, John Thompson and Gail Quests deepen the meaning of genocide by pointing out that there is a difference between genocide and civil war; genocide falls outside of legitimate warfare. Calling what happened in Rwanda a civil war is like calling the Holocaust of World War II a civil war. Anthropologist Nigel Eltringham writes,

> By drawing analogies with the Holocaust Rwandese legitimately refute the representation of the 1994 genocide as "a black and incomprehensible frenzy" in the "Dark Heart of Africa." No one would contend that the Holocaust—however brutal—was the outcome of primordial tribalism. It was a premeditated act in which irrational "savagery" gave way to its polar opposite, clinical state bureaucracy. (68)

This is not to say that the RPF was innocent; political scientist René Lemarchand estimates the RPF, in reprisal killings, murdered between 25,000 to 45,000 Hutus (166). The late human rights activist Allison Des Forges wrote, "There is little question that many such killings stemmed from a sense of uncontrolled rage by Tutsi troops, many of whom had lost members of their family during the genocide" (167). Nazi victims, no doubt, attacked Nazis when they could.

The false narrative of "civil war" obfuscates French and Chinese militaristic complicity; France and China were providing radical Hutus with enormous amounts of weaponry. Rwanda is one of the smallest countries in Africa, yet it had more arms than most. Isabelle notes that, because it would keep Rwanda a center of Francophone influence, France was eager to keep Hutus in power. After Rwanda gained its independence from Belgium in 1962, Stephen Kinzer, who wrote Paul Kagame's biography, *A Thousand Hills: Rwanda's Rebirth and the Man Who Dreamed It* (2008), explains that France formed ties with Rwanda, ties that "became steadily closer" (37). France considered Juvénal Habyarimana, the Hutu president of Rwanda from 1973 until his assassination in 1994, as "one of their most faithful allies" (37). As a reward, France mightily armed Habyarimana's extremist government, which carried out the genocide. The Belgian politician Alain Destexhe writes that French-supplied arms were:

> out of all proportion to the actual military situation and the defence needs of the country. . . . In 1993, Rwanda, a tiny country with a population of seven million was receiving 55 million French francs (or $10 million) of military aid annually, placing it sixth on the list of African countries receiving such aid. (52)

Lemarchand calls France's fixation on Rwanda "obsessive" (153). France perceived the Uganda-based RPF as Anglophone; France wanted to keep Rwanda Francophone. Kinzer confirms:

> During the early 1990s, France sold the Rwandan regime more than $20 million worth of weaponry and helped it buy five times that amount from arms dealers in Egypt and South Africa. When Egyptian financiers hesitated to extend credit to Rwanda, France's government-owned bank, Crédit Lyonnais, stepped in as guarantor. . . . It turned one of the world's smallest and poorest countries into the third-largest arms importer in Africa. (94)

Lemarchand asserts that French involvement emboldened *génocidaires*, making them believe they could "act with impunity" (154). By 1992, says Samantha Power, radical Hutus "had purchased, stockpiled, and begun distributing an estimated eighty-five tons of munitions, as well as 581,000 machetes—one machete for every third adult Hutu male" (337). Power also summarizes a Central Intelligence Agency study: By December 1993, "some 4 million tons of small arms had been transferred from Poland to Rwanda, via Belgium, an extraordinary quantity for a government allegedly committed to a peace process" (338). British investigative journalist Linda Melvern says that Rwanda, one of the smallest countries in Africa, was the continent's "third largest importer of weapons in Africa" (5).

Several informational texts for young readers claim the Rwandan genocide was a civil war, including John Isaac and Keith Greenberg's *Rwanda: Fierce Clashes in Central Africa* (1997), Kathleen Deady's *Rwanda: A Question and Answer Book* (2005), and Kari Bodnarchuk's *Rwanda: A Country Torn Apart* (2000).

Rwanda: Fierce Clashes in Central Africa is a picture book for elementary school children, and part of Blackbirch Press's Children in Crisis Series. *School Library Journal* recommends the book for grades one through four, and *Kirkus Reviews* recommends it for children ages six to ten. The format is typical of that for younger children—thirty-two pages with a small amount of text on each page. The cover depicts a sad-looking girl, with snot dripping from her nose, and linty, closely cropped hair. Isabelle's response: Why do photographs of African children focus so much on what is pathetic?

At the time of the genocide Isaac was a photographer for the United Nations (UN). Like his book on Bosnia, that he was UN photographer and on the ground in both Bosnia and Rwanda does not mean that he understood the realities of either genocide. The format is unusual for a children's book: Isaac, of course, took all the photographs, but he breaks Greenberg's narrative from time to time, speaking in the first person. Every time he appears, his photograph is included—seven photographs in thirty pages of text, creating a solipsistic tone that calls to mind Michael Apple's observation of Whites unaware of their privileges in speaking of those outside their culture: "[B]ut enough of you, let me tell you about me" (xi).

Isaac and Greenberg explain that after President Habyarimana's plane was shot down on April 6, 1994, "A bloody civil war broke out" (7). What broke out was not a civil war but a well-planned genocide. Unarmed Tutsis and moderate Hutus could not have imagined what was about to happen to them in the next 100 days.

The question of who shot down Habyarimana's plane remained unanswered until 2012, when French judges conducted an investigation and ruled that the missile was launched from the Knombe Military Barracks, a bastion of Hutu extremists (Republic of Rwanda, n. pag.). In 1994 radical Hutus accused Paul Kagame, head of the RPF, of shooting down Habyarimana's plane; other explanations were that Colonel Théoneste Bagasora, angered that Habyarimana had agreed to participate in the Arusha Peace Accords that would allow more Tutsi participation in political processes and the military, ordered the shooting. Roadblocks were set up *before* the shooting, and moderate Hutus in the government were immediately executed, suggesting advance planning. Isabelle said that, to oversee the peaceful integration of Tutsis in the government, there was a small bastion of the RPF in Kigali, which was immediately attacked when the plane crashed. Habyarimana was flying back to confirm that Tutsis would have more say in government, which was unacceptable to radical Hutus. Although they did not have access to the results of the 2012 investigation, Greenberg and Isaac might have explained the political complexity rather than wrongly assuming the conflict was a civil war.

Deady's *Rwanda: A Question and Answer Book* (2000), part of the Capstone Press Question and Answer Series, is thirty-two pages long and in a format typical of books for children approximately six to eight years of age. To represent a country that is 95 percent Christian, with Roman Catholics in the majority and Protestants in the minority, the cover of Deady's book is of a Muslim boy wearing a white *taqiyah*. Isabelle's reaction to the cover: Why do they have a little Muslim boy? Muslims are a small minority of Rwanda's population; you would hardly ever see anyone dressed like this. The choice of the cover reflects, in Edward Said's words "exoticism" of "the Other," as we saw with Pastore's book, *Chantrea Conway's Story: A Voyage from Cambodia in 1975* (2004): the Cambodian girl on the cover was depicted wearing the Chinese conical hat.

The title page of Deady's book lists a consultant—a professor of African history, Michele D. Wagner of the University of Minnesota—giving unwarranted muscle to Deady's statement that "The Hutu and the Tutsi fought a **civil war** in the 1990s. By the war's end in 1994, at least one million people had died" (7; emphasis in the original). In a very short book, Deady calls the genocide a civil war three more times; this questionable book has found its way into the recommended reading lists of many school districts, thus contributing to the possibility that English-speaking children will grow up thinking that most Tutsis and moderate Hutus were involved in the fighting when they were not and, having no weapons, could not.

The inability of authors to call the catastrophe a genocide instead of a civil war is hard to understand when they do not mince words in describing events and disease. Bodnarchuk, in *Rwanda: A Country Torn Apart* (2000), part of Lerner's World in Conflict Series, whose audience is middle-grade readers, graphically writes: "Dead and decaying bodies were piled high along the roadsides in Goma, Zaire—a town on Rwanda's northwestern border—awaiting trucks to deliver them to mass graves" (22). Given that description, and descriptions found in other children's books, it would not be too great a leap to use the word *genocide*. Isaac and Greenberg describe a refugee camp in Zaire: "Contaminated water had caused an outbreak of cholera—a disease that results in severe and dangerous cases of diarrhea. With the body drained of fluids, cholera victims become weak, go into shock, and sometimes die" (11). Clare Bradford comments that the "pseudo-medical terminology with which 'the body' of 'cholera victims' is described ... seems ... to reduce human experience and suffering to a medicalised, depersonalized entity" (Bradford, "Fwd: Re: Hello and Question"). To write "Dead and decaying bodies" and "With the body drained of fluids" yet to avoid the use of *genocide* and also promote the lie of civil war is most problematic.

European Racist Theories and Colonization Contributed to the Rwandan Genocide

Rwanda's colonialist history played a significant role in the genocide. Belgians perceived the taller and lighter-skinned Tutsis as more intelligent than Hutus and Twas and promoted the education of Tutsis to carry out Belgian administration. Immaculée Ilibagiza, in her book *Left to Tell: Discovering God amidst the Rwandan Holocaust* (2006), writes "The Belgians favored the minority

Tutsi aristocracy and promoted its status as the ruling class; therefore, Tutsis were ensured a better education to better manage the country and generate greater profits for the Belgian overlords" (14–15). In other words, European pseudoscientific racist theories helped maximize revenue for the Belgians. In 1933, Belgians began requiring Hutus, Tutsis, and Twas to carry identity cards, and the seeds of genocide were set in motion. Destexhe writes, "In the end it was the ethnic classification system of identity cards introduced by the Belgians that enabled the Hutu regime to carry out the genocide of Tutsis" (viii). Eltringham, who lived in Rwanda for three years to write his book *Accounting for Horror: Post-Genocide Debates in Rwanda* (2004), and Kinzer agree that the ethnic identity cards contributed to the genocide (26).

Deady presents Rwandan history in this breezy manner: "In 1959, fights broke out between the Hutu and the Tutsi. The Tutsi leaders lost their power. In 1962, Belgium gave up control," making Belgium seem neutral and benign (7). Isaac and Greenberg create a similar impression: "When Rwanda gained its independence from Belgium in 1962, the Hutus were in charge of the government. Tutsi rebel groups then formed, ready to take over the country by force," which could also create the impression that Belgium was innocent in the matter (6).

J. K. Pomeray's *Rwanda* (2000) presents Belgian colonizers as categorically beneficial. Pomeray writes,

> The colonists tried to develop Rwanda's economy and political system, as well as to set up education and health-care programs. Although these efforts succeeded in other colonies, they never developed to the extent planned in Rwanda. . . . Colonial development did, however, break up the Tutsi-dominated feudal system. (16)

Colonial development did not break up the Tutsi-dominated feudal system. Belgians used it and empowered it for their own profit. Colonists also did not try to make Rwanda more profitable for Rwandans: "The Belgians tried to make Ruanda-Urundi more economically self-sufficient by increasing the production of staple foods. They also planted more coffee for export and introduced modern farming methods" (42). Any planting that was done was for the colonists' own profit—not for the Rwandans. There is no mention of the huge economic benefit Rwanda conferred upon Belgium. There is no mention of Belgian King Leopold's ghastly exploitation of the region. Had Pomeray studied Adam Hochschild's *King Leopold's Ghost: A Story of Greed, Terror, and Heroism in Colonial Africa* (1998), Pomeray could not possibly have written about colonists in such a flattering way. Leopold was as deceptive as Milošević, creating the impression in Europe that he was doing good in Africa while despicably enriching himself at the cost of human life and human hands in the region. Hochschild includes many photographs of those whose hands were chopped off because they had not brought enough rubber and ivory to

King Leopold's pawns in the region. Professor and political activist Gerald Caplan writes:

> For one hundred ten years prior to the Rwandan genocide, no external power played a more deplorable role in Africa than Belgium—a tiny country responsible for giant crimes against humanity. Its impact on Congo, Rwanda, and Burundi was catastrophic. The turbulent history of the entire Great Lakes region in the twentieth century would have been profoundly different if it had not been for Belgian colonial rule. And in 1994, just as the genocide was exploding across Rwanda, the Belgian Government sought to bring pressure on the Security Council to withdraw (in its entirety) its six-month old UN Assistance Mission for Rwanda (UNAMIR). (173)

It is hard to know what is more outrageous: Pomeray's portrayal of Belgian colonizers, or the cover of his or her book (J. K. is not gender-specific). The viewer sees only a gorilla. Although mountain gorillas do live in Rwanda, Pomeray's book is supposedly about Rwanda's history and so-called "civil war" (100). To represent the topic of the book with the visual image of a gorilla dehumanizes the Rwandan people. African studies and children's literature scholar Vivian Yenika-Agbaw refers to "the issue of White people's obsession with linking Blacks and animals" (24). It is appalling that Pomeray continues this obsession.

David King's *Rwanda* (2006), although well-designed and filled with colorful photographs, also makes benign destructive colonial powers:

> The Belgians had a strict program for "civilizing" colonial peoples and they applied these ideas to Rwandans between 1916 and 1962, when Rwanda became an independent nation.
>
> During the nearly half century of Belgian rule the Europeans had considerable success in improving physical aspects of the colony. (73)

Steven Lynn writes that postcolonial criticism "considers the role that literature has played as an agent of oppression and repression, distortion and understanding. What did European imperialists say about the people they colonized?" (156). King accepts and promotes the European imperialist project. He does not question Belgian authority in civilizing "the Other" or the assumption that it was the Belgians who were civilized when, in fact, they weren't. That it took half a century for Europeans to make improvements is a falsehood. Belgium gutted its colonies, raping land and life. King's uncritical acceptance of the imperialist narrative is unfortunate for young readers, who might unwittingly accept the same narrative.

King captures that the Belgians switched sides, but he downplays the role of European racist ideology and the identity cards: "While the cards did not have a major influence on the genocide in 1994, they were one more indicator of who would be killed and who would be spared" (77), which contradicts the views of Rwandan genocide scholars. Toward the end of his book, King describes a current library initiative in Rwanda and patronizingly writes, "Supporters feel that the library can open a whole new world to young Rwandans and that literature can help develop a commitment to democracy and the peaceful resolution of ethnic conflicts" (102). This seems to imply that, if the victimized Tutsis and moderate Hutus had read more books, they could have "peacefully resolved" the genocide. But no amount of reading could have stopped the radical Hutus from carrying out their murderous agenda. Terry Eagleton, as I wrote in Chapter Three, might point King to the Nazis reading their Goethe in concentration camps.

The Genocide Was Not a Spontaneous Tribal Outburst

Like the Holocaust, the Rwandan genocide was well-planned, well-organized, and systematic. The *Interahamwe*, the radical Hutu militia, deliberately exploited what they knew the western media bias would be: Westerners would readily accept the stereotype of "the Other"—those African tribes who were always killing each other and that there was nothing anyone could do to stop them. Melvern writes, "In Rwanda, the perpetrators and organizers of genocide were secure in the knowledge that outside interference would be at a minimum" (4).

As seen in the Cambodian and Bosnian genocides, thrusting a nation into genocide only takes a malicious and sociopathic few. Like Pol Pot and Milošević and their small groups, so too in Rwanda. Lieutenant-General Romeo Daillaire, the force commander of UNAMIR, whose torturous story is told in his *Shake Hands with the Devil: The Failure of Humanity in Rwanda* (2005), recognized that what happened in Rwanda was not a tribal outburst. Kinzer heard Daillaire speak in Chicago: "Several times he returned to the essential point: that Rwanda's genocide was not an eruption of tribal violence stemming from ancient hatreds but the work of a few dozen calculating and supremely cynical politicians" (279).

"A few dozen calculating and supremely cynical politicians" helped by western conceptions of "the Other." Eltringham further widens the frame of "the Other": "While it is often suggested that social distinctions emerge from an innate human propensity to distinguish 'insiders' and 'outsiders' (Us and Them), one can argue that it proceeds equally from the 'innate propensity' of external analysts to distinguish between 'them' and 'them'" (8).

Them and them: Tutsis and moderate Hutus, the genocidal victims, were a "them" and the radical Hutus were a "them." Both were thoroughly "othered." The ethnic conflict was perceived as inevitable, as the *Interahamwe* knew it would be. While promoting this false stereotype, perpetrators simultaneously made full use of bureaucratic operations. Shortly after the genocide, British journalist Fergal Keane visited the Office of the Bourgmestre of Rusomo. He writes,

With the ethnic identity and address of every resident registered here at the commune building, the Interahamwe had a ready-made death list. . . . Anybody who imagines that the killing was an arbitrary and disorganized tribal bloodbath had better come here. I have no doubt that this is an index list for murder, prepared years in advance and held in readiness. (86)

Eltringham observes, "Preparations for the genocide had been a long time in the making, including the formation, arming and training of militias, the establishment of *Kangura* and *RTLM* and the preparation of target lists" (116). Power confirms, "Lists of victims had been prepared ahead of time. That much was clear from the Radio Mille Collines broadcasts, which read the names, addresses, and license plate numbers of Tutsi and moderate Hutu" (333). Melvern writes, "Far from being a chaotic tribal war, what happened in Rwanda was deliberate, carefully planned and clinically carried out by an extremist group using army units and gendarmes to drive people systematically from their homes and assemble them at pre-arranged places of slaughter" (5). Journalist Philip Gourevitch notes that Hitler memorabilia were found in Habyarimana's home (78).

In *Rwanda: Fierce Clashes in Central Africa* (1997), Isaac tells of a young boy named Innocent whom he met in a refugee camp; Isaac comments, "It was only because the adults in Rwanda decided to kill each other, that Innocent became a victim" (10), a statement that serves to eradicate history. Tutsis and moderate Hutus did not choose to kill radical Hutus. Even if they had (excepting the RPF), they did not have the arms. And, as Mohamed Adhikari explains, the film *Hotel Rwanda* similarly contributes to the notion of a tribal outburst. A journalist asks Paul Rusesabagina, the hotel manager played by Don Cheadle, for the cause of the violence. Rusesabagina replies, "Hatred . . . insanity," leaving out France's agenda in keeping Rwanda Francophone by providing extraordinary numbers of weapons; Belgium's exploitation of the region and infusion of racist theories into a country that formerly had none; radical Hutu beliefs, not shared by moderate Hutus and Tutsis; and the bureaucratic apparatus to carry out the genocide, among other possible explanations. The response of "madness" does a disservice to viewers, as does Isaac's assertion that all of the adults in Rwanda decided to kill each other, who may accept the explanation and not investigate other possibilities. Adhikari writes, "*Hotel Rwanda*'s simplistic approach to the genocide is more likely to perpetuate rather than dispel stereotypes of Africa as a place of senseless violence and roiling tribal animosity" (175).

Isabelle asked me one day, "There's violence everywhere. Why is African violence different?" Chinua Achebe might have responded: "'[There] is a desire— one might indeed say a need—in Western psychology to set Africa up as a foil to Europe, as a place of negations . . . in comparison with which Europe's own state of spiritual grace will be manifest'" (qtd. in Maddy and MacCann, 13). I recalled with Isabelle Beverly Hawk's work in *Africa's Media Image* (1992):

She identifies lingering colonialist infiltration of the language used in speaking about African violence, which is distinctive, with such phrases as "'tribal' or 'black-on-black' violence. . . . No one calls the violence in Northern Ireland white-on-white violence, or tribal bloodshed" (7–8). Nor has Nazi violence been described as white-on-white. Achebe's notion of "foil" makes sense. Simplifying what happened to "madness" or adults deciding to kill each other contributes nothing to the search for truth. Isabelle suggested that it is a call to reevaluate coverage of African conflicts now and in the future.

International Governments and NGOs Did Not Help

As Isabelle noted, toward the end of the genocide, satellites showed the world the locations to which refugees rushed at the genocide's end in July of 1994. Those same satellites had also showed the world the travesty of genocide that began a few months before, on April 6, 1994—a travesty that was ignored.

After the Arusha Accords of 1993, the UN sent Dallaire and UNAMIR to Rwanda. In response to his constant and urgent requests for more troops and under pressure from the Clinton administration to do nothing (see Power 334–335), the UN instead reduced Daillaire's already pathetically undermanned 2,500 unit to a mere 270. Daillaire still feels that if he could have had just 5,000 troops, the genocide could have been stopped. Internationally, there were calls for a cease fire, which was a sham. Except for small bastions of RPF-controlled territory in the north, Tutsis and moderate Hutus had no fire to cease.

The way Isaac and Greenberg present this to young readers is troubling: "The United Nations sent soldiers to stand between the warring sides. It also flew in relief workers to help the injured and the sick" (7), and "UN soldiers had come from France as well as from the African countries of Senegal, Guinea-Bissau, Chad, Mauritania, Egypt, Niger, and the Congo. They positioned themselves between the collections of Hutus and Tutsis on the road. As official peacekeepers, the soldiers made every effort to prevent further bloodshed" (26). Actually, they did not and could not. As "monitors"—not peacekeepers—their orders were *not* to open fire. What are young readers to make of this? That the Hutus and Tutsis were so savage and brutal that one of the strongest forces on earth could not stop them? There were no "warring sides," and the world had done exactly the opposite: By the end of April, France and Belgium had evacuated their expatriates. There were few White people left in Rwanda. The world stood by and silently watched the slaughter of moderate Hutus and close to 80 percent of the Tutsi population in Rwanda. There is no denying that the world knew, as much Rwandan scholarship has since shown. Isaac and Greenberg would have done better to focus on Daillaire's tireless—and unanswered—appeals to the world for help or, as Isabelle suggests, on Sengalese Muslim Captain Mbaye Diagne, who rescued many Rwandans, including Prime Minister Agathe Uwlingiyimana's four children after Uwlingiyimana was put to death.

It was close to the genocide's end when NGOs arrived at the country's borders. Isabelle explained that, on their way out of Rwanda, the perpetrators grabbed families (who, Isabelle says, were mostly those of perpetrators who played a role in the killing as well, by either refusing to save victims or by disclosing their whereabouts) as human shields, so that, in fact, the NGOs were feeding and saving more perpetrators than victims. Isabelle said, "They had a choice. It was a hard choice. But it was a choice they made." Destexhe comments, "Humanitarian workers are continually confronted with the same problem: how to aid the victims without becoming caught up in the power struggles of their oppressors, or, as William Shawcross puts it, how to feed the victims without also providing aid to their tormentors" (57).

Isaac's overreach misrepresents international aid to young readers, and contributes to ongoing "othering."

Like Holocaust Survivors, Rwandans Are Not "Over" the Genocide

Tom Streissguth's *Rwanda in Pictures* (2008), part of Lerner's Twenty-First Century Books' Visual Geography Series, is an informational text written for middle-grade readers. The book is well-laid out, with vivid photographs that reveal why mountainous Rwanda is called "land of a thousand hills." Streissguth, with over forty books to his credit, is a capable writer. Unlike other authors who hesitate to use the word, Streissguth calls what happened in Rwanda a genocide in his introduction. He gives a detailed and fair account of Rwanda's history.

His assertion that "Rwanda has largely recovered from the 1994 genocide" (33) is highly questionable. Thirty pages later, he reasserts: "Rwanda has largely recovered from the tragic events of the 1990s. The economy has grown steadily, and ethnic violence is waning. The country has held peaceful elections, and its troublesome militias have disbanded" (64). Actually they have reassembled in the Congo, which is currently undergoing its own catastrophe. When I read Streissguth's book in 2008 I asked Yvette what she thought. She responded,

> If that is how the author feels he . . . needs to learn . . . more about what we have to heal from. . . . There has been some remarkable progress but we as a country are still far away from using the term "healed." We are learning how to move forward with our wounds but I don't even think we will ever be healed. (Rugasaguhunga, "Re: Question")

Two years later, when I discussed the book with Isabelle, her immediate response was, "The Holocaust was over almost seventy years ago and people are still trying to come to terms with it, yet the Rwandans are 'over it'"!? Part of casting nonwesterners as "the Other" involves oversimplifying the complexity of human beings. In her *Unsettling Narratives: Postcolonial Readings of*

Children's Literature (2007), Bradford cautions against "the bland assumption that 'we' know what 'they' are like, and that 'they' are, after all, not very difficult to know" (226).

Lingering colonialism infiltrates the assumption that "Rwanda has largely recovered" from the genocide. In *Hopes and Impediments* (1988) Achebe writes,

> To the colonialist mind it was always of the utmost importance to be able to say: "I know my natives," a claim which implied two things at once: (a) that the native was really quite simple and (b) that understanding him and controlling him went hand in hand—understanding being a pre-condition for control and control constituting adequate proof of understanding. (71)

Having grown up in the American South, these words resonate with me. I well remember the resentment my relatives had when Yankees came down to interfere with our business during the Civil Rights movement. Over and over I heard, "We know our Blacks" (only *Blacks* is not the word we used). They were silly creatures, like children, who quickly got over things in their childish fashion and didn't mind being subjugated by their White superiors. Colonialism assumes the humanity of one group—the rulers and exploiters—and the less-than-human status of those colonized.

In *When Victims Become Killers* (2001), Mahmood Mandani interviewed radical Hutu killers. He asked one killer "how long he thought it would take for Hutus and Tutsis to forget." The killer responded, "It will probably take the time the earth has left" (246). That from the perspective of the killer.

Had Streissguth followed Linda Alcoff's suggestion of speaking *with* and *to* rather than *for* others, he might still have found silence—because of the deep and unknowable trauma of genocide. Journalist Jean Hatzfeld, in *The Antelope's Strategy: Living in Rwanda after the Genocide* (2009), observes:

> The difficulty or even impossibility of speaking to others about one's experience, of sharing it with someone who did not live through it, is a distinguishing—and very disturbing—characteristic. ... After a genocide, survivors and criminals alike usually keep quiet, reluctant to speak of their still-raw experience of human extermination. (76)

Keane visited an orphanage and witnessed a similar silence; of a young girl, he writes, "She made no sound at all but when she sat down she rocked back and forth incessantly. Nobody knew what had happened to her parents because she had not spoken since the day the RPF soldiers had found her wandering in the bush" (69). One of the caretakers at the orphanage told Keane, "'There are so many like her. So many who have lost their voices because of what they have seen'" (69). Similarly Cambodians, who lived in enforced silence for 3.5 years, took much time to finally begin to speak of their experiences. Even those of us who know trauma cannot begin to imagine the trauma of genocide unless we have experienced it ourselves.

In *My Father, Maker of the Trees: How I Survived the Rwandan Genocide* (2009), Eric Irivuzumugabe wrote fifteen years after the genocide's end: "For most genocide survivors, it is not easy to remember the days of the outbreak. Some of my family members are still too traumatized to share their account of survival. The pain is still raw. Flashbacks haunt the nights" (29). Irivuzumugabe adds, "It's estimated that 90 percent of all genocide survivors are still experiencing trauma at some level" (146). As Leydesdorff found with the women of Srebrenica, many Rwandan genocide victims remain frozen in trauma.

Francine Niyitegeka was nineteen-years-old at the time of the genocide. Six years later Hatzfeld recorded her words in his book *Life Laid Bare: The Survivors in Rwanda Speak* (2000):

> Since the genocide, I always feel hunted, day and night. In my bed, I turn away from the shadows; on a path, I glance back at forms following me. When I meet a stranger's eyes, I fear for my child. . . . I endure a kind of shame over feeling hunted like that a whole life long, just because of who I am. The moment my eyes close upon that, I weep inside, from misery and humiliation. (43)

To say that Rwanda has largely recovered revictimizes victims, especially children. Kinzer summarizes a UN report:

> 99.9 percent of Rwandan children witnessed violence during the spring of 1994. Ninety percent believed they would die. Eighty-seven percent saw dead bodies, 80 percent lost at least one relative, 58 percent saw people being hacked . . . and 31 percent witnessed rapes or other sexual assaults. (253)

The Organization of African Unity estimates that the genocide left approximately 300,000 to 400,000 children orphaned. Today those orphans are young adults who still struggle with the loss of their parents. A Kigali teacher told African Rights/Working for Justice:

> As time passes the impact deepens and becomes more and more visible. Those who were very young during the genocide, and who didn't know what was happening, have for now grown up in a bad environment where they feel the full weight of what happened. That can only increase their bitterness every day. They have never known love and cannot, therefore, love others in return. When you go to commemoration services in memory of the victims, you see clearly that the morale of survivors is on the decline. Their hearts are much more wounded. They are the living dead who, rightly, feel that they have been abandoned by their fellow citizens and the world. And on top of all that, comes the extreme poverty which

they face after having lost everything during the genocide. I don't know why the sorrow has increased instead of diminishing. I think in 1995, and until about 2000, they still hoped that justice would be done. But now, they have been disappointed and they have no hope of justice. And that affects them enormously. (3)

Seventy years from now, Rwandans, who are as worthy of respect as Holocaust survivors, will no doubt resemble Holocaust survivors who, now in their eighties and nineties, continue to grapple with their experience of the worst of humanity.

Recommended with Reservations: Children's and Young Adult Literature about the Rwandan Genocide

Nicola Barber's *Central Africa* (2005) is an informational text. With a two-page spread on each of the countries in Central Africa, the section on Rwanda is too brief to make much sense. While it does include the Belgian "about-face," which many books do not, the author also mistakenly calls the Rwandan Patriotic Front the FPR; it is usually called the RPF (28).

J. P. Stassen's graphic novel *Deogratias: A Tale of Rwanda* (2006) takes the approach of exploring the actions and thoughts of a young perpetrator of genocide. The protagonist commits the unthinkable by killing his friends and experiences profound self disgust. Stassen has chosen to live in Rwanda and has immersed himself in trying to understand perpetrators, especially youth. Although the novel is designated for young adults, it is as intense and disturbing as any text written for adults, particularly the scenes in which sadistic adults induce teenagers to carry out violence as well. Stassen's novel shows that it is in the world's best interest to support vulnerable families and communities; children growing up in a volatile environment are prone to put their trust, as the protagonist does, in adults who do not deserve it. Ellis Barowsky and I have written about this topic elsewhere:

> Unable to provide for their own safety, children depend heavily upon adults to ensure their survival. Under pervasively threatening conditions, children become emotionally vulnerable. ... When family and community structures ... frequently break down, children often struggle to re-establish a sense of order. They become prey to the manipulation of authority figures who offer the appearance of rescue and security. This vulnerability, paired with poverty and lost community resources, makes these children more likely targets for recruitment as child soldiers. (357)

Although I admire Stassen's effort and art, I place his book in this "with reservations" section. It crosses the line into making reading about trauma traumatic; it is a more appropriate graphic novel for adults than for children and teens, although it may perpetuate stereotypes even for adults in that Stassen focuses on the most violent aspects of Rwanda.

Isabelle read Nicki Cornwell's *Christophe's Story* (2006), a novella for young children, which is supposedly based on Cornwell's experience with refugees. Although the story has value—a Rwandan boy begins to work through his trauma through storytelling and help from a kind teacher—Cornwell gives in to the impulse to exoticize. About his experience in Rwanda, Christophe says, "[B]ad men came. They looked really scary. They were dressed in banana leaves and they had chalked their faces white. They carried knives and spears, and they burst into the house" (37). Isabelle thought the example of using the banana leaves as masks was an old practice, done in a time when people were ashamed of killing. Not in 1994—radical Hutus took pride in killing and did not bother with masks. Isabelle said they believed their actions would result in the end of all Tutsis; they didn't expect survivors. There were some reports in the International Criminal Tribunal for Rwanda of incidents where attackers wore masks of banana leaves; perhaps Cornwell made too much of these accounts. On a literary note, Cornwell overuses exclamation points.

Isabelle read and liked Hanna Jansen's *Over a Thousand Hills I Walk with You* (2002), as did I; Isabelle thought Jansen's fictionalized biography of her adopted daughter, Jeanne, gave a face to statistics.

Jeanne was nine-years-old at the time of the Rwandan genocide. The first half of the book is a recounting of her typical childhood, surrounded by her warm, loving family and servants. Jeanne knew little of the Hutu and Tutsi, and the genocide took her completely by surprise. She had heard her parents speak in hushed tones but had no way of knowing what lay ahead for Tutsis and moderate Hutus from April to July 1994.

When the genocide began she saw her mother and brother murdered before her eyes. A Hutu woman took Jeanne in and eventually she immigrated to Germany to become part of the Jansen family. Jeanne told her story repeatedly to her adoptive mother, who clearly adores her. Jansen's writing is poetic and evocative; Elizabeth Crawford won the Batchelder award for her translation of Jansen's book from the German. Jansen occasionally breaks the narrative with interludes where she speaks directly to Jeanne. Such breaks from the story line, Jansen felt, would make Jeanne's experience more real.

After the book was published, Hazel Rochman interviewed Jansen; Jansen says that Jeanne:

> felt an urgent need to tell about her witnessing the murder of her mother and brother, so she spoke about it again and again. It seemed to me as if she wanted to free herself from the terrible nightmares that drove her out of bed at night. . . . Once she told me that after sharing with me this way, she could feel like a complete person again. (42)

For those who wonder how survivors of genocide begin to recover, Jansen's loving attention to Jeanne is one way—the simple act of listening.

Brenda Randolph served on the Children's Africana Book Awards (CABA) committee in 2006 when *Over a Thousand Hills I Walk with You* was considered for an award. Randolph writes, "The book is a moving testament to the courage and resiliency of ... Jeanne" (79), and acknowledges that "Jansen does a masterful job of retelling Jeanne's story" (80). CABA sought the advice of genocide scholars, who told the committee that Jansen omits explanations of the cause of the genocide—the radical Hutus in power—and Lemarchand says, "'Rather than to look for age-old antagonisms between Hutu and Tutsi, the key to an understanding of the Rwandan apocalypse lies in the extent to which ethnic identities have been manipulated for political advantage by modern-day politicians'" (qtd. in Randolph, 80). Jansen, Randolph asserts, "reinforces the ethnic hatred idea with the statement: '[Death] was their constant companion. It had nothing to do with war, just with naked hatred, which had suddenly burst out and shown itself to them undisguised'" (81). Jansen's treatment of Hutu and Tutsi, Randolph says, in the words of political scientist Edouard Bustin, overdoes "'good guys and bad guys'" (qtd. in Randolph, 81). At the end of the book, Jansen's time line also leaves out the toxic effect of Belgian colonization and racism.

Still, Randolph does not discourage the book's use; she writes, "Whatever its omissions or missteps, the book depicts life before the genocide as experienced by many Rwandans. High school teachers who use Jansen's book should consider supplementing it with excerpts" (82). Here Randolph mentions Gerard Prunier, Andre Sibomana, and Immaculée Ilibagiza as resources.

I asked Yvette to comment on Jeanne's seeming lack of forewarning of the genocide. Yvette replied:

> I haven't read that book but I can see how some Tutsi lived in peace illusion. Most of uneducated Tutsi, or some of those in the villages, did not sense any danger. Even if some areas were more peaceful than others, every Tutsi regardless of [what] she/he saw, lived and experienced the dehumanization and discrimination in one way or another but some did not understand the worst was yet to come. I think this could be because of brainwashing ideas spread by the government and the militias that left many Tutsi believ[ing] that those who had been killed or jailed were the cause of their misery, the ones to blame. Some Tutsi did not empathize with the victims as they seriously believed they deserved what they were going through. .... Either Jeanne was too young or was a victim of that brainwashing. I was 14, my father barely spoke of politics but I could sense danger even if I could not imagine such horrible things to happen. (Rugasaguhunga, "E-mail message")

Jeanne's naivetë may have been the norm, but, as political scientist Michael Barnett observes about Rwanda (and, I'd add, about any country anywhere),

"Few dared to imagine the apocalyptic possibility of genocide. Genocide is not simply a low-probability form of violence that ranks at the bottom of any list of violent alternatives. It resides outside the realm of human imagination" (156). Most certainly it resides outside the realm of the imaginable for children. Albert Camus wrote of the phenomenon of universal shock in *The Plague*, over sixty years ago: "'There have been as many plagues as wars in history; yet always plagues and wars take people by surprise'" (qtd. in Felman and Laub, 1992, 97). So it was with nine-year-old Jeanne.

Recommended Children's and Young Adult Literature about the Rwandan Genocide

Novels

Of the books we read, Élisabeth Combres's *Broken Memory: A Novel of Rwanda* (2010) was Isabelle's favorite; she thought it the most realistic and beautifully written. She also thought that the book captured the feeling of being lost and confused, a state survivors found themselves in. The novel is based on accounts of the genocide Combres, a French journalist, collected from young survivors in 2004. First published in French, *Broken Memory* won several international awards (Figure 4.1).

The story tells of Emma, a Tutsi, who was five-years-old at the time of the genocide. She hides behind a sofa while her mother is killed by attackers; she then follows her mother's dying advice to flee. After days of walking and hiding, Emma finds Mukecuru, a kind Hutu woman, who risks her life by taking Emma in and raising her as her own. Hutus taking care of Tutsi children is based in fact; those who had lost everyone sometimes found "family" elsewhere. Now fourteen, Emma is still frozen in the past: "So she existed without really being there, not really alive and not dead, though she would sometimes feel like a corpse herself, buried in the mud at the foot of the garden" (21).

After the genocide, Rwanda initiated *gacaca* courts, grounded in Rwanda's traditional communal justice. The country was overwhelmed with former *génocidaires*, and its courts could not cope with all its prisoners. In the *gacaca* court, communities would determine what had happened and what should be done. One day Mukecuru says, "'They are coming, Emma'" (35), meaning those who had killed Emma's family were coming to their village to be tried by the *gacaca* court. Emma is deeply shaken and says, "'And the ones who survived, they might as well be dead, too'" (36). Mukecuru gently takes Emma into her arms and rocks her.

When the prisoners come to town, Emma expects the worst, but is surprised: "She had been prepared to see monsters, men with faces full of cruelty. Instead she saw simple peasants" (68). When the *gacaca* begins, Emma befriends Ndoli, a Tutsi boy who is almost deranged from what he experienced in the genocide. Combres writes, "She saw each mark the blows had left nine years earlier. The hollow on the right side of his skull where his hair was shaved. The thick scar that cut across the caramel skin of his forehead and pointed toward his left eye" (61). A doctor has come to town who begins to help Ndoli

Figure 4.1 Book cover from Élisabeth Combres; photograph by Robert Palumbo: *Broken Memory: A Novel of Rwanda*. Toronto, Canada: Groundwood, 2010.

recover and wants to help Emma, too. Mukecuru tells the doctor Emma must choose for herself. When Emma learns he might be able to help with her nightmares, which she has had for nine years, she becomes open to talking with him. Through her friendship with Ndoli, Mukecuru's undying love, and many conversations with the doctor, Emma begins to free herself from her horrifying past. The book ends with Emma, ten years later at age twenty-four, having returned to the village in which she was born and living in her deceased mother's home, looking "forward to the future with confidence" (131). Combres's author's note is helpful in contextualizing the genocide, and *Broken Memory* is a tribute to the victims and survivors of the Rwandan genocide.

Canadian author Eric Walters has over seventy books to his credit. In *Shattered* (2007), Ian, a high school student, forms a friendship with Jacques, a soldier loosely based on Romeo Daillaire. For a high school civics class, Ian, who comes from an affluent family, must carry out community service in a soup kitchen in Montreal. There he meets Jacques, who now has a drinking problem. Conversations with Jacques acquaint Ian with the Rwandan genocide and cause him to question Berta, his nanny from Guatemala, about the Guatemalan genocide as well. Berta gradually shares with Ian events that occurred in her life when she was about his age and the orphans she now supports with the salary she earns from Ian's parents. Through Berta and Jacques, Ian comes to an understanding of posttraumatic stress disorder and how it can be triggered by everyday objects in the environment. Standing on a bridge in a Canadian park, Jacques tells Ian the association he now makes with bridges:

"Do you know what I think of every time I cross this bridge?"
Of course I didn't know, but I didn't think he expected an answer.
"I think of bodies. A river full of bloated human bodies, dumped in a river, so thick that they formed a blockage across the river where it went under a bridge. And people had to haul those bodies out, drag them up onto the shore and dump them back into the river on the other side of the bridge to stop that log-jam of human beings from causing a flood. And each time they pulled out a body, another drifted down the river to take its place." (116)

Through Berta and Jacques, Ian's commitment to social justice becomes real—not solely an effort to get a passing grade. And, in time, Ian helps Jacques face alcoholism when he says:

Nobody is asking you to forget. . . . I'm asking you to remember those that you saved and to honour those you couldn't save. Giving up your life honours nobody, saves nobody. By living like this you're saying that life isn't precious. It *is* precious. Every life . . . including yours. Don't let Rwanda—don't let *evil*—claim one more victim. Don't let yourself be another casualty of Rwanda. (185–186)

The book ends on a hopeful note, suggesting that Jacques will stay sober and that Ian will continue working in the soup kitchen when it is no longer required.

Informational Texts

Frank Spalding's *Genocide in Rwanda* (2009), part of Rosen's Genocide in Modern Times Series, is a responsible informational text written for middle-

Figure 4.2 Book cover from Frank Spalding: *Genocide in Rwanda*. New York: Rosen Publishing, 2009.

grade readers (Figure 4.2). Early on Spalding acknowledges the pseudoscience that permeated Belgium's colonization of Rwanda. In recounting the history of Rwanda, he writes,

Figure 4.3   Book cover from Aimable Twagilimana: *Hutu and Tutsi*.

Belgians altered Rwanda's government by placing Tutsis—and only Tutsis—in positions of power. The Belgians believed that the Tutsis had more 'Caucasian' features than Hutus and were therefore more fit to rule. Blatantly racist beliefs such as these were not uncommon in Europe at the time. (10)

Spalding notes that, prior to 1933, there was flexibility between Hutus and Tutsis, and that they intermarried. Once Belgians required identity cards, Spalding acknowledges that the consequences would become "disastrous," alluding to the 1994 genocide (11).

Aimable Twagilimana, a native Rwandan, in *Hutu and Tutsi* (1998) provides information from a cultural insider's perspective. He discusses the history that led up to the genocide, including the Belgians' ethnic division of Hutus and Tutsis, a division that had not previously existed. He explains the counterfeit theories that informed their decision: The Tutsis, being lighter-skinned were deemed more intelligent. When the Belgians perceived it more financially advantageous to support the Hutus, their previously held beliefs of the Tutsis' superior intelligence was thrown to the wind. When the Belgians left, the inflammatory power structure remained. Twagilimana's style makes the books accessible to young readers (Figure 4.3).

Like his biography of Pol Pot, described in Chapter One, Andy Koopmans's *Rwanda* (2005) is another excellent informational text. He acknowledges the harm of colonialism: "With the coming to Africa of the book, the wheel, the hoe, and the modern rifle and cannon, foreigners also brought the vastly destructive transatlantic slave trade, oppression, discrimination, and onerous colonial rule" (n. pag.). Koopmans recognizes the toxicity of the Belgian edict of mandating identity cards in the 1930s, which lasted until the end of the genocide, and the racism behind the identity cards: "The predominant belief in Europe at the time was that the white race was superior; thus, in the minds of many Belgians, the Tutsis' appearance made them genetically superior to the Hutu and the Twa" (25).

Koopmans's account of the Belgian stance first toward Tutsis, then toward Hutus, reflects careful research. The threat the Arusha Accords of 1993 posed to radical Hutus is crystallized in this passage: "Despite the progress toward a new multiparty government, Hutu extremists did not want to share power with the Tutsis. These men—among them many government officials—planned a genocidal attack on the country's Tutsis and moderate Hutus" (29). Koopmans understands the efficient bureaucratic apparatus that had been mobilized to carry out genocide. And in contrast to Isaac and Greenberg, he understands the limited role played by the NGOs: "UN soldiers stationed in Rwanda were ordered not to respond. In fact, after 10 Belgian UN soldiers were killed in the violence the UN pulled out 90 percent of its forces, leaving many Tutsis to die unprotected" (29). In contrast to Streissguth's assertion that Rwandans are largely over the genocide, Koopmans conveys to young readers the trauma that continues: "The people of Kigali are still haunted by memories of the thousands of Tutsis slaughtered in the genocide, as well as the widespread and fierce fighting between the army and the Rwandan Patriotic Front (RPF) in 1990" (69). Koopmans's estimate of "thousands" is low, but recognizes that the impact of genocide on Rwandans is no less than it would be on any other group; Rwandans are as complex, and feel as deeply, as all other human beings.

Crossover Literature

To write her book *Stars of Rwanda: Children Write and Draw about Their Experiences during the Genocide of 1994* (2004), Wiljo Woodi Oosterom, founder of Silent Work: Sustainable Projects for the Forgotten Children of Africa, traveled to Rwanda to listen to children's stories and encourage them to create art. One of those interviewed, Pauline, had experiences similar to Jeanne in *Over a Thousand Hills I Walk with You,* because her childhood before the genocide was, like Jeanne's, relatively happy. Pauline told Oosterom, "My life before the tragic period was generally good, because I still had my parents and relatives. We were living our lives without any problems. The war turned everything upside down" (19). Linda Alcoff states, "Often the possibility of dialogue [with victims] is left unexplored or inadequately pursued by more privileged persons" (23). By talking with Pauline, and others, Oosterom explored and pursued dialogue. It should also be noted that the photographs in this book are beautifully rendered.

Rosalind Carr came from the United States to the Belgian Congo with her young husband in 1949. After their marriage ended, so in love with Rwanda was Carr that she stayed. At the time of the genocide, she took in orphans, and her biography tells of her efforts after the genocide to educate and nurture those children left alone. About the causes of the genocide, Carr ponders,

> I have asked myself a thousand times, how could such a thing happen in this time in our history? How could such a thing happen in a country that had known two decades of relative peace and prosperity? The Hutu and Tutsi populations in Rwanda shared a common language and a common culture. Hutu farmers and Tutsi cattle herders had coexisted in unity and cooperation. They lived side by side and intermarried. They were neighbors and friends. . . . There is no doubt that what happened in Rwanda was more than a spontaneous outpouring of tribal rage. What took place was a systematic campaign of extermination orchestrated by political leaders and backed by the military. (211)

Carr's observations are confirmed by Rwandan genocide scholars.

An after-effect of the Rwandan genocide that I have not found in the study of the other genocides is the renewal of religious faith as reflected in the following books. Two books that have been widely popular among young people in the United States, especially those in church groups, are Immaculée Ilibagiza's *Left to Tell: Discovering God amidst the Rwandan Holocaust* (2006). Ilibagiza, a Tutsi, was a college student home for a visit when the genocide began. After her family was murdered, Ilibagiza, along with seven other women, sought refuge with a Hutu pastor. Risking his own life for ninety-one days, he hid them in a tiny bathroom, placing a large wardrobe in front of the door so that the women would not be detected. Although Ilibagiza honestly describes the tensions of three months in a cramped bathroom—even the Hutu pastor has his moments of regret for taking the women in—Ilibagiza begins praying the rosary her father had given her and experiences a religious rebirth, for which she is now thankful. The Rwandan genocide did not shake her faith; after the genocide, she wrote:

> Staring into the night sky, I was again transfixed by the breathtaking beauty of the milky illumination cast by God's countless stars. The starlight was so intense that I could easily seek the road we'd arrived on. . . . I wondered if my family was safe and hiding somewhere nearby . . . or if they'd crossed over to the next life and now existed somewhere on the other side of the eternal galaxies above me. (3)

In 2008, she published a sequel: *Led by Faith: Rising from the Ashes of the Rwandan Genocide*. She now speaks internationally on the power of faith and forgiveness.

Another deeply religious book is Eric Irivuzumugabe's *My Father, Maker of the Trees: How I Survived the Rwandan Genocide* (2009). To stay alive, Irivuzumugabe had to live in a cypress tree for two weeks to avoid being detected. After the genocide, he became "born again" and now works with children orphaned by the genocide. He converted his brother, Mugabo, to Christianity. Mugabo says,

> Though I was ten years old, the genocide left me like an old man who had endured many wars of evil. I felt like a soldier who had never been relieved from battle. Everything looked different to me after the war, broken and empty. But I knew what Eric was telling me about God must be true. I had to forget the madness and move toward this Creator God he was telling me about. I knew Eric was telling me the truth but the climb toward God seemed like another long journey and I didn't know if I had the strength to follow. (98–99)

I asked Isabelle what she thought of the phenomenon of religious renewal after the genocide. Isabelle responded that she thought it was overstated, and worried that those incapable of forgiveness were deemed unstable, a judgment that fails to recognize forgiveness as a process. Isabelle also found condescending the expectation by outsiders that Rwandans should forgive—they weren't there when the genocide happened, so why monitor the recovery now? Francine, in Hatzfeld's *Life Laid Bare*, says, "I cannot glimpse much goodness in the hearts of those [who] now are returning to the hills, and I hear no one asking for forgiveness. In any case, I know there is nothing that can be forgiven" (42).

After the Holocaust, Primo Levi wrote, "'Today I think that if for no other reason than that an Auschwitz existed, no one in our age should speak of Providence'" (qtd. in Kidder, 177). Rabbi Steven Jacobs writes,

> All genocides challenge their religious victims. Believers, raised to appreciate the essential goodness and value of their own religious traditions, suddenly confront *génocidaires* who make a mockery of everything they hold sacred, and, in so doing, reveal the powerlessness of their belief systems in the face of such monstrous evil. ... but even to echo the Job of the Torah/Hebrew Bible—"Though He slay me, yet will I trust in Him; but I will argue my ways before Him" (Job 13:15)—is despite all evidence to the contrary, to affirm God in a godless world. It is to reject the momentary triumph of génocidaires in favor of the human community; it is to believe, despite everything, that tomorrow will be better than today, because it *must* be. (103; italics in the original)

Although Jacobs maintains his religious faith in spite of the Holocaust, it is a process that includes sheer force of will ("Though He slay me") (103). Ilibagiza and Irivuzumugabe do not shake their fists at the sky similarly.

While forgiveness and reconciliation are arguably good things, there is the danger of "painting over rust," as psychologist Ellis Barowsky says. "Despite the shiny covering of what appears to be a fresh coat of abilities, the underlying abrasion of emotional injury will ultimately break through" (Gangi and Barowsky, 358).

Besides the sheer number of books sold, that Ilibagiza is widely read is apparent in an interaction I had with José, a fifth grader already mentioned in my Introduction. Along with José's teacher and my undergraduate students, I had been conducting Book Clubs on books by Deborah Ellis: *Parvana's Journey* (2002), a novel about life under the Taliban in Afghanistan, and two informational texts: *Off to War: Voices of Soldiers' Children* (2008) and *Children of War: Voices of Iraqi Refugees* (2010). José was part of the latter group. While discussing the book, he turned to me and said, "This reminds me of *Left to Tell*."

Surprised, I asked, "You read that?"

"Yes," he said. "It was really good."

"How did you get that book?" I asked.

"My older brother gave it to me," he said. "It was really, really good."

That was all we had time for. As it was the end of the year, I did not get a chance to go back to the school to interview José further. This brief exchange points out that children will continue to read books meant for adults, as they always have.

Conclusion

Yenika-Agbaw writes, "because the majority of African children may not have access to these books, they are denied the opportunity to examine these cultural experiences and either agree with the depiction of their culture, or question/challenge inappropriate images of themselves that they may find. They therefore are **doubly marginalized**" (xvi; emphasis in the original). To convey to young readers that what happened in Rwanda was a civil war or a tribal outburst, to fail to mention Belgian colonization and the imposition of European racist theories on a country that had been fairly peaceful before the Europeans' arrival, and to assert that the Rwandans are over the genocide—all are forms of genocide denial. As Deborah Lipstadt poignantly observes, "'denial of genocide strives to reshape history in order to demonize the victims and rehabilitate the perpetrators, and is—indeed—the final state of genocide'" (qtd. in Balakian, 382). Isabelle says that the "only way to honor the genocide is to not allow it to be denied . . . it is a fundamental aspect of remembering the victims of a genocide . . . to never oversimplify or deny or reinvent the turn of events that led to their demise."

Works Cited

Achebe, Chinua. *Hopes and Impediments*. New York: Doubleday, 1988.

Adhikari, Mohamed. "*Hotel Rwanda*—The Challenges of Historicizing and Commercializing Genocide." *Development Dialogue* 50 (2008): 173–195.

African Rights/Working for Justice. *A Wounded Generation: The Children Who Survived Rwanda's Genocide*. Kigali, Rwanda: Author, 2006.

Alcoff, Linda. "The Problem of Speaking for Others." *Cultural Critique* 20 (1991–1992, Winter): 5–32.

Apple, Michael. Foreword. *White Reign: Deploying Whiteness in America*. Eds. Joe L. Kincheloe, Shirley R. Steinberg, Nelson M. Rodriguez, and Ronald E. Chennault. New York: St. Martin's, 1998.

Balakian, Peter. *The Burning Tigris: The Armenian Genocide and America's Response*. New York: HarperCollins, 2003.

Barnett, Michael. *Eyewitness to a Genocide: The United Nations and Rwanda*. Ithaca, NY: Cornell UP, 2002.

Bodnarchuk, Kari. *Rwanda: A Country Torn Apart*. Minneapolis, MN: Lerner, 2000. World in Conflict Ser.

Bradford, Clare. "Fwd: Re: Hello and Question." Message to Jane M. Gangi. 7 July 2008. E-mail.

———. *Unsettling Narratives: Postcolonial Readings of Children's Literature*. Waterloo, Ontario: Wilfrid Laurier UP, 2007.

Caplan, Gerald. "From Rwanda to Darfur: Lessons Learned?" Totten and Markusen, 171–179.

Dallaire, Romeo. *Shake Hands with the Devil: The Failure of Humanity in Rwanda*. New York: Carroll & Graf, 2005.

Deady, Kathleen W. *Rwanda: A Question and Answer Book*. Mankato, MN: Capstone, 2005. World in Conflict Ser.

Des Forges, Alison. *Leave None to Tell the Story: Genocide in Rwanda*. New York: Human Rights Watch, 1999.

Destexhe, Alain. *Rwanda and Genocide in the Twentieth Century*. New York: New York UP, 1995.

Ellis, Deborah. *Children of War*. Toronto: Groundwood, 2010.

——. *Off to War: Voices of Soldiers' Children*. Toronto: Groundwood, 2008.

——. *Parvana's Journey*. Toronto: Groundwood, 2002.

Eltringham, Nigel. *Accounting for Horror: Post-Genocide Debates in Rwanda*. London: Pluto, 2004.

Felman, Shoshana, and Dori Laub. *Testimony: Crises of Witnessing in Literature, Psychoanalysis, and History*. New York: Routledge, 1992.

Gangi, Jane M., and Ellis Barowsky. "Listening to Children's Voices: Literature and the Arts as Means of Responding to the Effects of War, Terrorism, and Disaster." *Childhood Education* 85.6 (2009): 357–363.

Gourevitch, Philip. *We Wish to Inform You That We Will Be Killed with Our Families: Stories from Rwanda*. New York: Farrar, 1998.

Hatzfeld, Jean. *The Antelope's Strategy: Living in Rwanda after the Genocide*. Trans. Linda Coverdale. New York: Farrar, 2009.

——. *Life Laid Bare: The Survivors in Rwanda Speak*. Trans. Linda Coverdale. New York: Other, 2000.

Hawk, Beverly G., ed. "Introduction." *Africa's Media Image*. Westport, CT: Praeger, 1992. 3–14.

Hochschild, Adam. *King Leopold's Ghost: A Story of Greed, Terror, and Heroism in Colonial Africa*. Boston: Houghton, 1998.

Hotel Rwanda. Dir. Greg Carson. Perf. Don Cheadle. MGM. 2004. Film.

Ilibagiza, Immaculée, with Steve Erwin. *Led by Faith: Rising from the Ashes of the Rwandan Genocide*. Carlsbad, CA: Hay, 2008.

Irivuzumugabe, Eric, with Tracey D. Lawrence. *My Father, Maker of the Trees: How I Survived the Rwandan Genocide*. Grand Rapids, MI: Baker, 2009.

Isaac, John (Photographer), and Keith Greenberg. *Rwanda: Fierce Clashes in Central Africa*. Woodbridge, CT: Blackbirch, 1997. Children in Crisis Ser.

Jacobs, Steven Leonard. "'Revisiting Again and Again the Kingdom of Night.'" Jones, *Evoking*, 101–103.

Jensen, Steven L. B., ed. *Genocide: Cases, Comparisons and Contemporary Debates*. Trans. Gwynneth Llewellyn. Njalsgade, Denmark: The Danish Center for Holocaust and Genocide Studies, 2003.

Jones, Adam, ed. *Evoking Genocide: Scholars and Activists Describe the Works That Shaped Their Lives*. Toronto: Key, 2009.

Keane, Fergal. *Season of Blood: A Rwandan Journey*. New York: Viking, 1995.

Kidder, Tracy. *Strength in What Remains*. New York: Random, 2009.

King, David C. *Rwanda*. Tarrytown, NY: Cavendish, 2006.

Kinzer, Stephen. *A Thousand Hills: Rwanda's Rebirth and the Man Who Dreamed It*. Hoboken, NJ: Wiley, 2008.

Lemarchand, René. "Comparing the Killing Fields: Rwanda, Cambodia and Bosnia." Jensen, 141–173.

Lynn, Steven. *Texts and Contexts: Writing about Literature with Critical Theory*. 2nd ed. Boston: Longman, 2011.

Maddy, Yulisa Amadu, and Donnarae MacCann. *Neo-Imperialism in Children's Literature about Africa: A Study of Contemporary Fiction*. New York: Routledge, 2009.

Mandani, Mahmood. *When Victims Become Killers: Colonialism, Nativism, and the Genocide in Rwanda*. Princeton, NJ: Princeton UP, 2001.

Melvern, Linda. *A People Betrayed: The Role of the West in Rwanda's Genocide*. London: Zed, 2000.

Organization of African Unity. "Rwanda: The Preventable Genocide." 2000. Web. 1 Apr. 2013. <http://www.africa-union.org/official_documents/reports/report_rowanda_genocide.pdf>

Pomeray, J. K. *Rwanda*. Philadelphia: Chelsea, 2000. Major World Nation Ser.

Power, Samantha. *"A Problem from Hell": America and the Age of Genocide*. New York: Basic, 2002.

Randolph, Brenda. "Picture Books Sweep the 2007 Children's African Book Awards." *Sankofa* 6 (2007): 74–84.

Republic of Rwanda. "French Judges Release Report on the Plane Crash Used to Start Genocide in Rwanda." 2012. Web. 1 Apr. 2013. <http://www.gov.rw/French-Judges-release-report-on-the-plane-crash-used-as-a-pretext-to-start-genocide-in-Rwanda>
Rochman, Hazel. "Talking with Hanna Jansen." *Book Links* (Sept. 2006): 42–43.
Rugasaguhunga, Yvette. Message to Jane M. Gangi. 24 Mar. 2008. E-mail.
———. "RE: question." Message to Jane M. Gangi. 26 Feb. 2008. E-mail.
Said, Edward. *Orientalism*. New York: Vintage, 1978.
Streissguth, Tom. *Rwanda in Pictures*. Minneapolis, MN: Twenty-First Century, 2008. Visual Geography Ser.
Summerfield, Derek. "The Social Experience of War and Some Issues for the Humanitarian Field." *Rethinking the Trauma of War*. Eds. Patrick J. Bracken and Celia Petty. London: Free Association/Save the Children, 1998. 9–37.
Yenika-Agbaw, Vivian. *Representing Africa in Children's Literature: Old and New Ways of Seeing*. New York: Routledge, 2008.

Recommended Children's and Young Adult Literature about the Rwandan Genocide

Combres, Élisabeth. *Broken Memory: A Novel of Rwanda*. Toronto: Groundwood, 2010.
Koopmans, Andy. *Rwanda*. Philadelphia: Mason Crest, 2005.
Oppong, Joseph R. *Rwanda*. New York: Chelsea, 2008.
Spalding, Frank. *Genocide in Rwanda*. New York: Rosen, 2009. Genocide in Modern Times Ser.
Twagilimana, Aimable. *Hutu and Tutsi*. New York: Rosen, 1998.
Walters, Eric. *Shattered*. Toronto: Puffin Canada, 2007.

Recommended with Reservations: Children's and Young Adult Literature about the Rwandan Genocide

Barber, Nicola. *Central Africa*. London: Smart Apple, 2005.
Cornwell, Nicki, and Karin Littlewood (Illus.). *Christophe's Story*. London: Francis Lincoln, 2006.
Jansen, Hanna. *Over a Thousand Hills I Walk with You*. Trans. Elizabeth D. Crawford. Minneapolis, MN: Carolrhoda, 2002.
Stassen, Jean-Philippe. *Deogratias: A Tale of Rwanda*. New York: First Second, 2006.

Recommended Crossover Literature about the Rwandan Genocide

Carr, Rosamond Halsey, with Ann Howard Halsey. *Land of a Thousand Hills: My Life in Rwanda*. New York: Viking, 1999.
Ilibagiza, Immaculée, with Steve Erwin. *Led by Faith: Rising from the Ashes of the Rwandan Genocide*. Carlsbad, CA: Hay, 2008.
———. *Left to Tell: Discovering God amidst the Rwandan Holocaust*. Carlsbad, CA: Hay, 2006.
Irivuzumugabe, Eric, with Tracey D. Lawrence. *My Father, Maker of the Trees: How I Survived the Rwandan Genocide*. Grand Rapids, MI: Baker, 2009.
Oosterom, Wiljo Woodi. *Stars of Kigali, Rwanda: Children Write and Draw about Their Experiences during the Genocide of 1994*. Kigali, Rwanda: Silent Work Foundation, 2004.

Chapter Five
Children's and Young Adult Literature of Darfur

Darfur was a backwater, a prisoner of geography.
—Julie Flint and Alex de Waal

In 2003 the Khartoum government in Sudan, led by President Omar Hassan al-Bashir, initiated a genocide that killed approximately 400,000 innocent victims in the Darfur region and displaced over 2 million civilians, who to this day (2013) live in miserable camps in Darfur and Chad. In Darfur, the attackers and the attacked for the most part shared the same religion: Islam. The Arab government in Khartoum and government-sponsored Janjaweed targeted the villages of Black Muslims.

As in Rwanda, the destructive forces of prior colonization were at work. From 1898 to 1953, the British controlled southern Sudan, while the Egyptians controlled northern Sudan. In the north, the predominant religion is Islam; in the south, it is either Christianity or a traditional African religion. In the 1950s, as more and more African countries gained independence, so too did the Sudan. The British, who had primarily occupied southern Sudan, deserted their former colony, agreeing with Egyptian leaders and Arab Muslims in the north to locate political power and governance in Khartoum. Once again, an artificial nation was cobbled together with uninformed guidelines created by ignorant, greedy outsiders. Because Darfur was not near the River Nile, as Khartoum was, and therefore not potentially profitable, the British favored Arab Muslim power in the northeast of Sudan. During its long colonial rule, Britain had done little to nothing for Darfur, a province in the far west of this huge country.

The north and the south fought the world's longest-running civil war, from 1983 until 2005, when the Comprehensive Peace Agreement was signed. On July

6, 2011, Africa's largest country, Sudan, split. The south, called the Republic of South Sudan, and the north, called the Republic of Sudan, are now two independent states. Although peace has become possible between the north and the south, the conflict in Darfur, which is part of the Republic of Sudan, continues.

In addition to the toxic British legacy, another cause of the conflict is, as journalist Julie Flint and social anthropologist Alex de Waal write, a "new political ideology in Darfur: Arab supremacism" (49). This ideology was fueled by Libyan president Muammar Gaddafi's "'Arab Gathering'" (50). Gaddafi wanted to create an Arab state by taking over, first, Chad, then the Darfur region of the Sudan; J. Millard Burr and Robert Collins add, "Qaddafi would dream of a single, united Arab nation stretching from 'Sind' [Pakistan] to the Atlantic Ocean" (75). As noted in my Introduction, an extension of the definition of genocide is that it requires an ideology to fuel it, and Gaddafi's ideology, which al-Bashir and his government embraced, helped fuel the genocide in Darfur. Samuel Totten and Erick Markusen conducted interviews with Darfuris; they tell of a Black African who had lost everything: the "*Janjaweed* screamed at him: 'You are not a real Sudanese, you're black. We swore to drive you away from this country on al-Bashir's . . . orders. We are the real Sudanese. No blacks need stay here'" (98). This was a shift from historic racist beliefs to land grabs and genocide. Burr and Collins explain,

> Arab superiority has been a characteristic of northern Sudanese societies for centuries but their determination to use force to seize the regional government and change its name . . . was hitherto unheard of in a society in which Arab nomads and African farmers had managed to coexist under a workable system that settled inter-tribal disputes. (283)

As with Bosnia and Rwanda, so, too with Khartoum; al-Bashir knew the West would be ready and willing to attribute the conflict to ancient ethnic conflicts when, in fact, farmers and nomads had had communal ways of solving their problems for many years.

Taxation without representation also led to the conflict. Khartoum, which collected the taxes, allotted little to schools, hospitals, roads, or government jobs in the province of Darfur. In 2000, young Black Muslim men distributed *The Black Book: Imbalance of Power and Wealth in Sudan*. Flint and de Waal write that the book "gave a detailed breakdown of where political and economic power in Sudan lay and documented how the state apparatus had been dominated, ever since independence, by a small group" (17).

To protest long-standing inequities and imbalances of power, in February 2003 the Darfur Liberation Front (DLF) and the Justice and Equality Movement (JEM) attacked government units in Darfur. "Two weeks later," writes historian Robert Collins, "the DLF changed its name to the Sudan Liberation Movement/Army (SLM/A)". In its *Political Declaration* the SLM/A accused Khartoum of "'systematically adher[ing] to the policies of marginalization, racial discrimination, exclusion, exploitation, and divisiveness'" (qtd. in

Collins, 9). al-Bashir and the government in Khartoum responded savagely— with the genocide of Black African Muslims, especially the Massalit, Fur, and Zaghawa tribes. The SLM/A and JEM attacked soldiers and outposts of the Government of Sudan (GoS) soldiers. The GoS butchered civilians.

In Darfur, Arab Muslims are mostly nomads and herders; in times of drought, Black Africans, who are mostly farmers, allowed, albeit begrudgingly, Arab Muslims' livestock to graze on their lands. Droughts and encroaching desertification have made the arrangement much more contentious, pushing the herders more and more to the south of Darfur. Eighty-year-old Seikh Heri Rahman said in 2005,

> We did not know the word *Janjawiid* when we were young. . . . The Arabs came here looking for pasture, and when the grass was finished they went back. They used up our grass, but they took good care of the gardens and the people. There were no robberies, no thieves, no revolution. No one thought of domination; everyone was safe. We were afraid only of lions and hyenas. Now there is nothing but trouble, all over Sudan. . . . We no longer recognize this land of ours. (qtd. in Flint and de Waal, 134)

Also, historically, Black African Muslims and Arab Muslims have intermarried, much like Hutus and Tutsis, thus making distinctions sometimes difficult to detect.

The Janjaweed originated from a war in Darfur from 1996 to 1998, caused by Khartoum's replacement of African Muslims with Arab Muslims in government positions in Darfur and from Khartoum's conscription of Massalit young people to fight on the north's side in the civil war with the south. When Darfuri soldiers rebelled, Khartoum recruited the Janjaweed; a report called "The Masalit Community in Exile" describes their methods:

> Most attacks took place late at night, when villagers were sleeping. Upon reaching a village, the attackers typically began by setting fire to all the houses. Villagers who managed to escape the flames were then shot by the Arab militias as they fled their homes. The timing of most attacks coincided with the agricultural harvest. By burning the fields just before they were ready to be harvested, or while the crop lay on the ground after first being cut, the militias destroyed the year's crop and exposed Masalit farmers to starvation. (qtd. in Flint and de Waal, 59–60)

Such night attacks are reminiscent of those carried out during the siege of Sarajevo, and the destruction of the food source is similar to European Americans' slaughter of the buffalo to deliberately starve American Indians. Knowing how to kill in this manner served the *génocidaires* well once the genocide in Darfur began.

Although there were peace agreements in Darfur in 2006 and 2010, the violence continues. In March 2009 the International Criminal Court (ICC) charged al-Bashir with five counts of crimes against humanity. Tom Andrews, president of United to End Genocide, writes that because al-Bashir has since 2009 acted with impunity, the consequences have been lethal: "The failure of the international community to bring President Bashir to justice has resulted in the ongoing commission of atrocities against the Sudanese people" (Andrews, "Breaking: Bashir to Travel to Chad. Demand His Arrest").

Speaking with and to Darfuris

This was not possible for me in writing this book, so I read accounts published by those for whom it has been possible. I also talked with Hawi Debelo, who is from Ethiopia; Ethiopia borders Sudan, and Hawi has friends from Sudan. Hawi was the Work-Study assistant in our department, the best we ever had. She now lives and works in New York, and her comments are included here.

Problematic Children's and Young Books about the Darfur Genocide

Melissa Leembruggen's *The Sudan Project: Rebuilding with the People of Darfur, A Young Person's Guide* (2007) is the first picture book published on the Darfur genocide. The book is an abecedarian, meaning the narrative is organized by the alphabet: A is for this, B is for that, and so on. When Leembruggen gets to "Jj," she writes, "Janjaweed is a funny word./ It's not a plant or flower. / It's a group of men with guns,/making war and taking power" (n. pag.). The photograph on which this rhyme appears is of one of barrenness, a part of the land on which there was once a village, but without the debris of destruction. I shared the book with Hawi, who said,

> The book is in a way educational because I learned about The Sudan Project and what the United Methodist Committee Relief is doing for the people suffering from the conflicts in Darfur. ... However, I was very disappointed by the approach the author took to describe certain terms. The one that struck me the most is the phrase "Janjaweed is a funny word. ... " I thought it was very insensitive of the author to say that Janjaweed is a funny word knowing that it's a name given to a group of men who heartlessly take the lives of innocent people every day. It completely undermines the seriousness of the situation in Darfur and it's not fair to the people who have suffered and still suffer through the war. I can't even begin to imagine what it feels like to be in the shoes of those children who are in constant fear of losing a family member or their own lives and it's very saddening to know someone else finds humor in the word "Janjaweed" which triggers such fear in those children. (Debelo, "Re: Darfur")

I was with Hawi when she read this book and could see the pain in her eyes; she comprehended the connotation Leembruggen imposed on the word *Jan-jaweed*, a connotation victims and survivors would never make. To them *Jan-jaweed* would evoke what *Nazi* would have evoked during the Holocaust for Jews, Roma, homosexuals, and individuals with disabilities.

In addition to Hawi's response, there is the insight of a ten-year-old boy, Morgan (a pseudonym). Courtney Ryan Kelly and I have conducted workshops with fifth graders on "problematic books," for example, Lynn Reid Banks's *The Indian in the Cupboard*. As Marilyn Cochran-Smith says, we would never say *"The Jew in the Cupboard"* or *"The Black in the Cupboard"* (100). (Please see more on the problematic books workshop in Mary Ann Reilly's, Rob Cohen's, and my *Deepening Literacy Learning: Art and Literature Engagements in K-8 Classrooms* and in Chapter Seven of this book.) In the workshop, we included *The Sudan Project*. Responding to "J is for Janjaweed," Morgan noted that the genre—a jingle—was inappropriate for describing genocide. I have shared this workshop with many teachers, and no adult grasped that genre was significant in writing about genocide. It took a child to realize the disservice literary genre can be to suffering human beings.

A jingle and a joke not only demean but cannot begin to represent the terror. Flint and de Waal write,

> The *Janjawiid* not only murdered. They also targeted women with sexual violence—a feature of the war in the Nuba mountains, but seldom before seen in Darfur. Rape was so ubiquitous that it appeared to be an instrument of policy to destroy the fabric of the targeted communities and perhaps even to create a new generation with "Arab" paternity. "These rapes are . . . orchestrated to create a dynamic where the African tribal groups are destroyed," an aid worker said. "It's hard to believe that they tell them they want to make Arab babies, but it's true. It's systematic." Nor was sexual violence limited to rape. Early in 2003, a young woman called Mariam Ahamad was stopped at a roadblock and forced to watch while *Janjawiid* cut the penis off her 21-day-old son, Ahmad. The child died soon after in her arms. (108–109)

Leembruggen's book would be better left unwritten than to diminish the atrocities suffered by the people of the Darfur.

The cover of Leembruggen's book is also problematic: a photograph of a beaming young Black woman holding what we learn from the text are tarps and blankets from the United Methodist Committee on Relief. Although the young woman is no doubt grateful for the good work of the Methodists, the photograph seems to downplay the horrific situation she is in. Catherine Magno and Jackie Kirk use visual research methods to analyze photographs of girls selected by North American and European development agencies to raise money, and the way that the photographs mediate "information and the construction of knowledge about other parts of the world" (352). They wonder "in what ways a photograph 'truthfully' depicts a particular girl's complex lived experience in the moment the image is shot" (351). The cover of *The Sudan Project* fails to capture this young woman's reality. Magno and Kirk cite Lutz and Collin's notion that photographs can allow viewers to "'achieve idealization of the other, permitting the projection of the ideal and happy life'" (qtd. in Magno and Kirk, 356). The young woman in the photograph appears both joyful and grateful, which might allow viewers to assume that all that is needed for her problems to be solved is an outside group's assistance and distribution of blankets. Vivian Yenika-Agbaw reminds us, "Africans are perceived by the outside world as children who need to be constantly told what to do, and how to do it; they continue to live under perpetual threat and patronage from their Western benefactors" (xvi). And Clare Bradford, to whom I referred in Chapter Four on Rwanda, is worth citing again as she cautions against "the bland assumption that 'we' know what 'they' are like, and that 'they' are, after all, not very difficult to know" (226). The cover oversimplifies this young woman's life and hopes and does not recognize the strengths and knowledge she possesses. Flint and de Waal write:

> Darfur's people are resourceful and resilient. Extracting a living from this land requires unrelenting hard work and detailed knowledge of every crevice from which food or livelihood can be scratched. A woman living on the desert edge will know how to gather a dozen varieties of wild grasses and berries to supplement a meagre diet of cultivated millet and vegetables, along with goat or camel's milk. She will know the farms and village markets within a hundred miles or more, and will not hesitate to walk or ride such distances to buy, sell or work. (1)

As with Bosnia, and indeed as with all of the countries we have looked at in evaluating books on genocide, we must recognize in Darfur the cultural strengths that existed before its people, through no fault of their own, became targets of genocide.

Another problematic book is Patricia Levy and Zawiah Abdul Latif's *Sudan* (2008). It is an informational text not specifically about the genocide, yet the authors in their introduction nevertheless misrepresent the conflict: "Sustainable progress will be difficult until the opposing sides can live peacefully together. Until Sudan's differences are reconciled, this vast country and its friendly, hospitable people will suffer the pain and hardships of war and famine" (5). Imagine this being written of Germany in the 1940s: "Sustainable progress will be difficult until Nazis and Jews can live peacefully together. Until Germany's differences are reconciled, this vast country and its friendly, hospitable people will suffer the pain and hardships of war and famine." The Sudanese government in Khartoum, like the Nazi regime, has carried out a genocide of its own people. The expectation that Darfuri people could—and should—reconcile with their executioners is patronizing and demeaning.

Levy and Latif handle British colonialism lightly: "During the British administration the two halves of the country had been kept separate, but with the new pro-Egyptian party in power, southern elements began to see a threat to their control over their own affairs" (28). Britain appears neutral when, in fact, it was complicit, much as the Belgians were in Rwanda, in creating an elite ruling class located in northern Khartoum. Flint and de Waal explain that, before 1916, Darfur had been a "powerful" kingdom for three centuries (8). As Darfur was absorbed into the British Empire, an imbalance of inequities commenced and persisted to the beginning of the genocide in 2003. Flint and de Waal observe:

> In 1935, Darfur had just one elementary school, one "tribal" elementary school and two "sub-grade" schools. This was worse than neglect: British policy was deliberately to restrict education to the sons of chiefs, so that their authority would not be challenged by better-schooled Sudanese administrators or merchants. In the health sector, things were no better. There was no maternity clinic before the 1940s, and at independence . . . Darfur had the lowest number of hospital beds of any Sudanese province. (13)

Levy and Latif describe the Darfur genocide as, simply:

> Having felt long ignored in the peace process, two new rebel groups, the Sudan Liberation Army (SLA) and the Justice and Equality Movement, attacked in 2003 seeking greater autonomy for the Fur, Masalit, and Zaghawa tribes. The government responded by arming Arab militias, the Janjaweed (JOHN-ja-weed), to put down the insurrection. More than 200,000 Arab and non-Arab people in the region were killed, and more than 2 million people fled from their homes. (30)

The authors do not use the word *genocide*; although it is true that some Arabs were killed, most of the victims were Black Muslims. Readers must wait nine more pages to get a fuller picture: "[I]n Darfur, the government and rebel forces have committed atrocities, murdering, raping, and driving millions of people from their homes into refugee camps" (39). But even this report is questionable; although it is true that rebel forces rebelled, I have not read accounts of rebel forces (the SML/A) committing atrocities, murdering, and raping. Returning to Frank Chalk and Kurt Jonassohn's definition as cited in my Introduction, although conflict is never unambiguous, genocide is usually one-sided; in this case, the perpetrators are the Khartoum government, the Janjaweed, and criminal recruits.

In a chapter called "Lifestyle," discussing famine, the authors write, "As the nation struggles to recover from the war, the raging ethnic warfare in the Darfur region sees an estimated 2.7 million people, including 1.8 million children, at risk from malnutrition" (83). The genocide in Darfur is not "raging ethnic warfare"; to call it thus would be like calling what happened during the Holocaust "raging ethnic warfare." Framing the Darfur genocide as ethnic warfare implies that both sides have fairly equal access to arms. What has happened is outside the scope of legitimate warfare, another example of the extension of the definition of genocide mentioned in my Introduction. Although Yulisa Amadu Maddy and Donnarae MacCann are writing about fiction in their book *Neo-Imperialism in Children's Literature about Africa* (2009), this insight seems equally true for nonfiction: When authors cast events in Africa with a simple lens, as Levy and Latif do, they deny children "the complex and enriching worldviews" to which they have a right (77).

Also problematic is Sean Connolly's informational text *Sudan* (2008), part of Rourke's Countries in Crisis Series. The large point size and few words on a page seem to indicate that this book is for second- or third-grade students. The sentences are shorter than those found in other books on genocide for children: "Families struggle across a dry and dusty landscape. Mothers carry tiny babies. Skinny children walk beside them in the dirt. These families are **refugees**. They have been driven away from their villages by armed men riding horses and camels" (4; emphasis in the original). Because the book is written on such a simple level, the question has to be asked whether it should be written at all. Does it provide enough support for the child? Would a seven- or eight-year-old child wonder whether armed men riding horses and camels might invade their world?

On the second page of Chapter One, "Conflict and Hunger," there is a sidebar: "WHAT IS A FAMINE? A big problem facing western Sudan is famine. A famine is more serious—and deadlier—than a food shortage. A famine may last months or even years" (5). What is to be gained by calling genocide famine and thus misleading young readers? The tone changes on the next page, however, when, in another sidebar, Connolly includes a quotation from the *New York Times* Op-Ed Page: "Throughout Darfur . . . villages have been bombed and their inhabitants killed, **raped** and forced into government-run **concentration camps** . . . agencies have been denied access to most of the displaced" (qtd. in Connolly, 6; emphasis in the original). Without an explanation of why rape and concentration camps are bolded, or why the conflict is occurring, Chapter One ends, and Chapter Two, "Old Divisions," begins.

Connolly makes British colonialism seem benevolent: "To help educate the people, the British opened Gordon Memorial College in Khartoum in 1902. Most of the college's students came from the Muslim and Arabic-speaking north of Sudan" (17). Connolly does not help young readers understand the deliberate inequity implied in this statement. Of course the British set up a college—so they could maximize profits near the Nile. Had Darfuris lived near the Nile, the British would most likely have set up colleges for them, too. Connolly also does not help young readers understand how British intrusion and favoritism, much like Belgium's intrusion and favoritism in Rwanda, exacerbated hostilities among groups.

Although Connolly is correct that rebel groups in Darfur, out of long-standing frustration, began the attacks in 2003, he does not help readers see the disproportionate savagery on the part of the Sudanese government. He writes, "In response to the rebel groups, the government armed local Arab **militia**. These gunmen were not the official army. But it was their job to deal with the rebels" (38; emphasis in the original). Connolly should have added that it was not just the rebels who were slain but innocent civilians as well. He continues, "Villages have been burned. Wells have been poisoned. Farms have almost turned into desert" (38). The use of passive voice does not make clear to young readers that the government and the Janjaweed are the ones burning and poisoning. It is also not clear how the wells are poisoned. The Janjaweed make a practice of throwing Black African human bodies into wells so that there is no water source for those who escape from their raids and are left behind. He does include U.S. Secretary of State Colin Powell's assertion that "'**genocide** has been committed in Darfur'" (qtd. in Connolly, 41; emphasis in the original).

Despite Powell's declaration of genocide in 2004 and despite the diplomatic efforts that his declaration prompted, little was accomplished internationally on Darfur's behalf. Gerald Caplan writes,

> [t]he first lesson from Rwanda—the harsh unwelcome reminder . . . was that global powers-that-be are capable of almost infinite callousness and indifference to human suffering if geopolitical or political interests are not at stake. Calls for forceful intervention based strictly on humanitarian grounds, as we have learned the hard way once again in Darfur, are simply irrelevant to those with the means to intervene. (173)

Although there have been some efforts, Darfur did not, and does not, hold enough geopolitical interest for other nations to ensure that the violence will stop.

James Pipe's *Hoping for Peace in Sudan: Divided by Conflict, Wishing for Peace* (2013) is a multigenre informational text that includes letters and photographs. In the early pages Pipe focuses on the civil war between north and south; then he introduces Darfur, which he does not call a genocide. Instead, Pipe writes that the people of Darfur "had been having issues over land and water" (18), which does not take into account the Arab Gathering or long-standing inequities set in motion by the British. Pipe writes,

> In 2003, the black Muslim rebels attacked government troops and police stations in Darfur. They demanded more rights and a share of the money from the region's many valuable oil fields. The government's response was swift and brutal. It supplied local Arab nomads with horses, camels, and weapons. Although these raiders, known as "janjaweed" (Arabic for "horse and gun"), soon defeated the rebels, they kept on raiding.

Supported by the Sudanese army and air force, they destroyed village after village, burning, looting, and killing many people. In Darfur, more than 300,000 people died as a result of the attacks, many from hunger and disease. (18–19)

This is partially correct—the rebel attacks and the swiftness and brutality of Khartoum's retaliation. However, 300,000, many dying from hunger and disease, underestimates the number of murders. Pipe's letters are fictional; it would have been more effective if the letters were from real people. Pipe makes no attempt to analyze the deleterious effects of colonization. He writes, "The British colonized part of Sudan in the late 1800s, but in 1956, modern Sudan declared its independence. Soon after, a civil war started between the people living in the south and those in the north" (5). This seems to locate all responsibility for the civil war in the people of Sudan. And additionally, *genocide* is not in his glossary but *civil war* is; calling what has happened in Darfur a civil war misrepresents the tragic occurrences in that country and is a form of genocide denial. Pipe recommends to young readers Leembruggen's callous *The Sudan Project*, a clear example of how the creation of myth can compound itself in children's and young adult books.

Francesca DiPiazza's *Sudan in Pictures* (2006) is part of the same Visual Geography Series as Tom Streissguth's *Rwanda in Pictures*. DiPiazza opens her book with the end of the civil war between the north and the south in 2005: "Since the nation's independence from Great Britain in 1956, southerners have struggled against the dominance of the more industrialized north" (4), which might lead readers to believe that it was the north's industrialization—not Britain's betrayal—that caused the southerners' problems.

She explains the peace agreement between the north and the south, then introduces the genocide:

> Excitement over the peace agreement was dampened by an ongoing, separate war in the west of Sudan. In the region of Darfur, thirty ethnic groups, all Islamic, have a history of competition for scarce resources, such as land and water. The ethnic tensions erupted into violence in 2003. Hundreds of thousands have been killed or have died from starvation and disease. More than one million have lost their homes and their livelihoods. The United Nations (a world peace-keeping organization) declared the situation in Darfur to be the largest humanitarian disaster in the world. (7)

DiPiazza explains to readers what the United Nations is, but does not explain that what happened in Darfur was a one-sided genocide. To name the conflict "ethnic tensions" is reminiscent of the conversation Isabelle and I had in the Rwanda chapter on "African" violence. Westerners too easily believe the myth of ethnic conflict. DiPiazza does not contextualize the genocide—a deliberate attempt to wipe out Black Muslims by the Sudanese government and the Janjaweed, informed by an Arab supremacist ideology, and as retaliation against the SML/A and the JEM, who dared to protest gross inequities. She abruptly moves on, "Sudan is Africa's largest country, covering 8 percent of the continent" (7). This is helpful information, but not after blithely introducing a genocide, and not naming it but instead attributing cause to what was not cause.

Later DiPiazza effectively includes a passage from Paul Theroux's travel book *Dark Star Safari: Overland from Cairo to Cape Town*, which, through a story about a broken-down car, portrays strengths that had long been in the culture:

> Three men stood by the old car in the hot bright desert, the only features in the landscape. Ramadan conferred with them and the men explained their dilemma, which was obvious: a blowout, no spare tire, no traffic on the road; they needed a new tire. They got into our truck and we drove them about fifty miles and dropped them off at a repair shop in a small town way off the road. The lengthy detour of an hour and a half was considered normal courtesy, like the rule of the sea that necessitates one ship helping another in trouble, no matter what the inconvenience. And here the desert much resembled a wide sea. (qtd. in DiPiazza, 44)

Instead of feeding only the perception of African violence ("ethnic tensions erupted into violence in 2003"), DiPiazza might have included accounts, of which there are many, of Black Muslim farmers allowing nomadic Arab Muslims' livestock to graze on their lands. Perhaps part of supporting the child reader is revealing the strengths of a culture. As we saw in Bosnia, it was a country of many strengths, preyed upon and ignited into bloodshed by Slobodan Milošević and his henchmen. So too in Darfur. Just as U.S. ambassador to Yugoslavia Warren Zimmerman had no doubt that, had Milošević's parents committed suicide before his birth instead of after, he would not be writing about the end of Yugoslavia, I have little doubt that, had al-Bashir not been born, there would not have been a genocide in Darfur. Children must be helped to recognize those who deceive and who recruit criminals to carry out their malevolent agendas.

The following sections of DiPiazza's book include magnificent photographs of "The Land"; "The History and Government" section is accurate. DiPiazza shows the harm Britain did to the country by favoring the northeast and marginalizing the south. The section on Darfur includes the attacks of the Janjaweed: "The janjaweed attacked non-Arab civilians, often with government backup, including aerial bombing of villages" (33). Her use of past tense might lead readers to believe the genocide was over in 2006, when it wasn't: "Darfur's total population of 6 million suffered heavily during the conflict. An estimated 100,000 lost their lives in the violence, and another 180,000 died from hunger and disease" (33). When her book was published in 2006, the geno-cide was in full force, and the estimates of those who died were many more than DiPiazza suggests. Finally, on the following page in a sidebar, DiPiazza introduces the word *genocide*, citing Colin Powell's use of the term in 2004. Darfur is not much mentioned in the remaining thirty-five pages of the book. Although the book provides helpful information on some aspects of Sudan, what DiPiazza writes on Darfur is not one of those aspects.

Recommended with Reservations: Children's and Young Adult Literature about the Darfur Genocide

In *George Clooney and the Crisis in Darfur* (2009), part of Rosen's Celebrity Activists Series, Tamara Orr begins with biographical information on Cloo-ney, and how he became involved in the Darfur conflict. She writes at the very beginning that Clooney has won the "'sexiest man alive'" award several times, which detracts from her purpose. Orr does not need to patronize young read-ers with the enticement of sex to care about genocide. Her third paragraph informs readers of the nearly half a million Darfuris killed and the more than 2 million displaced from their homes and villages. Her words, "Yet the world has remained largely silent and unmoved in the face of this horror," do not take into account the hundreds of chapters in high schools and colleges of Students Taking Action Now: Darfur (STAND), Genocide Intervention Network, and Save Darfur (7). Over a dozen aid workers were killed in 2006 trying to help in Darfur. Although Clooney's work is to be admired, he is not the sole savior. Later in her book, Orr seems to contradict herself, as she describes the massive efforts of millions of people to get the United Nations and the United States to act. In a time line, others are mentioned: Oxfam had to pull out of the Sudan when workers were killed, and Save the Children lost workers as well.

The first chapter is devoted to Clooney's early life, his move from Kentucky to California, and his rise to fame as an actor. The second chapter describes the situation in Darfur, but when the author explains other genocides, she makes mistakes. In a table, she places the date of the Rwandan genocide as 1984 (it occurred in 1994), and she profoundly oversimplifies the Bosnian genocide: "Due to the conflict of the three main ethnic groups (Serbs, Croats, and Muslims) . . ." (34). Ethnic conflict is the myth; national Serbian aggres-sion is closer to the truth.

Orr's Chapter Four, "Returning Home and Alerting the World," is a com-pelling one. She brings together the work of individuals from around the world, including Amnesty International's release in 2007 of *Instant Karma: The Campaign to Save Darfur*, which brings together musicians to sing John Lennon's songs, with all royalties going to Darfur. Clooney and the cast of *Ocean's Thirteen* donated the film's $9.3 million profits; Clooney has inspired other philanthropists to contribute to Darfur.

When I was teaching a genocide course in 2007, a student turned to me and asked, "Why do we know more about Britney Spears than the genocide in Darfur?" (about which most of them had never heard until they took the course). I responded: "Genocide doesn't sell." Clooney is aware of this, and Orr aptly includes a quote (one of Clooney's many in the book): "'We need to focus global attention on the plight of the 2.5 million civilians who have fled their homes. Rather than talk about who I'm dating, let's talk about saving lives'" (75). Orr also cites Ishmael Beah on Clooney: "'He has used his fame to speak wholeheartedly for those who cannot speak, with genuine concern and insight and a deep commitment and selflessness that is rare but does not have to be'" (qtd. in Orr, 76). Orr ends by helping readers know how they can act and recommends an excellent resource for activism, Don Cheadle and John Prendergast's *Not on Our Watch: The Mission to End Genocide in Darfur and Beyond* (2007). In a sidebar, Orr includes the story of Massachusetts high school student Nick Anderson who, with his friends, raised more than $300,000 for Darfur. Anderson traveled to Darfur and talked with teens there: "'They want to move forward with their lives and build structures that are made of bricks, not of plastic sheets. . . . Everyone I encountered was really gung-ho about rebuilding. They just need the tools, and we as Americans can help provide those things'" (qtd. in Orr, 87). Orr discusses the work of an England-based organization, Kids for Kids, which has spread to the U.S. and has provided seeds and livestock to help the people of Darfur rebuild their lives.

Although Orr's book is flawed in her knowledge of other genocides (why write about them without researching them?), hers is an noteworthy biography of George Clooney, who has used his fame and wealth in the service of others and has motivated others to act on behalf of Darfur.

Michael Schuman profiles another celebrity who has used her fame to help Darfur—Angelina Jolie. In his biography *Angelina Jolie: Celebrity with Heart* (2011), Schuman explains Jolie's humanitarian interests: "When actor Angelina Jolie was filming *Lara Croft: Tomb Raider* in Cambodia in 2000, she had some time to see the country. Civil war had raged through much of Cambodia in the 1970s. Weapons had included land mines, which are explosive devices placed just below the ground" (5). Although it is admirable that Jolie started a campaign to alleviate the land mine problem in Cambodia, it is unfortunate that Schuman labels the Cambodian genocide a civil war. The approximately 3 million people who were killed, overworked, and starved to death did not have weapons with which to defend themselves from the Khmer Rouge.

The next four chapters of the book are about Jolie's life, including no-holds-barred passages on the cutting she did of herself and her boyfriend in her teen years, the fractious relationship she has had with her father, actor Jon Voight, and the many films in which she has appeared. In 2001, Jolie made a goodwill trip to Sierra Leone and Tanzania. The UN Refugee Agency thought Jolie sincere and not motivated by publicity; her trips have, Schuman says, inspired "tons of inquiries from young people" (55). Jolie has donated millions of dollars to various needy countries and pays all her expenses on her trips. She adopted a Cambodian baby in 2001.

The chapter on Darfur and the Janjaweed contains little, although accurate, information:

> Darfur is a district in the western part of the African nation of Sudan. Some residents of Darfur, mainly black Africans, are victims of genocide at the hands of the government of Sudan. The Sudanese militia, known as the Janjaweed, are mainly of Arabic descent. The Janjaweed were conducting raids against the civilians of Darfur. They uprooted Darfur residents from their homes. The Janjaweed also committed violent crimes against the people of Darfur, including rape and murder. The situation in Darfur had caught the attention of the world. Yet no one seemed to be able to do anything about ending the genocide. (75–76)

Schuman is to be admired for his concise synthesis of the genocide and for using the word *genocide*. Nonetheless, to call a chapter "Darfur and the Janjaweed" when it is primarily about Jolie's personal life seems misleading.

In 2004 Jolie went to Chad to hear stories of refugees from Darfur. Schuman's account of that trip is intermingled with the saga of Jolie and Brad Pitt, who was married to Jennifer Aniston before beginning a relationship with Jolie. Together, Pitt and Jolie adopted a baby from Ethiopia, and in 2005, Jolie won the United Nations Global Humanitarian Action Award. In 2007 Jolie made another goodwill trip to the area. Schuman underestimates the number of Darfuris who have died ("two hundred thousand people") but is correct in his estimation of the number of refugees and correctly identifies those who had forced them to flee: "the Janjaweed militia had driven 2.5 million people from their homes" (96). Schuman ends with the statement that until peace is achieved, "one can expect Angelina Jolie and her family in any country in the world, either making a movie or working for the well-being of others" (106).

Also recommended with reservations is Jane Levey's *Genocide in Darfur* (2009) in Rosen's Genocide in Modern Times Series. Levey begins with a very brief history of genocide leading up to Darfur and truthfully writes, "Government soldiers and Janjaweed militias forced more than two million Africans from their homes. As many as 500,000 Africans may have died. The Darfur genocide has been called the worst humanitarian crisis in the twenty-first century" (8). In writing a history of genocide in a few pages, one can miss the complexities, as she does with Cambodia. Her paragraph on that genocide, though concisely summing up Pol Pot's role, does not mention the outside international forces that pushed ordinary Cambodians into the arms of the Khmer Rouge. So, too, with her paragraph on Bosnia, which fails to reference Serbian nationalist aggression and underestimates the number of those slaughtered—"thousands"—when it was hundreds of thousands (13). And her paragraph on Rwanda omits international and colonialist involvement in setting off the genocide, that Tutsis were for the most part unarmed, and that there were moderate Hutus who suffered as much as the Tutsis. Levey might better have begun with Chapter Two, where she describes Raphael Lemkin's life's work of creating a name for the crime governments commit when they kill their own people: *genocide*. Levey also explains the establishment of the ICC in 1998, voted into existence by sixty nations, to try those accused of genocidal acts.

Levey also gives an excellent explanation of the colonialist influence on the current situation in the Sudan: Before independence, Egypt ruled northern Sudan, where Islam and the Arabic language were encouraged, and Britain ruled southern Sudan, where Christianity and the English language were encouraged. At independence in 1956, Britain basically sold out its former colony by going along with Egypt in placing the most power in Khartoum in the north, contributing to the country's instability. In 1989, after various coups, Sudan's current president, Omar Hassan Ahmad al-Bashir, came to power. Like Pol Pot, Slobodan Milošević, and other *génocidaires*, al-Bashir promised one thing to the people and delivered another. Levey includes a photograph of a smiling, charming al-Bashir promising peace; underneath the smile and the charm were plans to destroy Black Africans, a difficult undertaking Levey points out, because Black Africans in the Sudan have intermarried with Arabs for generations. Levey helps young readers distinguish between radical and moderate Muslims and notes the moderates' protestations against extreme Islamist movements and gatherings in Sudan, including Osama bin Laden's stay there from 1991 until 1996.

Levey explains how military skirmishes in 2002 evolved into the genocide of civilians in 2003; like Milošević, al-Bashir freed criminals and recruited Janjaweed from Arab tribes to carry out his murderous agenda. Like the Serbs who protested Milošević's agenda, Levey writes, "some Arab tribes refused to take part in the genocide" (25). Rosen Publishing sets the reading level at grade six; the book is for grades nine to twelve. Some young readers may be challenged by this passage:

> The Janjaweed sometimes lined up men and boys and shot them in the back of the head. They tossed children into burning houses. They chained schoolchildren together and burned them alive. Women and girls were raped, often more than once. Some rape victims were killed, some were not. . . . In order to make their suffering worse, the Janjaweed sometimes branded rape victims so that everyone who saw them would know what had happened to them. (26–27)

Sensitive caregivers will have to decide whether the children with whom they work can handle this truthful passage; trauma may become traumatic for some young people.

In her final chapter, Levey introduces those who have responded to the genocide: actress Mia Farrow, who has traveled to Darfur and raised money; journalist Nicholas Kristoff, who won a Pulitzer Prize for his work on Darfur; Colin Powell, who publicly called what happened genocide; and professor of English Eric Reeves, who writes extensively about Darfur. Inspiringly, there are student-initiated groups that have tried to stop the genocide: Students Taking Action Now: Darfur (STAND) and Genocide Intervention Fund (GIF), thus showing young readers that they can initiate collective efforts to help victims of genocide.

Recommended Children's and Young Adult Literature about the Darfur Genocide

Informational Texts

John Xavier, in *Darfur: African Genocide* (2008) in Rosen's In the News Series, does not hold back; in his opening paragraph, he forcefully writes: "In recent years, the people of Darfur have been systematically attacked by the Sudanese army and by proxy-militia controlled by the Sudanese government. These militia bands are called the janjaweed" (4). He continues:

> The escalating violence in Darfur has resulted in an estimated 200,000 to 500,000 deaths since 2003. In other words, approximately one in twelve people have been killed from 2003 to 2006. Attacks on villages take the form of raids, where the janjaweed arrive on horses, camels, or in automobiles. They pillage the villages, stealing anything of value. The villagers are often raped and tortured, and many are murdered. These attacks are followed by aerial assault from the Sudanese military. Planes bomb the villages. (5)

Halima Bashir, in *Tears of the Desert: A Memoir of Survival in Darfur* (2008), the first memoir to be published in English on Darfur genocide, recalls a reverse order: First the planes, then the Janjaweed. Bashir grew up in a Zaghawa village in Darfur and lived through what Xavier describes. In her memoir, Bashir describes her village's experience: "Suddenly, the lead helicopter banked low over the village and there were a series of bright flashes and puffs of smoke from under its stubby wings. An instant later, the huts beneath it exploded, mud and thatch and branches and bodies being thrown into the air" (239). Following the helicopters, Bashir remembers, came the Janjaweed:

> The *Janjaweed* urged their horses forward, tossing blazing torches onto the huts, the dry thatch roofs bursting into flames. I kept glancing behind in fear at the flashes of gunfire and the flames that were sweeping through

the village like a wave of fiery death. I could hear the devil horsemen screaming like animals, a howling wave of evil and hatred tearing our village asunder. As they got closer and closer I could make out the individual Arabic phrases that they were chanting, over and over and over again.

"We're coming for you! To kill you all!"

"Kill the black slaves! . . . Kill the black donkeys." (240)

The helicopters return; perhaps Xavier based his account on this pattern: "Up ahead I could see the helicopters circling, turning for another attack run, and then there were further flashes and smoke, and bullets and rockets were tearing into the fleeing women and children, ripping bodies apart" (241). Bashir eventually became a doctor and often treated raped and mutilated girls, who were as young as seven. Bashir herself was raped. She eventually fled the country and is now a refugee living in the United Kingdom.

Although Xavier provides information on Sudan's economy, geography, food, and history, he frames the book around the Darfur genocide; his handling of British colonialism and its deleterious effects is strong. Xavier ends in a final chapter, "Why Darfur Matters to the Rest of the World," with a social justice theme, urging young readers to realize all of us are affected by genocide:

Human beings have more in common with one another than almost any other species on the planet. When scientists mapped the human genome in 2001, they discovered that all humans are 99.9 percent identical on a genetic level. That means the measurable difference between any two people on the planet is one-tenth of 1 percent. (46)

Xavier has written a balanced and well-researched text for young readers (Figure 5.1).

So, too, has Joseph Oppong in his book *Sudan* (2010), in Chelsea House's Modern World Nations Series. He acknowledges British colonialist influence, capturing how Britain "kept north and south Sudan separate, developing the fertile lands around the Nile Valley in the north, while neglecting the south, east, and Darfur to the west. Consequently, northern Sudan was well-educated, mostly Arabic speaking, and Muslim, and had solid political and economic infrastructures" (64). These British policies were to have catastrophic consequences throughout subsequent decades, as was this decision: "On January 1, 1956, the British handed political power over to a minority of northern Arab-Muslim elites" (65). Oppong includes the ICC charges against al-Bashir and his crimes against humanity, and an honest account of "killings, torture, rape, and imprisonment" (75). He is clear with young readers about the identity of the Janjaweed: "Most members are recruits from nomadic Arabic tribes, angry former soldiers, or criminal elements" (78). Oppong astutely includes the role of climate change in Sudan; desertification has meant the migration of more nomads into southern Darfur, a pattern not likely to change until global warming is addressed (75–85).

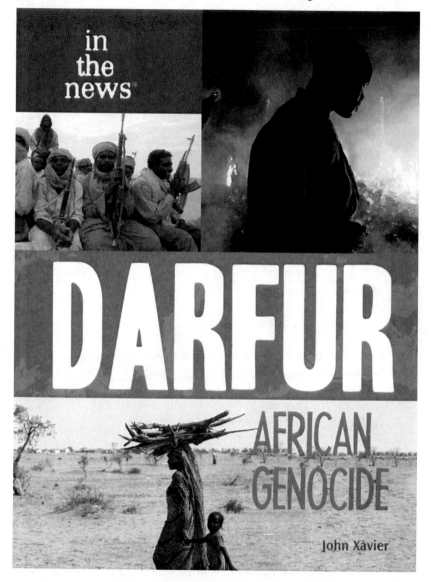

Figure 5.1 Book cover from John Xavier: *Darfur: African Genocide*. New York: Rosen Publishing, 2008.

Like Xavier and Oppong, Philip Steele has written, for the most part, an authentic and responsible account of the Darfur genocide in his *Sudan, Darfur and the Nomadic Conflicts* (2011). The recent publication date permits him to report on the Republic of South Sudan's declaration of independence from the Republic of Sudan. Questionable are his early remarks:

The different peoples making up Sudan have a long history of ethnic conflict. This has not just been between the north and the south, but between the various peoples living within these regions. For example, the region of Darfur, in the west of North Sudan, has seen violence since 2003, with villages destroyed and refugees fleeing the country. (7)

The use of the passive voice could leave readers wondering, Villages destroyed by whom? Refugees fleeing the country for what reasons? But Steele, a few pages later, makes up for the use of the passive voice, and clearly explains the "bombing of Darfur by government and attacks on civilians by Janjawid militias" (11). He puts al-Bashir front and center, where he belongs; Steele writes, "Bashir was accused of hiring local militias called the Janjawid to suppress the rebellion. The Janjawid attacked rebels and civilians with great brutality. They burned down villages, raped and murdered" (14).

He includes the death of Osama bin Laden and the 2009 indictment of al-Bashir by the ICC, and the ICC's call in 2010 for "Bashir's arrest for genocide—an attempt to destroy a whole people" (15). Additionally, Steele adds "as a result of the atrocities in Darfur, he became the first serving head of state in the world to be charged with genocide before the International Criminal Court" (23).

Steele also describes the legacy of colonization:

During the 1800s when the European empire builders drew up the borders of the new African colonies . . . they were often less concerned with the peoples they ruled than with their own political rivalries, or with resources and trade. Borders of territories often passed straight through historical homelands, dividing people and cultures. Ethnic conflict was sometimes used to prevent a united opposition arising, a policy referred to as "divide and rule." European rulers in Africa might recruit the army from one ethnic group, for example, and the civil service such as the government administration, from another. In Sudan little was done to improve economic conditions or provide education and security. (20)

This is the kind of explanation young readers need in order to understand many of Africa's problems, especially the genocides in Rwanda and Darfur. Steele writes that the UN and African Union jointly established a peacekeeping force in Darfur in 2008 but that conflicts continue. Steele's is a comprehensive and accurate text on the Sudan (Figure 5.2).

Short Stories and Poetry

What You Wish For: Stories and Poems for Darfur (2011) is not about Darfur; it is a collection of short stories and poems by popular young adult authors who

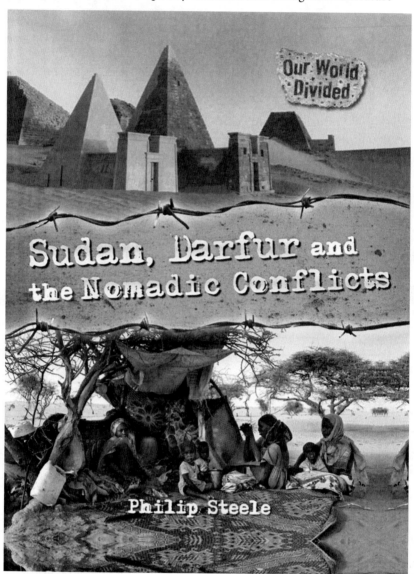

Figure 5.2 Book cover from Philip Steele: *Sudan, Darfur and the Nomadic Conflicts.* New York: Rosen Publishing, 2013.

contribute their royalties to libraries in refugee camps through the Book Wish Foundation, monitored by the UN Refugee Agency. Those authors are Alexander McCall Smith, Jeanne DuPrau, Jane Yolen, Meg Cabot, Sofia Quintero, Karen Hesse, Gary Soto, John Green, Ann M. Martin, Naomi Shihab Nye, Cynthia Voight, Cornelia Funke, Nikki Giovanni, R. L. Stine, Marilyn Nelson, Francisco X. Stork, Nate Powell, and Joyce Carol Oates. All of the stories and poems focus on wishes.

Smith's entertaining opening story, "The Strange Story of Bobby Box," is about a boy floating down a river in a box in Scotland and found by a fisherman. The police take Bobby to an orphanage, where he gets barely enough to eat; a farmer buys him and Bobby endures slave labor throughout his childhood years. He runs away from the farmer and is made to work as a lion tamer in a circus, where a loving childless couple find him, help him escape, and adopt him. Smith tells his young readers to "Never give up hope" (20).

The book has an unusual format; pictures of refugees from Darfur are interspersed between some of the stories and poems, giving information on their plight. A boy dressed in a torn shirt informs readers that two thirds of the refugees are children (n. pag.). There are photographs of refugees cooking and lining up for water. Another set of photographs shows children carrying out chores, such as collecting firewood; others show the open tents that serve as schools in the refugee camps. The World Food Programme is recognized for its provision of grain to refugees, and there are photos of the scorched-earth villages in Darfur that refugees were forced to leave.

Logan Kleinwaks's Editor's Note explains the situation in Darfur and the origin of the Book Wish Foundation. He connects the provision of libraries in refugee camps in Chad with the theme of the book: wishes. Books may help the wishes of Darfuri children come true. This is an impressive collection created by excellent writers and a caring editor.

Crossover Literature

Craig Walzer's *Out of Exile: Narratives from the Abducted and Displaced People of Sudan* (2009) gives voice to those whose voices might not have been heard, such as that of Nadia el-Kareem:

> I had a normal life like any girl in Darfur. I would help the cows and goats get food and water. I would clean the house and help my mother cook. I was happy. People who can stay with their parents should be happy. My cousin Muna was my best friend. We didn't really play together, but we would do chores around the house together, and when we finished we would sleep. . . . That is all I can tell you about my childhood. The experiences I have had now are enough to make me forget everything about my childhood. (136)

It is important to recognize that, until 2003, Darfuris led normal lives—as normal as can be in an impoverished area. Many had happy childhoods and best friends, and they loved their parents. The Janjaweed came to el-Kareem's village, killing her family and others in her village. She managed to hide and escape; in her search for safety, she met Mahmoud, who was kind to her and helped her. They eventually married and are now living in Egypt. el-Kareem is homesick and says, "I am very ready to go back to Sudan. There are no benefits to going back, and I know there could be risks. I still want to go to Darfur, even though it's dangerous. . . . But it's just better to die in my own country, in my home" (147).

Also in Walzer's book is Ahmed Ishag's story, whose memories of his childhood are like el-Kareem's memories: "My village in Darfur was beautiful. It was close to mountains, a valley, and a river. There were lemon trees, guavas, and mangoes. We planted okra and sugar cane. There were many animals around—donkeys, horses, camels, cows, goats, and even savage hyenas. It was a beautiful place to live" (199–200). There was much to love in Darfur, and many Darfuris, like most of us, cherish their land and homes.

Conclusion

Flint and de Waal write,

> The serial war criminals at the heart of Sudan's present government once sought absolute control in pursuit of an Islamic state. Now they seek power for its own sake. Today, as yesterday, the people they perceive to be challenging that power count for nothing. They can be subjugated, shot or starved without compunction. (134)

As with some other genocides, it is one man—al-Bashir—and his criminal government that have carried out the unwarranted destruction and displacement of the Darfuri people. Children who read about this tragedy need to know of the influence of colonialism and of the impact that a small group with malevolent intent can have.

Works Cited

Andrews, Tom. "Breaking: Bashir to Travel to Chad. Demand His Arrest." Message to Jane M. Gangi. 15 Mar. 2013. E-mail.

Banks, Lynne Reid. *The Indian in the Cupboard.* New York: Doubleday, 1980.

Bashir, Halima, with Damien Lewis. *Tears of the Desert: A Memoir of Survival in Darfur.* New York: Ballantine, 2008.

Bradford, Clare. *Unsettling Narratives: Postcolonial Readings of Children's Literature.* Waterloo, Ontario: Wilfrid Laurier UP, 2007.

Burr, J. Millard, and Robert O. Collins. *Darfur: The Long Road to Disaster.* Princeton, NJ: Markus Wiener, 2008.

Caplan, Gerald. "From Rwanda to Darfur: Lessons Learned?" Totten and Markusen, 171–179.

Cheadle, Don, and John Prendergast. *Not on Our Watch: The Mission to End Genocide in Darfur and Beyond.* New York: Hyperion, 2007.

Cochran-Smith, Marilyn. *Walking the Road: Race, Diversity, and Social Justice.* New York: Teachers College, 2004.

Collins, Robert O. "Disaster in Darfur: Historical Overview." Totten and Markusen, 2–24.

Connolly, Sean. *Sudan.* Vero Beach, FL: Rourke, 2008. Countries in Crisis Ser.

Debelo. Hawi. "Re: Darfur." Message to Jane M. Gangi. 11 Mar. 2013. E-mail.

DiPiazza, Francesca. *Sudan in Pictures.* Minneapolis, MN: Twenty-First Century, 2006. Visual Geography Ser.

el-Kareem, Nadia. "Life, Death, There's No Big Difference." Walzer, 135–147.

Flint, Julie, and Alex de Waal. *Darfur: A Short History of a Long War*. London: Zed, 2005.

Ishag, Ahmed. "We Wanted Israel's Protection. That Was All." Walzer, 199–236.

Leembruggen, Melissa. *The Sudan Project: Rebuilding with the People of Darfur, A Young Person's Guide*. Nashville, TN: Abingdon, 2007.

Levy, Patricia, and Zawiah Abdul Latif. *Sudan*. New York: Cavendish, 2008. Cultures of the World Ser.

Maddy, Yulisa Amadu, and Donnarae MacCann. *Neo-Imperialism in Children's Literature about Africa: A Study of Contemporary Fiction*. New York: Routledge, 2009.

Magno, Catherine, and Jackie Kirk. "Imaging Girls: Visual Methodologies and Messages for Girls' Education." *Compare* 38.1 (2008): 349–362.

Pipe, James. *Hoping for Peace in Sudan: Divided by Conflict, Wishing for Peace*. New York: Gareth Stevens, 2013.

Reilly, Mary Ann, Jane M. Gangi, and Rob Cohen. *Deepening Literacy Learning: Art and Literature Engagements in K-8 Classrooms*. Charlotte, NC: Information Age, 2010.

Smith, Alexander McCall. "The Strange Story of Bobby Box." Book Wish Foundation, 1–11.

Totten, Samuel, and Erick Markusen, eds. *Genocide in Darfur: Investigating the Atrocities in the Sudan*. New York: Routledge, 2006.

Walzer, Craig, comp. and ed. *Out of Exile: Narratives from the Abducted and Displaced People of Sudan*. San Francisco: McSweeny's, 2009.

Yenika-Agbaw, Vivian. *Representing Africa in Children's Literature: Old and New Ways of Seeing*. New York: Routledge, 2008.

Recommended Children's and Young Adult Books about the Darfur Genocide

Book Wish Foundation. *What You Wish For: Stories and Poems for Darfur*. Reston, VA: Author, 2011.

Oppong, Joseph R. *Sudan*. New York: Chelsea, 2010. Modern World Nations Ser.

Steele, Philip. *Sudan, Darfur and the Nomadic Conflicts*. New York: Rosen, 2013. Our World Divided Ser.

Xavier, John. *Darfur: African Genocide*. New York: Rosen, 2008. In the News Ser.

Recommended with Reservations: Children's and Young Adult Books about the Darfur Genocide

Levey, Jane. *Genocide in Darfur*. New York: Rosen, 2009. Genocide in Modern Times Ser.

Orr, Tamara. *George Clooney and the Crisis in Darfur*. New York: Rosen, 2009. Celebrity Activists Ser.

Schuman, Michael. *Angelina Jolie: Celebrity with Heart*. Berkeley Heights, NJ: Enslow, 2011. Celebrities with Heart Ser.

Recommended Crossover Literature about the Darfur Genocide

Walzer, Craig, comp. and ed. *Out of Exile: Narratives from the Abducted and Displaced People of Sudan*. San Francisco: McSweeny's, 2009.

Chapter Six
Comprehensive Books about Genocide for Children and Young Adults

Currently, approximately one billion children under the age of eighteen are growing up in regions affected by conflict.

—J. L. Powers

In this chapter I examine those books in which authors address multiple genocides. In my Introduction I wrote about the challenges authors face when they write outside their cultures. If they are White North Americans or Europeans, they may not be cognizant of the default to whiteness and the privilege and authority that brings. They may not know of Linda Alcoff's urging that, in representing others, they need to try to speak *with* and *to* rather than *for* others. When they address vastly different cultures and countries, they may produce historical slippages. From a postcolonial perspective, they may cast "the Other" as backward, degenerate, and unequal. On the other hand, they may achieve what Emmanuel Levinas terms respect for "the Other"—one who is treated ethically and deserving of the highest respect. In this chapter, we will see examples of both.

Problematic Comprehensive Books about Genocide for Children and Young Adults

Linda Altman's *Genocide: The Systematic Killing of a People* (2009) is comprehensive; it includes Native Americans, who are often omitted when victims of genocide are discussed. She takes into account the Ukrainian genocide, also called the Holomodor, when, in the early 1930s, millions of children and adults were starved to death by their own government.

To help young readers understand how genocide might occur, Altman quotes Adolf Hitler, from a text by George Seldes:

> The size of the lie is a definite factor in causing it to be believed . . . for the vast masses are . . . more easily deceived than they are consciously and intentionally bad. The primitive simplicity of their minds renders them a more easy prey to a big lie than a small one, for they themselves often tell little lies but would be ashamed to tell a big one. (qtd. in Altman, 73)

It is difficult to penetrate the mind of a *génocidaire*; this quote by Hitler is most revealing.

Unlike some of the authors examined in Chapter One, on Cambodia, Altman brings to bear Chinese and Soviet involvement in the Cambodian genocide. She quotes eyewitness accounts and states that up to "three million perished," recognizing the enormity of the genocide, which some texts on the Cambodian genocide do not (81).

Her treatment of Bosnia is less evenhanded. Bolded in a side box is this: "In the last decade of the twentieth century, instead of entering an era of peace, the world faced ethnic war—a war of people rather than governments" (84). As we have seen, Slobodan Milošević, his thugs, and Serbian nationalists were responsible for at least 90 percent of the violence, and they had access to the full force of the Yugoslav army that virtually ensured Serbian nationalist victory. Bosniaks had no access, and were subject to an arms embargo. This was not "a war of people"; it was a genocidal war of the Serbian government, led by a small group of amoral and criminal men.

Altman's chapter on Rwanda seems to perpetuate the myth that African violence is somehow more violent than that of other continents. I wonder if she could have written about Bosnia or Cambodia the way she writes about Rwanda: "a slaughter so terrible that it horrified even battle-hardened soldiers and seasoned war correspondents" (90). It is hard to imagine that what happened in Rwanda was any more terrible that what happens in other genocides; they are all horrifying. None is more civil than another. Altman also creates the impression that only Tutsis were killed, omitting that many, many moderate Hutus lost their lives as well; it is regrettable that Altman does not distinguish between moderate Hutus and the radical Hutu who carried out the genocide. In a sidebar she writes, "In Rwanda, the two major tribes, Hutu and Tutsi, share the same race, religion, culture, and language, yet from time to time peaceful relations have been broken by outbreaks of ethnic hatred" (92). There is no mention of German and Belgian colonization, of Belgium's racist legacy, or how France and other countries heavily armed radical Hutus.

Similarly, there are numerous inaccuracies in Lila Perl's *Genocide: Stand By or Intervene?* (2011). She reports that 100,000 died during the genocide in Bosnia. In this book I am citing 300,000 deaths because it is the number I see most frequently in academic literature, but I have read estimates as high as 500,000 killed. Perl describes those who live in the Balkans as "fierce and combative peoples," perpetuating the myth that somehow Bosnians are more violent than the rest of us (73). Yet a few pages later she seems to contradict herself, writing:

> For generations people of many ethnic backgrounds and several different religions, dwelling side by side, had enjoyed peaceful living conditions. Milosevic sought to disrupt this amity. To create a greater Serbia, Milosevic was prepared to cleanse the other republics of all but their Serb populations, even though Serbs were in the minority within them. (75)

It would have been better to describe Milošević, his cronies, and the criminals they recruited as "fierce and combative" and not make a blanket statement about all Bosnians.

Perl describes the beginning of the genocide (it was on April 6, not April 5): Serb snipers opened fire on peaceful protestors from atop the Holiday Inn in downtown Sarajevo. Perl depicts the crowd "as thousands of unarmed Sarajevo citizens of all faiths and nationalities [who] marched through the city protesting ethnic divisions and proclaiming tolerance" (77). It is sometimes overlooked that many Serbs protested Milošević's policies, and the peaceful protestors belie the fiction of a "fierce and combative" people.

Perl misrepresents the Rwandan genocide in several ways. About the lethal ethnic identity cards Belgium began requiring in the 1930s, she offhandedly writes, "The purpose appeared to be mainly administrative" (58). As we saw in Chapter Four, numerous Rwandan scholars believe that Rwandan identity cards sowed the seeds of genocide. Perl also fails to mention Belgian complicity in the struggles during the 1950s. Perl has written a well received book on the Holocaust, *Four Perfect Pebbles: A Holocaust Story* (1996). Perhaps Perl is better acquainted with that genocide than with others.

David Downing in his *Africa: Postcolonial Conflict* (2004) tries to cover all of Africa in sixty-four pages; of necessity he oversimplifies his topic. The title of one section, "Troubled Continent," is untoward (4); there are countries in Africa that are working well and have seen vast improvements in their quality of life. Specific to the Sudan, Downing acknowledges that Britain, in giving up claims on its former colony, forced an untenable match: the Muslims of the north and the Christians and animists of the south. This is helpful for young readers to know (12–13). Specific to Rwanda, Downing, like other authors, leaves out Belgian complicity. His is not a useful book.

Recommended with Reservations: Comprehensive
Books about Genocide for Young People

In Elizabeth Hankins's picture book *I Learned a New Word Today . . . Genocide* (2009), a fifth-grade immigrant boy, Javier Mendoza, keeps a journal. Each day he writes in his journal what he is learning in school about genocide: Armenia, the Holocaust in Europe, the Kurds in Iraq, Bosnia, Rwanda, and Darfur. The writing is a bit wooden and didactic, and in the section on *Hotel Rwanda* Hankins does not seem cognizant of the criticisms of the film. But the book does introduce readers ten years of age and up to "Enough: The Project to End Genocide and Crimes against Humanity" (http://www.enough-project.org/). The introduction of so many genocides to ten-year-olds in one book seems overpowering.

Thom Winckelmann's *Genocide: Man's Inhumanities* (2009) opens with Darfur and references the Holocaust, the African slave trade, and indigenous peoples of the Americas. He introduces his book with questions he hopes to answer: "What exactly is genocide? How widespread is this problem? Does genocide still occur? Why is it important to learn about genocide?" (5). He begins to answer the questions by introducing Raphael Lemkin and his extraordinary work to create the word *genocide* and its definition.

In writing about Darfur in his introduction, Winckelmann does not perpetuate myths about black-on-black violence. He straightforwardly writes, "In early 2003, another conflict arose in the Darfur region of Sudan. The Darfur region is on the western side of Sudan. Its citizens have been oppressed by a brutal regime" (13–14).

His brief overview of the Armenian genocide is accurate. His chapter on the Holocaust contains graphic images and language: "Zyklon-B gas proved remarkably successful. Camp staff poured the gas into rooftop pipes atop shower buildings. The inmates went into the showers for 'decontamination.' The shower room doors were locked, and the victims were gassed to death" (32–33). The chapter on Cambodia also contains graphic images and language, summing up the genocide in ten pages. "Global Bystanders" is the title of the chapter on Rwanda, which Winckelmann would have better left unwritten, as it contributes to the "tribal outburst" myth and does not acknowledge that moderate Hutus also lost their lives: "Once the frenzy of killing began, 75% of Tutsis in Rwanda lost their lives. The Hutu killed more than 700,000 people in just six weeks" (49). This kind of writing does not capture the complexity of the Rwandan genocide; it is important for the world to know that it was radical Hutus from the north who orchestrated the genocide. In his "More Information" section, Winckelmann recommends Clare Pastore's *Journey to America: Chantrea Conway's Story*, presented in Chapter One of the present volume as the least reliable of sources on Cambodia.

Recommended Comprehensive Books
about Genocide for Young People

Essays

In her introduction to her collection of essays from around the world, *That Mad Game: Growing Up in a Warzone: An Anthology of Essays from around the Globe* (2012), J. L. Powers describes contrasting experiences of childhood:

> In the western world, we tend to think of childhood as a protected state—an idyllic time when children can play, go to school and enjoy life without being burdened with the cares of the adult world. One assumption behind this idea is that children should grow up in a safe and stable environment. Yet considering the daily realities of children worldwide, safety and stability are not the norm. Charles London . . . points out that there have been 14,000 wars in the last 5,600 years, and at least 60 wars since 1945. Children are far more likely to experience war at some point during their childhood than they are to grow up without it. Currently, approximately one billion children under the age of eighteen are growing up in regions affected by conflict. In fact, even in the U.S., many children are growing up in neighborhoods affected by so much gang violence that they are essentially growing up in a war zone. (14–15)

For Powers, the stories we tell ourselves matter, and she cites London's work in Serbia after the Bosnia and Kosovo genocides. Upon London's request, Serbian children told and drew stories for him about why their country had gone to war. Their narrative went back to the Battle of Kosovo that took place in 1389; Serbia has for over 600 years believed Kosovo belonged to it. Powers comments, "Their pictures demonstrate the way propaganda, idealism and ideology are embedded within stories" (15), and argues that "positive narratives that position all of us as citizens of a diverse and complex world" must be created to push against "destructive narratives" (16).

The collection includes essays by authors from Cambodia and Bosnia. Peauladd Huy was eight-years-old when the Cambodian genocide began. She opens with: "Mid-morning sun pushes holes in the canopy of our neighbor's mango and milk fruit trees. The winds are scarce, the leaves at a standstill. Then, sarong unfurled, Mother's feet are shuffling left and right. Her shoulders rock side to side and the baby's almost asleep" (103). As noted in my Introduction, aesthetic experience is rarely the purpose in texts about genocide for children and young people; in this passage Huy's sensory writing is informative and also has aesthetic appeal. For young readers, an effect of Huy's evocative writing can be the realization that Cambodia was for millions of people their beloved and comforting home—before the Khmer Rouge.

Huy's father had left Phnom Penh just before the arrival of the soldiers, and her family was stalling for time (her brothers were bribing the rebels with food) in hopes that her father would come back and the family could leave together. Because they were one of the last families to leave, Huy experienced the city in a way few could:

> The outside world is very eerie. It is like our whole world is picked clean of its inhabitants. No cars. No mopeds. No bicycles. The neighbor to the right is gone. The monks behind us in Wat Domrei Sar are all gone. No changing. Classrooms all empty. No students. No teachers. Everyone is gone. Strangely, with all this emptiness, there is a sense of confinement. We are watching them watching us. (104–105)

At gunpoint, they are made to leave without Huy's father. In labor camps, Huy experiences what so many did: hard labor, little food. Like the Serbian snipers who exhausted Sarajevans by firing all night, the Khmer Rouge also carry out their killings at night: "Village by village, people are taken out: the weak ones by nature and the not-so-weak ones carried off for execution, night after night. With the Khmer Rouge, everything is done in the dark" (110). One night, the Khmer Rouge come for Huy's mother, and she is never seen again. When the genocide ends, Huy returns to her home village: "There was nothing left, like we had never lived there" (118). She continues to hope for news of her parents, even after she immigrates to the United States. But the visual images of the killing fields end her hope: "The first time I saw those piles of bones was on my computer's screen many years later. I was so shaken. *There's your missing parents, your aunts and uncles and cousins*, I remember muttering to myself. *You can stop hoping now. Accept it. Stop fooling yourself. They're more than dead now*" (119; italics in the original). Despite giving up hope of ever seeing many family members again, Huy remains optimistic for the future of her children.

Nikolina Kulidžan's essay "Across the River" provides a Serbian perspective on growing up in Mostar. In her introduction, Powers writes that Mostar, as we saw with Sarajevo, was a "thriving city" whose population "were from three different ethnic/religious backgrounds—Muslim Bosniaks, Catholic Croats, and Eastern Orthodox Serbs" (65). Like Sarajevo, Mostar had been a model of multicultural tolerance. Kulidžan displays the love of place we have often seen in other war-torn countries:

> My hometown was my first true love. The smells of blooming linden trees and roasted chestnuts, the sounds of rambling railroad cars and rushing water, and the touch of the warm Mediterranean breeze all helped shape my senses and carve out in me a sense of identity. And when my family fled . . . losing Mostar became my first heartbreak. (66)

After the Serbs withdrew from Mostar in 1992, the Kulidžan family felt threatened by the Croats and Bosniaks who remained. She and her family escaped to Belgrade, where they lived in a "dinky studio apartment" (66); eventually Kulidžan became an exchange student in the U.S. and revisited Mostar in 2000.

Kulidžan affirms what we learned in Chapter Three on Bosnia: Intermarriage was common. She writes,

> My aunt Jasna and uncle Neđo have only recently returned to Mostar from Germany, where they had lived as refugees since 1993. They are an ethnically mixed couple: he is a Serb and she is a Bosniak. . . . Uncle Neđo and Aunt Jasna have done their best to put on a happy face for my visit, but they cannot conceal the fact that Mostar is a broken town and not the place they once loved so much. (69)

Kulidžan also writes of the destruction of the Mostar bridge built by the Ottomans in the sixteenth century:

> I remember my shock one November evening in 1993 when footage of the destruction of the bridge was played and replayed on Serbia's evening news. From a hill to the south, the Croatian artillery fired with flawless accuracy, reducing the centuries-old monument in a matter of minutes to rubble and dust that was swallowed by the river. . . . the bridge belonged to every resident of Mostar, Croats, and Serbs, no less than Bosniaks. (72)

The bridge has since been rebuilt.

Kulidžan, a Serb, has an affair with a Croat man while she is visiting Mostar.

Informational Texts

Jane Springer's *Genocide* (2006) is authentic and accurate; it achieves Levinas's respect for "the Other." I have used it as a text in many classes, motivating my former students to use it later in their own classrooms with their students. The book is part of their Groundwood Guide Series, of which Springer is the editor.

Groundwood Guides are advertised for ages fourteen and up. Young adults and their teachers will have to decide whether Springer's *Genocide* (Figure 6.1) is manageable for all teen readers. Here in reference to Darfur is the opening paragraph:

> Bombed-out mud huts in a parched desert landscape. A two-year-old boy, face in the sand, beaten to death. Corpses stuffed into wells. An adult skeleton, wrists still tied behind its back. Anguished African women and small children in crowded refugee camps. (7)

Giving details of the modus operandi of destruction, Springer explains that typically government planes bomb villages and are then followed by the Janjaweed, who:

> round up the men and boys and take them out of the village. If the hostages are lucky, the janjaweed and soldiers just shoot them. More often they torture them first. Sometimes they chain them together and burn them alive. . . . Many girls and women are kidnapped and brutally gangraped, often in front of their families. (8)

Springer points out that the western media are inclined to portray this genocide and others as "'tribal conflict,'" but Springer negates this portrayal with a clear, concise explanation of the factors that led to this genocide. She then introduces readers to the idea of human rights, which leads straight to Raphael Lemkin, the development of the word *genocide*, and the United Nations' adoption of the Convention on the Prevention and Punishment of the Crime of Genocide.

Springer next reviews those historical events that qualify as genocides, starting with Biblical accounts of destruction. Other groups of people include the Carthaginians, American Indians, the Congolese under King Leopold's rule, and the Herrero in what is now Namibia. Orders from Berlin to annihilate the Herrero are well-documented; 64,000 of a total population of 80,000 died. The next major genocide is that of the Armenians, 1915–1918; in this regard Springer quotes Hitler, "'Who today remembers the extermination of the Armenians?'" (qtd. in Springer, 40). In making his plans to exterminate Jews, homosexuals, the disabled, and Roma, Hitler knew that the Turks had suffered no legal consequences in carrying out the genocide of the Armenians so inferred he could carry out a genocide in Europe with impunity.

Springer states her view that African enslavement was genocide, citing David Stannard who "'estimates that between 36 and 60 million men, women and children died *before* they ever started work as slaves'" (qtd. in Springer, 36; italics in the original). She calls the USSR's starvation of Ukrainian peasants in the early 1930s genocide; 7 million died, 3 million of whom were children (39).

Readers of this book have probably gathered that I am in agreement with Warren Zimmerman, who thought that if Slobodan Milošević's parents had committed suicide before his birth instead of after, there would not have been a genocide in Bosnia, and that I think similarly of Pol Pot in Cambodia and Omar al-Bashir in Sudan. In Chapter Four of Springer's book, "Theories of Genocide," Springer's counterargument to the "one evil man" view (41), for which I have no answer except, possibly, mob mentality, is: "This theory does not explain how hundreds, thousands or even millions of people in a society are drawn into participating in a genocide" (42). It is hard to explain why there were so few "Righteous Gentiles" during the Holocaust, and how genocidal, radical Hutus were able to gain so many adherents in Rwanda; Lars Waldorf estimates "200,000 killers" in the *Interhamwe* (103). She continues,

"And it does not take into account or investigate the political, economic and social situations that might lead to genocide" (42). In this book, I have tried to consider "the political, economic and social situations" that contribute to genocide; I still think that in some of the genocides it took only a wretched few to mobilize forces, yet acknowledge Springer's line of reasoning about why so many participate in carrying out genocide.

Springer points to varying agendas: the exploitation of natural resources (the Herrero and others), the creation of an ideal society (the Holocaust, Cambodia), or power and control (Rwanda). She also acknowledges that perpetrators use the cover of "civil war" for the crime of one-sided genocide, as we have seen happen in Bosnia, Rwanda, and Darfur:

> Genocide is often described by the perpetrators as part of a civil war, or a war between armed factions within a country. But again, this is usually just an excuse for killing the victims with impunity. . . . The government claims that it is defending the national state by "fighting" with victims, who are unarmed. This has happened in Darfur. Civil war is also used as a reason for not intervening to help the victims. (45)

Hitler said, "'The size of the lie is a definite factor in causing it to be believed'" and that "'a big lie' is more easily believed than a small one'" (qtd. in Altman, 73). Referring to genocide as "civil war" is the big lie.

Besides the ruse of "civil war" as a reason for failure to intervene, there is also racism. Springer refers to Major Brent Beardsley, an aide to Romeo Dallaire in Rwanda, who "argues that the lack of response to the genocides in Rwanda and Darfur suggest that Western 'white' governments do not consider the death of an African to be equal to the death of a white person" (46).

Springer refutes the notion that genocides can explode spontaneously; they are, instead, well-planned and thought out. Great preparation goes into what Barthes calls creating myths by turning history into nature, as noted in my Introduction; Springer says,

> The planners manage to take away people's rights by reinforcing an "us-them" situation built on old conflicts, racism or ethnocentrism and making it seem "natural" or "right" that the target is brutally discriminated against. . . . The underlying logic is that if people in the targeted group are not human, then they can be killed without remorse. (57)

In his book *The Burning Tigris: The Armenian Genocide and America's Response* (2003), Peter Balakian gives other examples from the Holocaust and Armenian genocide of making groups of people "not human":

> In ways that were similar and anticipated the Nazi race-hygiene ideology of the 1930s, which depicted the Jew as a "harmful bacillus" and

"bloodsuckers" infecting the German nation from within (Hitler called the Jew "a maggot in a rotting corpse" and a "germ carrier of the worst sort"), pan-Turkist ideology envisioned the Armenian as an invasive infection in Muslim Turkish society. . . . Mehmed Reshid [a Turkish physician] . . . likened Armenians to "dangerous microbes," asking rhetorically, "Isn't it the duty of a doctor to destroy these microbes?" (164)

Figure 6.1 Book cover from Jane Springer: *Genocide*. Toronto, Canada: Groundwood Books, 2006.

Springer illustrates this objectification of other people with Radio Mille Collines, which repeatedly and beguilingly referred to Tutsis as "cockroaches" (59).

In a separate box, Springer displays Gregory Stanton's "Eight Stages of Genocide": classification, symbolization, dehumanization, organization, polarization, preparation, extermination, and denial (60). "Most important," writes Springer, is the notion that "the genocide can be stopped at each stage"—an assertion with which I wholeheartedly agree (60).

The remainder of her book covers specific genocides concisely and intelligently, making this an excellent text for high school and undergraduate courses. Her table, "Genocides through History," is most informative (120–125). Springer attains Levinas's concept of "the Other" by treating others ethically and respectfully with extensive and thoughtful research.

Brendan January's *Genocide: Modern Crimes against Humanity* (2007) addresses six genocides: the Armenian genocide, the Holocaust, and the genocides in Cambodia, Rwanda, Bosnia, and Darfur. In his introduction, he explains the difficulties of writing about genocide and offers this advice to young readers: "The author encourages the reader to do more research on this subject, to seek out other opinions and views, and to arrive at his or her own conclusion" (8).

January opens with Armenia and a brief history of the Ottoman Empire. The reduction of that empire contributed to the Turkish desire to destroy Armenians, who had lived in Turkey as a Christian community for centuries. Much like Milošević, angered by the loss of the countries of Slovenia and Croatia and therefore zealously aggressive toward Bosnia and Kosovo, so too were the Turks angered by the loss of Greece, parts of the Balkans, and Algeria in the nineteenth century. January devotes several pages to American ambassador Henry Morgenthau, who documented in writing much of the genocide. He wrote:

> *In a few days, what had been a procession of normal human beings became a stumbling horde of dust-covered skeletons, ravenously looking for scraps of food, eating any offal that came their way, crazed by the hideous sights that filled every hour of their existence, sick with all the diseases that accompany such hardships and privations, but still prodded on by the whips and clubs of their executioners.* (qtd. in January, 17; italics in the original)

The heroic Morgenthau, who was Jewish, communicated constantly with Washington and met with Mehmet Talaat (the same Talaat I wrote about in my Introduction, whose assassination and the subsequent trial of his murderer prompted Lemkin to devote his life to defining and creating an international law against genocide). Talaat could not comprehend a Jew's concern for Christians; January quotes Morgenthau's response: "'You don't seem to realize that I am not here as a Jew but as the American Ambassador. . . . I do not appeal to you in the name of any race or religion but merely as a human being'" (qtd.

in January, 18). Unable to stop the terror, Morgenthau resigned in protest in 1916. I did not hear of Morgenthau—or the Armenian genocide—until I was an adult. I appreciate January's coverage of both and would have liked to learn of him and the genocide sooner in my life. Morgenthau is an ethical mentor to us all. And there are no words for the enormity of the genocide—half of the Armenian population. January writes, "Of the nearly 2 million Armenians who were alive at the start of the war, 1 million had died in the genocide" (21). Current estimates are closer to 1.5 million.

In his second chapter, January introduces another mentor for millions, Raphael Lemkin, an inspiring person for all of us to know. Jean Paul Sartre once said, "'The world and man reveal themselves by undertakings. And all the undertakings we might speak of reduce themselves to a single one, making history'" (qtd. in Ladson-Billings and Tate, 214). Lemkin's undertaking was one of the greatest of all time and most certainly made history. As young people are making decisions about their own undertakings, knowing about Lemkin's could be influential. January's chapter on this great man is an essential one.

The next chapter is on the Holocaust. January's opening paragraph lends credence to Springer's assertion that genocides cannot all be attributed to the small, wrong group of men who are in the wrong place at the wrong time, manipulating "hundreds, thousands or even millions of people" to carry out genocide (42). He writes:

> The genocide of European Jews was possible because of anti-Semitism that reached back hundreds, even thousands of years. To the common people of medieval Europe, Jews were objects of suspicion, fear, and contempt. Jews, they thought, used the blood of Christian children in barbaric rituals. Jews were considered diabolical, secretive, sneaky, and dirty. . . . "What then shall we Christians do with the damned, rejected race of Jews?" asked the German priest and revolutionary Martin Luther in 1543. "Since they live among us and we know about their lying and blasphemy and cursing, we cannot tolerate them." (32)

January adds that Luther "urged the 'setting of fire to their synagogues and schools . . . so that no man will ever see a stone or cinder of them again'" (32). With this long-standing, dreadful leadership of a revered Protestant, perhaps it is no surprise few lifted a hand to help the Jews. The rest of the chapter seems comprehensive, and January includes a passage from *Night* by Elie Wiesel— the passage I noted in my Introduction that my son could not tolerate when he was twelve but which he later read on his own:

> Never shall I forget that smoke. Never shall I forget the little faces of children, whose bodies I saw turned into wreaths of smoke beneath a silent blue sky. . . . Never shall I forget those moments which murdered my God

and my soul and turned my dreams to dust. Never shall I forget these things, even if I am condemned to live as long as God Himself. Never. (qtd. in January, 53)

Horrific photographs of gas chambers and piles of bones are included. For some children and young adults reading about trauma may become traumatic.

January begins his chapter on Cambodia with Lemkin's arrival at the Nuremburg trials, where he hoped to introduce the concept of genocide. Although the authorities at Nuremburg convicted Nazi criminals, it was not on charges of genocide. Disappointed but still determined, Lemkin raced to New York, where the UN was in the process of coming together as a world organization that might have some leverage in cases of genocide. After enormous effort, Lemkin's law came into being. The first test case would be Cambodia in 1975.

January tells of the emptying of Phnom Penh and bases much of his Cambodian chapter on Luong Ung's *First They Killed My Father: A Daughter of Cambodia Remembers*, which was discussed in Chapter One in the section about crossover literature. Like Andy Koopmans in his biography of Pol Pot, January emphasizes Pol Pot's secrecy. Like Michelle Lord in *A Song for Cambodia*, he tells of the murder of thousands of Buddhist monks, and he includes the staggering fact that the "United States sided with the Khmer Rouge" (73). January's chapter on Cambodia is truthful and concise and interwoven with the unfolding events that led to the United States becoming the "ninety-eighth nation to ratify" the United Nations Convention on the Prevention and Punishment of the Crime of Genocide in 1986.

The next genocide January considers is the Rwandan genocide. In his opening paragraphs he establishes the harm done by Belgium, especially by requiring identity cards in 1933. His version of the events is based on high-quality scholarship, including that of Fergel Keane, whose work I drew upon in Chapter Four. Significant is January's observation that "It soon became clear that this was not a spontaneous outbreak of violence caused by a sudden plane crash. The Hutu leaders had prepared. Relying on identification cards that labeled each citizen as Hutu or Tutsi they had methodically prepared lists of Tutsi to be eliminated" (83). The western press too easily led westerners to believe that it was a "spontaneous outbreak." It should be noted that several grisly photographs of skeletons, skulls, and bones are included in this chapter, as they were in the Cambodia chapter as well.

January opens his chapter on Bosnia by describing the work of forensic anthropologist Clea Koff in her book *The Bone Woman: A Forensic Anthropologist's Search for Truth in the Mass Graves of Rwanda, Bosnia, Croatia, and Kosovo* (2004), which I also read in preparation for writing this book. More than other books on children's and young adult literature on the Bosnian genocide, January highlights the Serbian practice of hiding bodies: Bosnian corpses were often taken to the interior of Serbia and buried there. There are also photographs of Serbian concentration camps with starving Muslim men and boys. As in his chapter on Armenia, January references a Jew standing up for someone not of his faith. Morgenthau, a Jew, stood up for Armenian Christians; Elie Wiesel, a Jew, writes January, stood up for Muslims in Bosnia: "'I have been in the former Yugoslavia last fall. I cannot sleep since what I have seen. As a Jew I am saying that. We must do something to stop the bloodshed in that country'" (qtd. in January, 100).

Koff's purpose in going to Bosnia was to ascertain how 8,000 men and boys were killed in Srebrenica in July of 1995. "All had been hit at close range by a high-velocity weapon," says January (105). Many had their hands tied behind their backs. Koff's work contributed to the evidence that would help the International Criminal Tribunal for the former Yugoslavia indict over 160 Serbian perpetrators. January closes this chapter with the genocide in Kosovo and NATO's move to stop it.

His next topic is the genocide in Darfur, which he describes as well as any book on Darfur discussed in Chapter Five. His profile of Dr. Jerry Ehrlich does not appear in other books for children and young adults on Darfur, and it is well-worth including. At age sixty-nine, in 2004, Dr. Ehrlich went to Nyala, Darfur, with Doctors Without Borders. There he provided whatever health care he could, especially focusing on children. He also gave the children paper and crayons, and encouraged them to draw; Ehrlich became the first to help the rest of the world see what was going on in Darfur through children's eyes. When he left Darfur, he slipped the children's drawings inside his *New York Times* so they would not be taken away by the Sudanese government in the airport. Several of the drawings are reproduced in January's chapter: planes bombing, men shooting, people dying, dead, or about to die. The chapter ends with the words of Bill Schulz of Amnesty International, "'How far have we really come [since the genocide in Rwanda]? . . . The Sudanese government has been emboldened by international inaction. They think they can get away with murder, and frankly there's every reason to believe they are right'" (qtd. in January, 131).

Multigenre Text

Sybella Wilkes collected stories and art work from refugee children in Kenya for her book *One Day We Had to Run! Refugee Children Tell Their Stories in Words and Paintings* (1994). Although she focuses on the strife in Ethiopia, Somalia, and the effects of the civil war between the north and the south in Sudan, at the end she mentions Rwanda, whose crisis was unfolding as her book went to press in 1994. She vividly describes Rwandans leaving their country: "For miles and miles, people could be seen walking through torrential rains" (56). Because the book is almost twenty-years-old, the statistics are out of date in describing refugees in Africa, but the stories will never be out of date. Chol was nine-years-old when soldiers from the north attacked his village in southern Sudan. He told Wilkes:

> It was something like an accident when I ran away from my village. We were playing at about 5 o'clock when these people, the soldiers, came. We just ran. We didn't know where we were going to, we just ran. . . . We didn't know where our mother or father were, we didn't say good-bye. When there is shooting, when you hear BANG! BANG! BANG!, you don't think about your friend or your mother, you just run to save your life. . . . In the day the sun is hot and your feet burn. So we walked at night when it is cold, because then you don't say all the time, 'I want water, I want water.' To rest we stood under trees, but you can die of hunger if you give up and just lie under a tree. (16)

Although not about Darfur, Chol's story resonates with what Darfuri children's stories must be. Wilkes's is a valuable and accessible book for upper elementary, middle school, and high school students.

Conclusion

Writing about multiple genocides is a difficult task, as the books described in this chapter show. The authors face the same challenges, as outlined in my Introduction, that I face: missing innuendoes and the tacit knowledge cultural insiders are more likely to have than I am, as well as the time to explore all the experts—political scientists, historians, anthropologists, and journalists—write about the genocides. All of us who write about multiple genocides by necessity underresearch; it is not possible to grasp in a lifetime all the complexities of genocide. Jane Springer and Brendan January complete the task as well as possible.

Works Cited

Altman, Linda. *Genocide: The Systematic Killing of a People*. Berkeley Heights, NJ: Enslow, 2009.

Balakian, Peter. *The Burning Tigris: The Armenian Genocide and America's Response*. New York: HarperCollins, 2003.

Downing, David. *Africa: Postcolonial Conflict*. Chicago: Raintree, 2004.

Koff, Clea. *The Bone Woman: A Forensic Anthropologist's Search for Truth in the Mass Graves of Rwanda, Bosnia, Croatia, and Kosovo*. New York: Random, 2004.

Ladson-Billings, Gloria, and William Tate, eds. *Education Research in the Public Interest: Social Justice, Action, and Policy*. New York: Teachers College, 2006.

Perl, Lila. *Four Perfect Pebbles: A Holocaust Story*. New York: Greenwillow, 1996.

———. *Genocide: Stand By or Intervene?* New York: Cavendish, 2011.

Waldorf, Lars. "Revisiting *Hotel Rwanda*: Genocide Ideology, Reconciliation, and Rescuers." *Journal of Genocide Research* 11.1 (2009): 101–125.

Recommended Children's and Young Adult Comprehensive Books about Genocide

Huy, Peauladd. "Ways of the Khmer Rouge." Powers, 103–120.

January, Brendan. *Genocide: Modern Crimes against Humanity*. Minneapolis, MN: Twenty-First Century, 2007.

Kulidžan, Nikolina. "Across the River." Powers, 65–74.

Powers, J. L., ed. *The Mad Game: Growing Up in a Warzone: An Anthology of Essays from around the Globe*. El Paso, TX: Cinco Puntos, 2012.

Springer, Jane. *Genocide*. Toronto: Groundwood, 2006. Groundwood Guide Ser.

Wilkes, Sybella. *One Day We Had to Run! Refugee Children Tell Their Stories in Words and Paintings*. Brookfield, CT: Millbrook, 1994.

Recommended with Reservations: Children's and Young Adult Comprehensive Books about Genocide

Hankins, Elizabeth. *I Learned a New Word Today*. Toronto: Key, 2009.

Winckelmann, Thom. *Genocide: Man's Inhumanities*. Yankton, SD: Erickson, 2009.

Chapter Seven
Teaching Genocide

The information that is out there, the art, the music, the literature is enough on its own. They tell their own stories that need no more stressors or emphasis. Let the books tell their story, let the music sing its songs, and let the art show to the world what has happened. . . . Numbers and peoples and all details came up . . . but they were not lectured to us, there was a sense of self-discovery in the material that made it more influential.

—Richard Dunn

Richard Dunn was a student in my course "Genocide in Literature and Art" and captures in this epigraph why teaching genocide through literature and art can be powerful. In this chapter, I discuss ways in which I and others have taught genocide with grades five through higher education. None of this chapter is meant to be prescriptive; teachers and professors must decide what is appropriate for their students. I begin by discussing current policies that will make teaching genocide through literature and art less likely, despite its enormous potential.

Current Educational Policies and the Teaching of Genocide

In the United States, to be eligible for federal money from the U.S. Department of Education's Race to the Top (RTTT) program, forty-six states have, since 2010, hastily accepted the Common Core State Standards (CCSS); David Coleman and Sue Pimental are the primary "architects" of the English Language Arts (ELA) standards (National Governors Association Center for Best Practices, Council of Chief State School Officers). Coleman has never taught in the K–12 schools. The CCSS ELA standards dictate that elementary school children, to become "college and career ready," will read 50 percent informational texts and 50 percent literary texts. Middle and high school students, to become "college and career ready," will read 70 percent informational texts and 30 percent literary texts. Coleman has gone on to becoming president of the College Board, where he hopes to bring similar emphases to higher education.

In the study of genocide, there is reason for concern about these percentages. In a remarkable book, *Evoking Genocide: Scholars and Activists Describe the Works That Shaped Their Lives* (2009), genocide scholar Adam Jones interviewed fifty-eight genocide scholars and human rights activists to understand the origin of their dedication to the field of genocide studies. Professors, deans, researchers, education and museum directors, writers, a rabbi, a reporter, and one doctoral candidate discuss the texts and works of art that inspired them to do the work they do. Fine arts and literary texts dominate the most influential works that provoked them to work on genocide and human rights; for these professionals, who are clearly "college and career ready," the percentages are the opposite of what the CCSS demand: About 21 percent of the texts are informational; 74 percent of the texts are literature and the arts. Of those that might be called informational or nonfiction, there is one autobiography, one biography, four memoirs (Elie Wiesel's *Night* is mentioned twice), one diary, one document, one essay, one multidisciplinary history, one philological study, one report, and one survivor testimony.

Of literary texts, there is one letter, six novels, one play, three poems, and one short story (27 percent of the literature and fine arts category). Of the fine arts, there is one documentary, one set of drawings, twelve films, one *LEGO®* Concentration Camp construction, one monument, one mural, one museum, one painting, seven sets of photographs, one political cartoon, one sculpture, two songs, and one *Star Trek* episode (72 percent of the literature and fine arts category). There were two "genres" outside of the informational, literary, and fine arts descriptors: one "history," which was in fact a fabrication, and one contributor was deeply moved by the ruins she saw of a synagogue in Vienna.

The CCSS mentions music once, as appropriate for students in the seventh grade, and song is mentioned once for students in the second grade. Films based on literary texts are acceptable for seventh and eighth graders. Photographs are mentioned twice. Documentaries, drawings, LEGO® construction, monuments, murals, museums, paintings, political cartoons, sculpture, and television episodes are not mentioned.

The ages of the fifty-eight individuals Jones interviewed ranged from seven to the adult years: thirty-four reported being adults when they encountered the work that inspired them to their life's work—the study and participation in genocide prevention and human rights. Four were undergraduates, twelve were in their teens, five were children under the age of thirteen, and three did not report their ages.

Clearly, the fine arts and literary texts, together, which constitute 74 percent of the influential works, are of major importance to genocide scholars and human rights activists. See Table 7.1 for the specific works.

Table 7.1   Meaningful Works for Genocide Scholars and Human Rights Activists

Genocide Scholar and/or Human Rights Activist	Work That Moved Him or Her to Study Genocide and Human Rights
Professor Atenea Acevedo, as an adult	Marie Uchytilová and Jiří Hampl's *Monument to the Child Victims of War*, in Lidice
Researcher Diane F. Afoumado, at age eleven	Hans Peter Richter's novel *Mon Ami Frédéric* (1963)
Professor Joyce Aspel, as an adult	Raul Hillberg's multidisciplinary history *The Destruction of the European Jews* (1961)
Professor Paul Bartrop, as a graduate student	Stefan Lorant's memoir *I Was Hitler's Prisoner* (1935)
Professor Helen Bond, as an adult	Hans Knopf's photograph of Raphael Lemkin (1951)
Professor R. Charli Carpenter, as a teenager	"I, Borg," Episode 223 of *Star Trek: The Next Generation* (1992)
Professor Ward Churchill, at age nineteen	Buffy Sainte-Marie's song "My Country 'Tis of Thy People You're Dying" (1966)
Education Director Sara Cohan, at age seventeen (Cohan, "Re: question")	Peter Balakian's poem "History of Armenia" and the testimony of her grandfather, an Armenian genocide survivor
Professor and Dean G. Jan Colijn, as a teenager	Harry Mulisch's personal essay *De Zaak 40/61 (Case 40/61)* (1962)
Professor John Cox, as an undergraduate	Diego Rivera's mural "Le Gran Tenochtitlán" (1945)
Professor Marcia Esparza, as an adult	Jonathan Moller's photographs from Guatemala (2004)
Professor Stephen Feinstein, as an adult	Zbigniew Libera's *LEGO® Concentration Camp* (1995)
Professor Jonathan Friedman, as an adult	Tim Blake Nelson's film *The Grey Zone* (2002)
Professor Donna-Lee Frieze, as an adult	Radu Mihaieanu's film *Train of Life* (1998)
Professor Lee Ann Fujii, at age seventeen	Amnesty International's Cambodia Photo Exhibit

(Continued)

Table 7.1 Continued

Genocide Scholar and/or Human Rights Activist	Work That Moved Him or Her to Study Genocide and Human Rights
Professor Alexander George, as an adult	Judy Ellis Glickman's sculpture "Execution Wall" (1990) at the Auschwitz Concentration Camp in Poland
Professor Simone Gigliotti, as an undergraduate	Jackie Farkas's film *The Illustrated Auschwitz* (1992)
Professor Eric Gordy, as an adult	Hannah Arendt's report *Eichmann in Jerusalem* (1963)
Professor Fred Grünfeld, as an adult (Grünfeld, "Re: question")	Elie Wiesel's novel *The Town beyond the Wall* (1964)
Professor Wendy Hamblet, as an adult	Tony Kaye's film *American History X* (1998)
Professor Michael Hayse, around age eighteen	Günter Grass's novel *The Tin Drum* (1959)
Founding Director of the Center for Holocaust, Genocide and Peace Studies Viktoria Hertling, at age thirteen	Gotthold Ephraim Lessing's play *Nathan the Wise*
Professor William Hewitt, as a teenager	Viktor Frankl's memoir *Man's Search for Meaning* (1946)
Research Fellow Winton Higgins, as an adult	Pierre Sauvage's documentary *Weapons of the Spirit* (1989)
Professor Alex Hinton, age unspecified	Octavio Paz's poem "Hermandad" (1988)
Professor Steven Leonard Jacobs, at age thirteen (Jacobs, "Re: question")	Elie Wiesel's memoir *Night* (1958)
Professor Adam Jones, as an adult (Jones, "Re: question")	Midnight Oil's anthem "Hercules" (1985)
Professor Ani Kalayjian, as an adult	J. Michael Hagopian's film *Voices from the Lake* (2003)
Museum Education Director Nina Krieger, as an adult	Armin T. Wegner's photographs and letters
Professor Scott Laderman, as an adult	Roland Joffé's film *The Killing Fields* (1984)
Professor Benjamin Lieberman, as an adult	Books by survivors, such as Primo Levi and Dawid Sierakowiak
Professor Fiona de Londras, as a teenager	Alexander Ramati's novel *And the Violins Stopped Playing: A Story of the Gypsy Holocaust* (1985), which she rereads every year
Professor Pam Maclean, as an adult	The Or-Sarua Synagogue ruins in Vienna
Professor Daniel Magilow, as an adult	Early photos of Saddam Hussein and Adolf Hitler

(Continued)

Table 7.1 Continued

Genocide Scholar and/or Human Rights Activist	Work That Moved Him or Her to Study Genocide and Human Rights
Professor Henry Maitles, age unspecified	Primo Levi's autobiographies and poetry
Professor Jens Meierhenrich, as a teenager	Victor Klemperer's philological study *The Language of the Third Reich* (1947)
Reporter Jina Moore, at age seven	Anne Frank's diary *The Diary of a Young Girl* (1952)
Professor Thomas Nagy, as an adult	1991 U.S. Defense Intelligence Agency Document "Iraq Water Treatment Vulnerabilities"
Shayna Parekh, as an undergraduate	Greg Barker's film *Ghosts of Rwanda* (2004)
Professor Edward Paulino, as an undergraduate	Ambassador R. Henry Norweb's letter to Franklin Delano Roosevelt
Author Jack Nusan Porter, as a graduate student	Magnus Hirschfeld, the man, and the film *Different from Others* (1919)
Professor Christopher Powell, at age sixteen	Roland Joffé's film, *The Mission* (1986)
Professor Eric Reeves, as an adult (Reeves, "Re: question")	Paul Jeffrey's photo of a Darfuri girl, and Ursula K. LeGuin's dystopian short story "The Ones Who Walk Away from Omelas" (1975)
Dean Stefanie Rixecker, at age twelve	Francis Ford Coppola's film *Apocalypse Now* (1979)
Professor John K. Roth, in his early thirties	Elie Wiesel's memoir *Night* (1958)
Professor Victoria Sanford, as an adult	Crime Scene Photos of Guatemala (2006)
Professor William Schabas, recommended by his father when he was twelve	Franz Werfel's novel *The Forty Days of Musa Dagh* (1933), based on the Armenian genocide
Professor Dominick Schaller, in high school	Binjamin Wilkomirski's fabricated autobiography *Fragments* (1995)
Doctoral candidate Russell Schimmer, as an adult	A Landsat photo of Dili, East Timor (1999)
Professor Jacques Sémelin, as a graduate student	Auschwitz-Birkenau State Museum, Oświęcim, Poland
Professor David J. Simon, at age ten	Pablo Picasso's painting "Guernica" (1937)
Professor Robert Skloot, as an adult	Ján Kadár and Elmar Klos's film *The Shop on Main Street* (1965)
Professor Christopher Taylor, as a graduate student	Cartoon in *Kangura*, Rwanda (1993)

(Continued)

Table 7.1   Continued

Genocide Scholar and/or Human Rights Activist	Work That Moved Him or Her to Study Genocide and Human Rights
Professor Ernesto Verdeja, as a graduate student	Gitta Sereny's biography *Albert Speer: His Battle with Truth* (1995)
Professor Joseph Robert White, as an adult	Karl Schwesig's charcoal drawings, titled *Schlegelkeller* (1983)
Writer Benjamin Whitmer, who continues to reread the book, in his early twenties	Cormac McCarthy's novel *Blood Meridian* (1985)
Professor John Zimmerman, as an adult	Walter Sanning's fabrication of Holocaust denial, *The Dissolution of Eastern European Jewry* (1983)
Professor Lior Zylberman, age unspecified	Alejandro Agresti's film *The Act in Question* (1993)

Source: Adam Jones, *Evoking Genocide: Scholars and Activists Describe the Works That Shaped Their Lives.*

Although Dominick Schaller cites Binjamin Wilkomirski's fraudulent autobiography *Fragments* (1995) as the work that has most powerfully affected him, he adds that in high school Primo Levi's autobiographies and Paul Celan's poetry held more significance for him. Schaller writes, "It was the artistic and refined way in which these two authors transformed their terrible experiences into literature that fascinated me" (119). For Diane Afoumado, it was a novel that led her to her current work. She says,

> It is no exaggeration to say that if I had not read *Mon Ami Frédéric* as a teenager, I would not now be working for the United States Holocaust Memorial Museum, or have worked for France's Commission for the Study of the Seizure of Properties Belonging to Jewish People, the Commission for the Compensation of Victims of Spoliation, and the Holocaust memorial in Paris. This makes me wonder whether, and to what extent, the choices we make in our life are truly "our own." What I do know is that after more than fifteen years studying the Holocaust, I cherish this book and its lessons more than ever. (79)

Author Joan Aiken observes, "'[F]iction—fact implanted in a story—does have a way of becoming knit into the mental processes much more easily, much more permanently, than facts on their own, unrelated, ever can'" (qtd. in Kokkola, 53). For Afoumado, a fictional work about the Holocaust became "knit" into her mind and heart "much more permanently"—and much more inspiringly—than had she read an informational text about the Holocaust. Given the current educational climate, educators will have to swim against the tide to ensure that young people have access to fictional and artistic works about genocide.

Significantly, it was also a novel he read as a child that propelled Raphael Lemkin to learn all he could about crimes against humanity. Lemkin wrote:

> In my early boyhood, I read *Quo Vadis* by Henry Sienkiewicz—this story is full of fascination about the sufferings of the early Christians and the Romans' attempt to destroy them solely because they believed in Christ. Nobody could save them, neither the police of Rome nor any outside power. It was more than curiosity that led me to search in history for similar examples, such as the case of the Hugenots, the Moors of Spain, the Aztecs of Mexico, the Catholics in Japan, and so many races and nations under Genghis Khan. The trail of this unspeakable destruction led straight through modern times up to the threshold of my own life. I was appalled by the frequency of the evil, by great losses in life and culture, by . . . [the] impossibility of reviving the dead or consoling the orphans, and above all, by the impunity coldly relied upon by the guilty. (qtd. in Schaller and Zimmerer, 3)

It is emotional engagement that can propel people of all ages to look for more information about a subject. Lemkin's reading of the fictional *Quo Vadis* led to his acquiring vast knowledge, and possibly to his creation of the word *genocide*. Jane Springer observes that Lemkin, in addition to his immense erudition on crimes against humanity, "learned to speak nine languages and read another five" (20). That this brilliant, influential man would credit a work of fiction, *Quo Vadis*, with provoking him to devote his life to ending genocide, is most noteworthy in this day and age, when percentages of fiction and nonfiction for children and young adults are dictated. If the Common Core State Standards had directed Lemkin's education—50 percent informational text in the elementary grades and 70 percent informational text by secondary grades—would there be a word for genocide, a consciousness of genocide? I am opposed to percentage mandates, but if we must have them, it seems they should be weighted the other way around.

Teaching Genocide

Access

As the scholars and human rights activists in Jones's study shows, access to many texts and works of art have been crucial for genocide scholars and human rights activists. And, as Hamida Bosmajian said in my Introduction, there must be "first stories of a thousand and one recountings to prevent the reduction of collective memory" (248). In this book, I have tried to indicate books that honor the victims of genocide, and that are respectful and responsible, to which young people should have access.

How likely is it books on genocide will be shared on a wide scale? The aggregate of research on multicultural literature in schools is not encouraging. The marginalization of multicultural literature is apparent in children's literature textbooks (Scroggins and Gangi), booklists (Gangi *Booklists*), awards (Gangi *Inclusive*), classroom collections (Gangi and Ferguson), school book fairs and book order forms (McNair *Innocent* and *Representation*), literacy textbooks (Gangi *Unbearable*), transitional books (Hughes-Hassell, Barklay, and Koehler), board books (Hughes-Hassell and Cox), and young adult book covers (Hart). Of 171 text exemplars in Appendix B of the Common Core State Standards, there are eighteen authors of color. Taken as an aggregate, it is apparent that children of color continue to be marginalized in schools' curricula in the U.S. To their credit, the authors of the Common Core have worked with Collaborative for Equity in Literacy Learning at my college, Mount Saint Mary College in Newburgh, New York, to expand multicultural selections for Appendix B.

In the meantime marginalization places an unbearable burden on children of color and the poor: Developing reading proficiency requires, for most children, books to which they can make connections. In Rudine Sims Bishop's words, all children must have both "mirror" and "window" books (n. pag.). In most cases, reading begins with "mirror" books; children must be able to activate their prior knowledge to gain new knowledge. An imbalanced collection—of mostly White books and few multicultural books—besides unfairly advantaging White children as they launch into their reading lives, may influence White children, if they grow up thinking the world centers on them, to develop increasingly narcissistic thinking. Research on the marginalization of multicultural literature could shed light on the way much of the world seems to respond to genocide; in the case of Rwanda, the world had almost no response at all. When White children of the West read mostly about themselves, they may learn not to concern themselves with others. Teachers and the professors who teach them must work to ensure that children of color and children of war and genocide are represented in the curricula.

Self-Care

As discussed in my Introduction, sustaining the child must be part of the writer's intent in writing about genocide for children and young adults. So too in teaching genocide; instructors must support students.

I ask college students to take care of themselves as we study the gravest of subjects. When the subject gets to be too much for them, I encourage them to go to those places and people where they feel safe. An analogy: On airplanes, caretakers are directed to put on their own oxygen masks before helping children. In the study of genocide, we have to keep our own oxygen masks on and back off when we need to. I am honest with students: I am not sure that at their age I would have taken such a course. We set out to learn about the worst abuses of humankind; it would be better to space those learnings out, if necessary, than not to study genocide at all. If they feel the need, they are to "back off." Later in the semester, I receive e-mails with the subject line of "backing off," and the message, "Dr. Gangi, I just can't take it this week." Students do not abuse this privilege of not attending class, and the instruction to take care of themselves is one thing former students still mention as imperative.

The same for the reading: If it gets to be too much, they are to stop. In a course for undergraduate honors students, I paired works of art and literature with chapters from Samantha Power's *"A Problem from Hell": America and the Age of Genocide*. We noticed that in her chapter on Bosnia, her writing takes on an especially grisly tone not as evident in chapters on other genocides; this change may be explained by the fact that she had been in Bosnia at the time of the genocide, making it an especially severe experience for her. Toward the end of the semester, the topic of nightmares came up: Almost all of us had nightmares at some point in the semester. (For one student, the nightmares did not stop and, because they affected her work in other courses, she dropped the class with my full support.)

Genocide in Literature and Art

Teaching genocide through the arts seems particularly effective because, as Richard Dunn says in the epigraph, there is a "sense of self-discovery." For philosopher Maxine Greene, the arts are a way to "invent ways of freeing people to feel and express indignation, to break through the opaqueness, to refuse the silences" and, thus, "teach in such a way as to arouse passion" (441). The intense experience of the arts and literature in the study of genocide produces an array of responses.

Although he writes about teaching music, Keith Swanwick's understandings in *Musical Knowledge: Intuition, Analysis and Music Education* (1994) can inform the study of genocide. He writes,

> Instruction without encounter, analysis without intuition, artistic craft without aesthetic pleasure; these are recipes for educational disaster. Meaningless action is worse than no activity at all and leads to confusion and apathy, whereas meaning generates its own models and motivation and in so doing frees the student from the teacher. Thus we take charge of our own learning; there is no other way. (159)

If I simply instruct and do not give students time to encounter literature and the arts on genocide on their own and with each other, the pursuit may become meaningless; the victims may become as described in my Introduction, in Paul Slovic's words, "human beings with the tears dried off." This did not happen for Richard and other students; even after the course was over, some volunteered their time to share their outstanding multimedia presentation on Darfur in area high schools, and as I wrote in the Acknowledgments, some students went on to human rights law and other areas related to genocide.

But some time must be spent "instructing." Again Swanwick provides guidance on how to create deep experiential learning, while simultaneously introducing to students horizons and knowledge of which they know not. In *Music, Mind, and Education* (1988), Swanwick says,

> [T]his tension between instruction and encounter is both inevitable and fertile. These apparently contradictory aspects of human learning are the positive and negative poles between which the electricity of educational transactions flow. . . . But it is encounter that characterizes the left hand side: sensory impression, personal expression, structural speculation and symbolic veneration. Here, the student needs to be left alone with possibilities, many of which will exist thanks to some instructional framing. (135)

Teachers of genocide must balance this tension, allowing learners time for their own encounters while giving instructional framing. Teachers must also help students find their voices to respond to genocide, both personally and socially. To deepen students' sense of the possibilities of multimodal forms of expression, I assign Tom Romano's chapter "A Place to Start" from *Blending Genre, Altering Style: Writing Multigenre Papers* (2000), a book that helps readers to learn how they might concurrently express themselves through poetry, essays, playwriting, and other genres.

For each genocide, I also share how literature and the arts can, used wrongly, promote genocide. Like Terry Eagleton, aesthetician John Briggs recognizes that creativity, which includes the arts, can have a dark side. He writes,

> [O]f course, creativity has brought humanity many dreadful things, too. Along with the uses of fire and the insights of religion have come innovative means of torture and destruction; violently escapist entertainment; and the unintended consequences of technology, where an ostensibly advantageous invention can quickly transform into a demonic influence. (xviii)

Here I discuss ways I have instructionally framed through the arts the genocides of enslaved Africans, especially during the Middle Passage; also included are the genocides of American Indians, Armenians, Jews, homosexuals, Roma, and the disabled in the Holocaust, Cambodians, Iraqi Kurds, the Maya of Guatemala, Muslims of Bosnia and Kosovo, Tutsis and moderate Hutus in Rwanda, and Black Muslims in Darfur. I begin with how I have taught genocide in higher education; high school teachers can modify the material to suit their students' needs. I highly recommend Facing History and Ourselves; this site has many resources, including videos, on teaching genocide. I then share the ways I and others have taught genocide, fifth grade and up, in the K–12 schools.

The Middle Passage

Overview

Scholars disagree on whether African enslavement, sometimes called the Black Holocaust, qualifies as genocide. David Bradley writes:

> between ten and twelve million Africans were brought to the New World between 1510 and 1865 . . . and that while losses sustained during the Middle Passage were much lower than is commonly believed (. . . 13 percent to 19 percent), those incurred during the capture, the march to the coast, and the sojourn in the "barracoons" (hence the term "coon") awaiting transport were substantial enough to raise overall mortality to between 30.4 percent and 39.25 percent, indicating that between 14,367,000 and 19,753,000 Africans were actually kidnapped. (206–207)

According to Bradley, 4 to 9 million Africans could have died during the Middle Passage. Jane Springer's estimates are far higher: 36 to 60 million (two thirds to three fourths of those captured). The deliberate weeding out of the weak, the sick, and the old seems to fit the definition of *genocide*: "Killing members of the group." Only the strongest survived; the rest were thrown overboard. Sharks followed the slave ships.

The Middle Passage through Literature and Art

While playing recordings of spirituals, I silently turn the pages for students to view the illustrations in Tom Feelings's *The Middle Passage: White Ships/ Black Cargo* (1995), Julius Lester and Jerry Pinkney's *The Old African* (2005), Julius Lester and Rod Brown's *From Slave Ship to Freedom Road* (1998), and/ or Jackie Napoleon Wilson's *Hidden Witness: African-American Images from the Dawn of Photography to the Civil War* (1999). Students who come into the course with notions that African enslavement could not have been genocide begin to change their thinking. Holocaust scholar Michael Bernard-Donals writes, "Much of the work done in the last several years on visual rhetoric has rightly concluded that the visual—photographic and screen images, paintings and other plastic arts—provides a corrective to the language of narrative that can only go so far to account for multiple human experiences" (381). In my Introduction I wrote about the difficulties of having only words with which to describe genocide and the literature of genocide. Narrative, as Bernard-Donals points out, has its limits. These images deepen our understanding of human experience.

We read Alice McGill's short story "Moon Time Child" (2004). The story tells of a young enslaved girl who is approaching her first menstrual cycle ("moon time"), which means that she will become the sex slave of the White master. Part of the definition of *genocide* is "Causing serious bodily or mental harm to members of the group." An enslaved African girl who must dread her first menstrual cycle because her White owner will systematically rape her to produce more slaves, more than fits the definition of *genocide* as "causing serious bodily or mental harm."

Also to be considered are the continuing effects of enslavement on young Black men. The United States has the highest incarceration rate in the industrialized world. The National Association for the Advancement of Colored People (NAACP) writes that "African Americans now constitute 1 million of the 2.3 million incarcerated population" (n. pag.). It seems that the bodily and mental harm of African enslavement continues to the present.

Problematic Representation

In the same way that art and literature can evoke action, empathy, and motivation for further learning, so too can literature and art dehumanize and perpetuate stereotypes. Tambay has posted online Nora Case's *Ten Little Nigger Boys* (1907), which is an atrocious use of literature and art. In her book *Brown Gold: Milestones of African-American Children's Picture Books, 1845–2002* (2004), Michelle Martin reproduces other versions of *Ten Little Nigger Boys*, a book that was printed and reprinted throughout Reconstruction. These visuals can help students see that literature and art can be a double-edged sword; they are not only forms of expression in response to inhumanity and ways to honor victims but can also contribute to the dehumanization of groups. As Bosmajian wisely says, books cannot be ice axes for children in the way that Franz Kafka would like to see books for adults as ice axes for the frozen seas within us. As books should not be ice axes for children, neither should they be ice axes for groups of children, in this case Africans and African Americans.

American Indians

Overview

At the time of European arrival, there were approximately 10 to 12 million American Indians in North America. As a result of genocide and disease, there were 1 million remaining by 1900 (Loewen 1995). As cited in Chapter One, on Cambodia, in reference to Nancy Graff's assertion that "almost everyone" in the United States is an immigrant, Joseph Bruchac demonstrates that the slaughter of the buffalo was a genocidal act—a deliberate cutting off of American Indians' food supply, as was the deliberate infection with the smallpox virus of blankets given to American Indians.

Students typically underestimate the number of enslaved Africans there were at the time of the Emancipation Proclamation, usually guessing 4,000 instead of the 4 million there were. Similarly, they estimate that there were a few thousand American Indians prior to European arrival, not the 10 to 12 million that historians now estimate. Few students I have met in higher education have heard of the Indian Boarding Schools, which fit part of the definition of genocide in the United Nations Convention on the Prevention and Punishment of the Crime of Genocide: "Forcibly transferring children of the group to another group." At first, the U.S. government and missions built schools near reservations with the slogan "Kill the Indian, save the man." "Killing the Indian" didn't work; when children were in schools close to their parents, they still spoke their languages and practiced their cultural mores. Schools were then deliberately built hundreds of miles from children's homes and they were forcibly taken there. So many children died of tuberculosis that a sanatorium had to be built in Iowa to house them until their deaths. Children were so poorly fed that, instead of gaining weight, as children should throughout their childhoods, these children lost weight.

Taking into account boarding schools, massacres, and slaughter of the buffalo, genocide was carried out against the American Indians over several centuries. This heinous past was carried out on America's own soil, which is important to remember in studying other genocides, especially those in Africa, where we are inclined to blame violence on tribal outbursts or, as in Bosnia, ancient ethnic hatreds.

The Genocide of American Indians through Literature and Art

For a brief overview of the Indian Boarding Schools we read Sonja Keohane's "The Reservation Boarding School System in the United States, 1870–1928" (2009). While students are viewing photographs and art, I play Chief Joseph Fire Crow's "Cheyenne Honor Song" (2000), which commemorates the forced removal of the Northern Cheyenne, a removal that they courageously resisted. The photographs and art can be selected from the following:

- Joseph Bruchac's *Crazy Horse's Vision* (2000), illustrated in the style of Native American Ledger Art by S. D. Nelson
- Nancy Plain's *The Man Who Painted Indians: George Catlin* (1997)
- Joseph Bruchac's *Navajo Long Walk: The Tragic Story of a Proud People's Forced March from Their Homeland* (2002), illustrated by Shonto Begay
- Russell Freedman's *An Indian Winter* (1992), with paintings by Karl Bodmer from 1833–1834

Literature choices are Joseph Bruchac's *Lasting Echoes* (1997) and Bruchac's historical fiction novel *The Winter People* (2002). *Lasting Echoes* includes excerpts from speeches and other forms of communication from the nineteenth century by both Indians and non-Indians. *The Winter People* is based on true events; it is the story of a massacre that took place in 1759 in Odanak, an Abenaki village in Quebec, and one young man's bravery as he set out to bring back his mother and sister, whom the "Bostoniaks" (Europeans) had captured. I have used this novel in many classes, from middle school to higher education; students are affected by it.

An excellent film for in-class or out-of-class viewing is *The Mission* (1986). The musical score by Ennio Morricone of this film, starring Jeremy Irons and Robert DeNiro, is haunting. For genocide scholar Christopher Powell, who was interviewed in Jones's *Evoking Genocide,* seeing *The Mission* when he was sixteen-years-old launched him into the field of genocide studies. The film was directed by Roland Joffé, who also directed *The Killing Fields,* which has been cited by genocide scholars as being influential. In the film, during the eighteenth century Jesuit priests try to protect indigenous peoples who live near the Iguazu Falls (on the Brazilian and Argentinian border) from Portugese slavers; the priests are not successful.

Problematic Representation

We also looked at demeaning images of Indians in children's literature, which exist in abundance: John Archambault and Bill Martin's *Knots on a Counting Rope* (1987); Lynne Reid Banks's *The Indian in the Cupboard* (1980); Susan Jeffers's *Brother Eagle, Sister Sky* (1991); and Ann Rinaldi's *My Heart Is on the Ground* (1999). (See Oyate's website, "Resources: Oyate's Additional Criteria," on how to evaluate these books.) Probably no group is more denigrated in children's literature than American Indians. Dehumanization might not only contribute to genocide but also prevent observers, past or present, from caring.

Armenia

Overview

As we saw in Chapter Six, Brendan January's book *Genocide* describes how the decline of the Ottoman Empire contributed to the Turkish massacre of Armenians, who had been a close community of Christians living in Turkey for centuries. The Armenians had become a strong middle class there, which threatened Turks. After World War I began, Interior Minister Mehmed Talaat, on April 24, 1915, ordered the execution of Armenian intellectuals and professionals. He and his Committee of Union and Progress (a committee name of Orwellian proportions if ever there was) knew that the world's attention would not be focused on a population of 2 million Armenians dwelling in the hinterlands of Turkey. By 1918 1.5 million Armenians had been killed.

The Armenian Genocide through Literature and Art

A book I have assigned often in various classes is David Kherdian's *A Road from Home: The Story of an Armenian Girl* (1979), which is the biography of

Kherdian's mother, Veron. Kherdian is an exquisite writer; his book deservedly received the Boston Globe-Horn Book Award for Excellence in Children's Literature in 1979 as well as the Jane Addams Book Award; it also received a Newbery Honor in 1980. It is hard not to care deeply about Veron as a young girl. One of the questions I ask students is: What images are particularly powerful to you? Usually they mention the scene where Veron, along with other Armenian survivors, had escaped to the seacoast city of Smyrna when the Turks attacked. There was no escape for the Armenians. Kherdian writes:

> By night the entire city was ablaze. We were packed, nearly half a million human beings, in an area a mile and one-half long and no more than one hundred feet wide. The buildings were crashing down into their own gutted cavities, the sound mixing with the howling wind and the crack of rifle fire. Men, as well as a few women and children, were swimming out to the huge ships, but except for the Italians, no one would take them aboard. The English ships were pouring boiling water down on the swimmers. (196)

The passage conveyed the desperate plight of the Armenians, who had already gone through the utterly unbearable.

Other choices are Kerop Bedoukian's *Some of Us Survived: The Story of an Armenian Boy* (1978). His "Historical Note" is particularly informative, giving the history of the area and contributing factors to the genocide. He writes:

> Though Armenians suffered under Turkish rule—the fate of all conquered peoples—they managed to keep their Christian faith, their cultural identity, and their strong family unity, in spite of the fact that in many places they were not allowed to speak their native language. Eventually the Armenians achieved considerable status in the Ottoman Empire. The Turks, who were warriors by choice, considered peaceful pursuits degrading, and relegated all such matters to the Armenians, who became their manufacturers, teachers, architects, lawyers, doctors, and bankers and gradually came to be regarded as the most loyal ethnic group in the Ottoman mosaic of nations. (236)

Bedoukian explains that Turks began to question Armenian loyalty during the Russo-Turkish war in the late 1870s, when Russia took parts of Turkey:

> Smoldering beneath the surface was the debtor/creditor relationship that had developed over the centuries as the Turks allowed the Armenians to control the money and business interests of the empire. ... This, combined with religious differences, aggravated the conflict between the races and set the stage for the genocide that was to follow. (237)

Adam Bagdasarian's *Forgotten Fire* (2000) is a fictionalized biography of his uncle, Vahan Kenderian, who was a child during the Armenian genocide. As in other stories, like Élisabeth Combres's *Broken Memory*, children who have lost their parents sometimes find surrogate parents. Ara Sarkisian took in Vahan and tried to help him see how he could go on despite his great losses. Sarkisian says,

> "You are looking for a home, for a family. Do you know where your real home is? Your real home is here." He pointed at his heart. "Who you are and what you believe in is your real home, the only home no one can take from you, the only home that will last." He held up his hands. "There is nothing these hands can hold that is worth having. They cannot hold the moonlight, or the melody of a song, or even the beauty of a woman. They can touch her face, but not her beauty. Only the heart can hold such things."
>
> "Time takes everything, Vahan. But your heart, your character, your faith, do not belong to time. So build your home here," he said, touching his chest. "And make that home strong, make that home beautiful. Then you will always be safe, and you will never be alone." (188)

This beautiful passage is an example of a writer, Bagdasarian, sustaining the young reader.

Also of interest is Charlotte Perkins Gilman's work on behalf of the Armenians; Gilman is best-known as the author of the classic feminist short story "The Yellow Wallpaper." In 1903, she wrote a short piece, "International Duties," in a journal called *Armenia*. Gilman foresees the battle Raphael Lemkin will fight on the issue of state sovereignty. She writes,

> Up to this age the largest social concept common to us was that of the nations. . . . Each "sovereign state" was held to be sole arbiter of the destinies of its people, and no other state had any right to interfere. Whatever oppression, injustice, cruelty went to a civilian inside the borders of a given country, might call for individual disapprobation among citizens, but not for national recognizance. (11)

She calls it "a disgrace to a civilized world to have within it any nation committing such revolting crimes as those of Turkey" (13), and calls upon America to lead in stopping the Armenian genocide.

I have paired these readings with "Race Murder" (on the Armenian genocide), the first chapter in Samantha Power's *"A Problem from Hell": America and the Age of Genocide*.

Problematic Representation

Turkish scholar Taner Akçam defied the Turkish government's policy of denying the Armenian genocide and was subsequently adopted by Amnesty International as a prisoner of conscience. In his book *A Shameful Act: The*

Armenian Genocide and the Question of Turkish Responsibility (2006), Akçam describes how literature aroused Turks to despise Armenians:

> Poems about the lost territories appeared in the press, with lines like "Alas, alas" and "Thou art not satisfied" and titles like "Rancor": "Oh, my father, who rests peacefully in his grave and who earned a name/now the name of his children is Joyous Revenge". . . . Even children were imbued with a desire for revenge. (116)

As a child growing up when the Ottoman Empire became weaker, losing battle after battle, Akçam remembers, "We children were immersed in the bitterness of a defeat which we could accept no more than the adults, who had learned to bow their heads with their gaze averted. Every song spoke of strange vengeance marches" (116). The Turkish poet Ziyap Gökalp wrote poems with aggressive themes, such as "'Run, take the standard and let it be planted once again Plevna/Night and day, let the waters of the Danube run red with blood'" (qtd. in Akçam, 117).

The Holocaust

Suggested by author Michelle Ule, I play Henryk Górecki's "Lento e Largo— Tranquillissimo" from his Symphony No. 3 (Symphony of Sorrowful Songs); Górecki's musical tribute to the Holocaust is one of the most heartrending pieces of music ever written. The libretto was scrawled on the wall of a Gestapo prison:

> No, Mother, do not weep,
> Most chaste Queen of Heaven
> Support me always.
> "Zdrowaś Mario."

Zdrowaś Mario is a Polish prayer that begins with Ave Maria. Beneath is the signature of Helena Wanda Błażusiakówna, and the words "18 year old imprisoned since 26 September 1944."

While playing Górecki's symphony, I show the pictures from Roberto Innocenti's picture book *Rose Blanche* (1985) and Ruth Vander Zee's picture book *Erika's Story* (2003). In *Rose Blanche,* the coming of the Nazis to her town is told through a young girl's eyes. She follows their trail to just outside of town, where she sees a concentration camp. Over time, she befriends the prisoners, and feeds them through barbed wire fence. When the Allies arrive, Rose goes back to the concentration camp to see what has become of the prisoners. They are gone, and Rose disappears.

Erika's Story, illustrated by Roberto Innocenti, is based on a true story of a baby whose mother threw her from a train headed to a concentration camp. When the mother realized that her baby had no hope of survival, she was forced to make such a choice. Righteous Gentiles found the baby and raised her as their own. This combination of sound, story, and visual images can be emotionally moving.

I have used Roald Dahl's short story "Genesis and Catastrophe" with middle school students and undergraduates. It is a true story of Adolf Hitler's mother, who had numerous miscarriages before giving birth to him. Dahl captures the heart-wrenching pain of losing child after child and, finally, when a new baby lives, the sad irony that the first child who lives in the Hitler family grows up to become the leader of the Nazi party. I have scripted parts of the story for readers' theater; students find the story and the format of readers' theater engaging.

I highly recommend James Cross Giblin's biography *The Life and Death of Adolf Hitler* (2002). It is well-researched and contains many excellent photographs; I have assigned the book to middle school students and undergraduates multiple times.

The U.S. Holocaust Memorial Museum has many excellent resources for teaching the Holocaust.

Cambodia

In addition to what is provided on Cambodia in Chapter One of this book, I suggest that students view, either in or out of class, *The Killing Fields* (1984), directed by Roland Joffé, who also directed *The Mission*; both films have prompted scholars to study genocide. *The Killing Fields* tells the story of Dith Pran, an aide to *New York Times* reporter Sydney Schanberg in Cambodia. Pran is played by Dr. Haing Ngor, a Cambodian survivor. When in April 1975 all foreigners were ordered out of Phnom Phen, including Schanberg, Pran and his wife and children had to remain behind. Schanberg was tormented as he watched Pran and his family being marched out of the city. Although he eventually escaped to a refugee camp in Thailand, Pran undergoes all of the suffering of the Cambodian genocide described in Chapter One.

Problematic Representation

In his biography of Pol Pot, Philip Short shows how the Khmer Rouge used art to incite violence. Short writes of The Democratic Kampuchea National Anthem, "which Pol sanctioned if not actually wrote":

Bright red Blood covers the towns and plains
of Kampuchea, our Motherland,

Sublime Blood of the workers and peasants,
Sublime Blood of the revolutionary men and women fighters!
The Blood changes into unrelenting hatred
And resolute struggle,
[Which] . . . frees us from slavery. (qtd. in Short, 248)

Sadly, the genocide saturated Cambodia with the blood of those slaughtered in the killing fields. The Tuol Sleng Museum has posted photographs from S-21 online.

Bosnia

In addition to what is presented in Chapter Three, on Bosnia and Kosovo, I suggest Danis Tanović's film *No Man's Land* (2001). The film won the Golden Globe for Best Foreign Language Film in 2002, the Cannes Film Festival award for Best Screenplay in 2001, and the Oscar in 2001 for Best Foreign Film. The cinematography captures the exquisite loveliness of Bosnia. As with the Maya, who loved their land and who were deeply and spiritually connected to it, so with Bosnians. It was impossible not to love the magnificent countryside; if nothing else, *No Man's Land* can help viewers see how heart-wrenching it must have been for Bosniaks to be removed from their homes.

The plot is agonizing: Two soldiers, a Bosnian and a Serb, are stranded together in the trenches. Another Bosnian soldier is lying over a spring bomb, which will go off if he moves. Although the soldiers find some commonalities in their situation, the film ends fatally.

Rwanda

In addition to what is presented in Chapter Four, I recommend the film *Munyurangabo* (2009). Munyurangabo is a young Tutsi boy orphaned during the genocide. The film opens with Munyurangabo stealing a machete in a Kigali market. He accompanies his Hutu friend, Sangwa, to Sangwa's village on their way to seek justice for the killing of Munyurangabo's parents. Sangwa's parents disapprove of their Hutu-Tutsi friendship and eventually Munyurangabo continues alone to his village, where he discovers the Hutu man responsible for his parents' deaths. The man is on his deathbed, dying from AIDS. Unaware of who Munyurangabo is, the man begs for water. Munyurangabo wrestles with his conscience and, after some time has passed, goes back with water for the dying man. Sangwa, overcoming his parents' disapproval, rejoins his friend at the end of the film. The film features Rwandan actors and authentic dance and was filmed on location in Rwanda.

Robert Lyons and Scott Straus's *Intimate Enemy: Images and Voices of the Rwandan Genocide* (2006) is a moving collection of photographs of killers, including a child as young as eight. I also recommend Richard Salem's *Witness to Genocide, the Children of Rwanda: Drawings by Child Survivors of the Rwandan Genocide of 1994* (2000). The photographs, drawings, and writings of the children of Rwanda make this a powerful collection.

Darfur

In addition to what is presented in Chapter Five, I would if I could command the world to listen to Julia Bloom's "Darfur Moon," which former student Kim O'Toole shared with me. Bloom wrote this "lullaby" for the children of Darfur, and it is haunting. She has posted it on the Internet for free. While playing Bloom's song, the illustrations Dr. Jerry Ehrlich collected from children in Darfur can be shown (SUNY Digital Repository).

Representing Genocide in Classrooms

I have assigned students to develop expertise in one genocide and represent their learnings to their classmates (and, sometimes, the community) in a multimedia format. Students can share their knowledge through multiple symbolic forms, most of which I model in class, including:

- Oral interpretation of prose through readers' theater or choral reading of poetry
- Musical selections
- Clips of films and/or documentaries
- Photographs
- Art

Genres from which students can draw materials on individual genocides include biographies, autobiographies, and memoir; fiction; informational texts, including scholarly texts and journals; poetry; picture books; plays; journalism; and Internet resources. The playwright Friedrich Durenmatt said: "No one single playwright, but the sum of all the playwrights of all ages can reflect an approximately satisfactory picture of this world" (135). To approximate an understanding of genocide, readers and viewers must have access to multiple genres and sources.

Upper Elementary, Middle, and High School: Teaching Genocide

I do not support the study of genocide until children are in the fourth or fifth grade, and then in supportive ways. There are those who question difficult and challenging books for even nine- and ten-year-olds, to which I respond: We line them up to buy the most violent video games, or see violent action films. Surely children with the guidance of sensitive teachers can handle beginning to learn the stories of genocide, "the first of a thousand stories."

When Deborah Ellis's *Three Wishes: Palestinian and Israeli Children Speak* was published in 2004, the Canadian Jewish Congress asked Boards of Education in Canada to remove the book from schools; they thought the book might encourage children to imitate suicide bombers. In response, Ellis wrote this letter to the editor of the *Toronto Star*:

> We mark and mourn military deaths but the deaths of civilians go unnamed, uncounted, and passed off as extra-collateral damage, part of the acceptable risk of achieving our objectives. Some children are so precious, we would gladly die rather than see them harmed. Other children are considered worthy only of slavery, eating garbage, and being human punching bags. This is the world that we, as a human community, have created. We're happy with it. If we weren't, we would have changed it, since we certainly have the ability to do so. We like being ignorant. We like being greedy, and we like having an underclass of throwaway children. We created this mess, so why be delicate about having our handiwork reflected in our literature for young people? If children are tough enough to be bombed and starved, then they are also tough enough to read about it. (A18)

We have a world in which, since 1945, millions of children have been victims of genocide. Those who did not die lived to see acts of atrocity no child should see. Responsible authors who write about genocide not only give those children "mirror" books but provide "window" books to more privileged children. Ellis continues,

> I believe anything we subject children to should be reflected in our literature for young people, limited only by the skills of the writer to present these crimes in a sensitive, respectful way. Otherwise, we are adding to the silence and the disappearance of the victims.
>
> The books we read as children stay with us our entire lives, taking root in our minds, helping us to decide who we will become. Free access to information, to a wide variety of voices and experiences, is essential to us being able to decipher the complexities of a crazy world—and to understand that the world is complex. I have done many school talks around my books about children in war. Kids can handle the truth about what is being done to other children. It's adults who get squeamish. They say, "We must protect our children from such things," when really they are protecting themselves from having to answer the question: "What are you doing to make the world better?" (A18)

I have often worked with fifth graders using Ellis's books for Book Clubs. One girl loved Ellis's books so much—she started with fiction then moved to informational texts—that she begged me for every book Ellis had ever written, which in 2010 was twenty-four books.

Having worked with fifth graders, their teachers, and my undergraduates for a semester, Courtney Ryan Kelly and I conducted problematic books workshops with several fifth-grade classes in urban schools. We approached the workshop from a critical literacy perspective; our goal was, in Allan Luke and Peter Freebody's words (as already presented in my Introduction) for fifth graders to "critically analyze and transform texts by acting on knowledge that texts are not ideologically natural or neutral—that they represent particular points of views while silencing others and influence people's ideas" (n. pag.). I referred to this workshop in Chapter Five, on Darfur, and quoted Morgan, one of the fifth graders, who recognized the inappropriateness of using a jingle to describe genocide. Our college's Institutional Review Board approved our work with the children for those semesters, and parents signed permission slips for their children's responses to be used.

In the workshop, I shared problematic books with the children. They chose the ones they wanted to analyze; they could work alone, with a partner, or in a larger group. Their teacher, Courtney, and I circulated throughout the classroom, giving help as needed. In addition to the problematic books mentioned in the American Indian section of this chapter, I included Tom Streissguth's *Rwanda in Pictures* (2008) (discussed in Chapter Four, on Rwanda) and Melissa Leembruggen's *The Sudan Project* (2007) (discussed in Chapter Five, on Darfur), and others that are demeaning to girls, women, Asian Americans, and Latino/as. Courtney recorded the conversations of the children, later transcribed; I took field notes, and a week after the workshops went back to the schools to collect the children's written responses.

In the selection of problematic books, two were on genocide. As cited in Chapter Five, on Darfur, Morgan (all names are pseudonyms) said, "I don't think that is something that should be told in rhyming verse. To me rhyming is playful and fun. That is belittling what is happening." Of Streissguth's book, Jimmy said, "It says everything is over and it is really not."

After the children examined problematic books, we gathered together to discuss the workshop:

Gangi:	Is this workshop valuable for fifth graders?
Gladys:	Yes, it will help future writers. When I become a writer, if I can remember this far back, I'll remember to include more than one side of the story.
Jimmy:	It makes you think of another's perspective.
Gangi:	Do the authors who write these books mean to hurt other people's feelings?
Class Buzz:	No! No, of course not.
Tiffany:	Some are careless in their words and writing. They should think before they write or talk.
Karen:	There's hidden racism in books.

They were asked to write what they had learned from the problematic books workshop and replied:

Mayra:	Now because of the lesson we had, I realize the books can be offensive. Maybe the authors don't mean it but they should get their facts straight.
Rosa:	I learned some books can be hurtful. . . . I didn't notice bias but now I will be more careful.
Tiffany:	We learned that authors carelessly just put things in their books without researching them first without getting their facts straight first.
Samantha:	I wanted to tell you not everything from a book is true. . . . I wonder if any of my other friends no [know] problemateic [sic]; if they do maybe we have to fix things. Your friend Samantha.

A future area of research would be to focus on one genocide and have children read both problematic and respectful books on that genocide.

Educators have approached genocide in other ways. In the book, *Not on Our Watch: The Mission to End Genocide in Darfur and Beyond* (2007) Don Cheadle, who played Paul Rusesabagina in *Hotel Rwanda*, and John Prendergast write about Barbara Vogel's work with her fifth-grade students in Aurora, Colorado:

> In February 1998 . . . Vogel . . . read an article to her fifth-grade class about Sudan, the human rights abuses in the south, and the efforts of Christian Solidarity International. Vogel was an associate at the American Anti-Slavery Group, an organization founded in 1994 by Dr. Charles Jacobs that works tirelessly to combat contemporary slavery around the world. Vogel's students were so affected by the tragedy of Sudan that they launched the Slavery That Oppresses People (S.T.O.P.) campaign, aiming to raise enough money to redeem one thousand slaves. One of the children asked, "Haven't we learned anything from the past?" They sold lemonade, T-shirts, and used toys and wrote a letter to the local paper, who commissioned a story on their campaign. The class's efforts eventually garnered the attention of the *CBS Evening News,* which, in turn, led to donations of over $50,000. The class also began an awareness campaign writing letters to national and international leaders urging an end to the slavery in Sudan. Other schools followed Vogel's class's example. "My goal is to show the power of children, to show that children want to help, and to show adults what children can do," says Vogel. (119)

Although not specific to the Darfur genocide, Cheadle and Prendergast include the activism of these children as an example of what can be done from halfway around the world.

Interviewing authors in real or virtual time is another way of introducing young people to genocide. A teacher of nine- and ten-year-old students used the first chapter of Adam Jones's *Genocide: A Comprehensive Introduction*. He writes, "I was pleased to be interviewed over Skype," a resourceful move on the part of these children's teacher (Jones, "Re: question").

Mary Ann Reilly and Rob Cohen used art conversations and collage to explore genocide with "economically privileged" eighth graders (384), about which they wrote a book chapter, "Sowing Seeds of Social Justice through Performative Pedagogy: Middle School Students Explore Genocide" (2008). They ground their work in Mikhail Bakhtin's notion of double-voiced discourse. He writes, "'Two embodied meanings cannot lie side by side like two objects—they must come into inner contact; that is, they must enter into a semantic bond'" (qtd. in Reilly and Cohen, 384). Before this double-voiced exploration, the students had completed I-Search papers on the specific genocide that they had chosen to study.

First Cohen read aloud an excerpt from Sybella Wilkes's *One Day We Had to Run: Refugee Children Tell Their Stories in Words and Paintings*, which was discussed in Chapter Six. As he read, the music *Spem in Alium* was played in the background. After Cohen's reading, students conversed through art conversations; they worked in pairs, silently fingerpainting in response to Cohen's reading for about twenty minutes.

After the cleanup, Cohen asked the students to write for ten minutes to "reflect on what you put in your painting, what you were thinking, what this whole process meant" (386). Reilly and Cohen write that when the students gathered together again, Kerry said of herself and her partner Sam's painting, "'This side is where the main genocide is going on' . . . . She pointed to the darkened portion of the painting. 'And then like the line down is like the paths the people were taking or trying to get to the safe land. Like they kept getting to places but the places kept being invaded by other people'" (387). After the discussion, the students wrote poems based on their paintings, which Reilly and Cohen reproduce in their chapter. They also include a table of the twenty-five genocides the students studied in Cohen's class, of which most of them had never heard. Reilly and Cohen write, "Through writing and I-Search essay, finger painting, composing and performing multivoiced poems, and constructing the virtual museum, performative space is created in the classroom. It is within such spaces students' beliefs about genocide and the culture they live in are unsettled" (395). Reilly and Cohen cite Kevin Kumashiro:

> All students come to school with partial knowledges. In some ways they may not know much about marginalized groups in society, but even when they do know about the *Other*, that knowledge is often a mis-knowledge, a knowledge of stereotypes and myths learned from the media, families, peer groups, and so forth. (qtd. in Reilly and Cohen, 391; italics in the original)

Through multiple performative approaches, Reilly and Cohen sought to unsettle misknowledges; in so doing, "some seeds were sown" (396).

Tim Salem, who was assistant principal at Danbury High School in Danbury, Connecticut, worked with high school students to produce two DVDs, *The Promise* (2006) and *Child of Hope: Darfur Dreams of Peace* (2008), both on Darfur. Among other influences, these videos had the effect of convincing Connecticut's then governor, Jodi Rell, to divest from the Sudan. When Salem visited my college class, one student wrote: "I was particularly moved by the Danbury High School students. If a group of high school students can get involved and make such a big impact then anyone can."

Parents can also introduce their children to genocide. Brendan January, whose book was discussed in Chapter Six, tells of Arielle Wisotsky, whose mother took her to the U.S. Holocaust Museum, where she learned about Darfur. In response, "she and two friends founded a nonprofit organization called Help Darfur Now" (129). These high school students raised tens of thousands of dollars, much of it going to Doctors Without Borders. The action of one young woman, Arielle, has inspired middle school and high school students in other states to start their own chapters of Help Darfur Now.

Conclusion

Resources for teaching genocide are not lacking; what may be lacking in some areas is the will. In the United States, in a highly questionable move, the U.S. Department of Education (USDOE) has insisted that teachers' evaluations be tied to their students' test scores. There is no research to support this experiment; with such a policy, teachers will be less likely to teach what is not on the test, and genocide is not on the test. Many groups throughout the U.S. are protesting USDOE policies; hopefully, change will come and there will be fewer obstacles to teaching genocide—the "first stories of a thousand and one recountings."

Works Cited

Acevedo, Atenea. "The Multiple Meanings of Lidice." Trans. Margaret Schroeder. Jones, *Evoking*, 70–72.
Afoumado, Diane F. "A Tale of Two Children." Jones, *Evoking*, 77–79.
Aspel, Joyce. "The Processes of Destruction." Jones, *Evoking*, 91–93.
Bartrop, Paul R. "Where It All Began." Jones, *Evoking*, 55–57.
Bernard-Donals, Michael. "Forgetful Memory and Images of the Holocaust." *College English* 66.4 (2004): 380–402.
Bishop, Rudine Sims. "Mirrors, Windows, and Sliding Glass Doors." 1990. Web. 31 Mar. 2013. <http://www.rif.org/us/literacy-resources/multicultural/mirrors-windows-and-sliding-glass-doors.htm>
Bond, Helen. "'You and I, We Must Change the World.'" Jones, *Evoking*, 156–160.
Bosmajian, Hamida. *Sparing the Child: Grief and the Unspeakable in Youth Literature about Nazism and the Holocaust.* New York: Routledge, 2002.

Briggs, John. Introduction. *Creativity and Compassion: How They Come Together.* Eds. John Briggs and Paul Hackett. Wayne, NJ: Karuna, 2012. xvii–xx.

Carpenter, R. Charli. "'The Enemy We Seek to Destroy.'" Jones, *Evoking*, 247–251.

Cheadle, Don, and John Prendergast. *Not on Our Watch: The Mission to End Genocide in Darfur and Beyond.* New York: Hyperion, 2007.

Child of Hope: Darfur Dreams of Peace. Dir. Tim Salem and Danbury High School Students. 2006. Web. 17 July 2013. <http://www.youtube.com/watch?v=Sjnv_i80Mb8>

Churchill, Ward. "'A Bargain Indeed.'" Jones, *Evoking*, 18–22.

Cohan, Sara. "My Grandfather's Testimony." Jones, *Evoking*, 27–31.

———. "Re: question." Message to Jane M. Gangi. 2 Aug. 2012. E-mail.

Colijn, G. Jan. "Eichmann, Mulisch, and Me." Jones, *Evoking*, 161–163.

Cox, John M. "Lost Worlds." Jones, *Evoking*, 8–10.

de Londras, Fiona. "Confronting the *Porrajmos*." Jones, *Evoking*, 142–144.

Durenmatt, Friedrich. *Writings on Theatre and Drama.* London: Jonathan Carpe, 1976.

Ellis, Deborah. "Kids Are Tough Enough for the Truth." *Toronto Star* 22 Mar. 2006: A18.

———. *Three Wishes: Palestinian and Israeli Children Speak.* Toronto: Groundwood, 2004.

Esparza, Marcia. "Photography, Memory, and Denial." Jones, *Evoking*, 204–209.

Facing History and Ourselves. "Educator Resources." 2013. Web. 2 Apr. 2013. <http://www.facing.org/educator-resources-0>

Feinstein, Stephen C. "Genocide and the Shock Process in Conceptual Art." Jones, *Evoking*, 148–151.

Friedman, Jonathan C. "The Holocaust as the Holocaust." Jones, *Evoking*, 108–113.

Frieze, Donna-Lee. "The Wealth of All Humanity." Jones, *Evoking*, 139–141.

Fujii, Lee Ann. "At Seventeen." Jones, *Evoking*, 185–187.

Gangi, Jane M. Letter. *Reading Today* Oct./Nov. 2005: 22.

———. "Inclusive Aesthetics: The Vanguard of Small, Multicultural Presses." *Children's Literature Association Quarterly* 30.3 (2005): 243–264.

———. "The Unbearable Whiteness of Literacy Instruction: Realizing the Implications of the Proficient Reader Research." *Multicultural Review* 17.2 (2008): 30–35.

Gangi, Jane M., and Aimee Ferguson. "African American Literature: Books to Stoke Dreams." *The Tennessee Reading Teacher* 34.2 (2006): 29–38.

George, Alexander. "At the Wall." Jones, *Evoking*, 137–138.

Gigliotti, Simone. "There's No Place Like Home." Jones, *Evoking*, 145–147.

Gordy, Eric. "Ugliness and Distance." Jones, *Evoking*, 164–168.

Greene, Maxine. "In Search of a Critical Pedagogy." *Harvard Educational Review* 56.4 (1986): 427–441.

Grünfeld, Fred. "Re: question." Message to Jane M. Gangi. 30 Aug. 2012. E-mail.

———. "The Role of the Bystander." Jones, *Evoking*, 97–100.

Hamblet, Wendy C. "Different Kinds of People." Jones, *Evoking*, 242–246.

Hart, Kate. "Uncovering YA Covers." 16 May 2012. Web. 31 Mar. 2013. <http://www.katehart.net/2012/05/uncovering-ya-covers-2011.html>

Hayse, Michael. "A Boy Who Refused to Grow Up, and One Who Did." Jones, *Evoking*, 73–76.

Hertling, Viktoria. "Lessing's Wisdom." Jones, *Evoking*, 84–86.

Hewitt, William. "Trauma and Transcendence." Jones, *Evoking*, 129–132.

Higgins, Winton. "The Moral Capital of the World." Jones, *Evoking*, 152–155.

Hinton, Alex. "Brotherhood." Jones, *Evoking*, 252–253.

Hughes-Hassell, Sandra, and Ernie J. Cox. "Inside Board Books: Representations of People of Color." *Library Quarterly* 80.3 (2010): 211–230.

Hughes-Hassell, Sandra, Heather A. Barkley, and Elizabeth Koehler. "Promoting Equity in Children's Literacy Instruction: Using a Critical Race Theory Framework to Examine Transitional Books." *American Association of School Librarians.* 2010. Web. 17 July 2013. <http.www.ala.org/aaslpubsandjournals/slmrl>

Jacobs, Steven Leonard. "Re: question." Message to Jane M. Gangi. 27 July 2012. E-mail.

———. "'Revisiting Again and Again the Kingdom of Night.'" Jones, *Evoking*, 101–103.

Jensen, Steven L. B., ed. *Genocide: Cases, Comparisons and Contemporary Debates.* Trans. Gwynneth Llewellyn. Njalsgade, Denmark: The Danish Center for Holocaust and Genocide Studies, 2003.

Jones, Adam. "Apocalypse Soon." Jones, *Evoking*, 195–199.

———. *Genocide: A Comprehensive Introduction.* 2nd ed. New York: Routledge, 2010.

———. "Re: question." Message to Jane M. Gangi. 30 July 2012. E-mail.

Jones, Adam, ed. *Evoking Genocide: Scholars and Activists Describe the Works That Shaped Their Lives.* Toronto: Key, 2009.

Kalayjian, Ani. "Conspiracy of Silence." Jones, *Evoking*, 45–48.

Kokkola, Lydia. *Representing the Holocaust in Children's Literature.* New York: Routledge, 2003.

Krieger, Nina. "'The Desire to Communicate Something of My Torment.'" Jones, *Evoking*, 35–42.

Laderman, Scott. "Beyond Good and Evil." Jones, *Evoking*, 188–190.

Lemarchand, René. "Comparing the Killing Fields: Rwanda, Cambodia and Bosnia." Jensen, 141–173.

Lieberman, Benjamin. "Warning: Here There Be Experts." Jones, *Evoking*, 43–44.

Loewen, James W. *Lies My Teacher Told Me: Everything Your American History Textbook Got Wrong.* New York: New, 1995.

Maclean, Pam. "Not the Holocaust Memorial." Jones, *Evoking*, 87–90.

Magilow, Daniel. "Children's Photos." Jones, *Evoking*, 219–221.

Maitles, Henry. "Keeping Memory Alive." Jones, *Evoking*, 114–117.

McNair, Jonda C. "Innocent Though They May Seem: A Critical Race Theory Analysis of Firefly and Seesaw Scholastic Book Club Order Forms." *MultiCultural Review* 17.1 (2008): 24–29.

———. "The Representation of Authors and Illustrators of Color in School-Based Book Clubs." *Language Arts* 85.3 (2008): 193–201.

Meierhenrich, Jens. "The Language of Klemperer." Jones, *Evoking*, 122–128.

Moore, Jina. "The Attic and the Imagination." Jones, *Evoking*, 80–83.

Nagy, Thomas J. "A Reluctant Genocide Activist." Jones, *Evoking*, 215–218.

National Association for the Advancement of Colored People. "Criminal Justice Fact Sheet." 2013. Web. 2 Apr. 2013. <http://www.naacp.org/pages/criminal-justice-fact-sheet>

National Governors Association Center for Best Practices, Council of Chief State School Officers. *Common Core State Standards.* Washington DC: Author, 2010.

Parekh, Shayna. "A Simple Task." Jones, *Evoking*, 230–234.

Paulino, Edward. "Discovering the Haitian Massacre." Jones, *Evoking*, 49–54.

Porter, Jack Nusan. "Sexuality and Genocide." Jones, *Evoking*, 65–69.

Powell, Christopher. "The Wound at the Heart of the World." Jones, *Evoking*, 11–17.

Power, Samantha. *"A Problem from Hell": America and the Age of Genocide.* New York: Basic, 2002.

The Promise. Dir. Tim Salem and Danbury High School Students. 2006. 17 July 2013. Danbury High School. Web. <http://www.youtube.com/watch?v=o67BmBEAGmM>

Reeves, Eric. "Re: question." Message to Jane M. Gangi. 13 Aug. 2012. E-mail.

———. "'A Single Child.'" Jones, *Evoking*, 254–256.

Reilly, Mary Ann, and Rob Cohen. "Sowing the Seeds of Social Justice through Performative Pedagogy: Middle School Students Explore Genocide." *Growing a Soul for Social Change: Building the Knowledge Base for Social Justice.* Charlotte, NC: Information Age, 2008. 383–398.

Rixecker, Stefanie. "The Horror." Jones, *Evoking*, 191–194.

Romano, Tom. "A Place to Start." *Blending Genre, Altering Style: Writing Multigenre Papers.* Portsmouth, NH: Heinemann, 2000. 7–14.

Roth, John K. "Will Only the Darkness Remain?" Jones, *Evoking*, 104–107.

Sanford, Victoria. "Images of Impunity." Jones, *Evoking*, 210–214.

Schabas, William. "Werfel, *Musa Dagh* and the Armenian Genocide." Jones, *Evoking*, 32–34.

Schaller, Dominick J. "Identity and Contested Authenticity." Jones, *Evoking*, 118–121.

Schaller, Dominick, and Jürgen Zimmerer. *The Origins of Genocide—Raphael Lemkin as a Historian of Mass Violence.* New York: Routledge, 2009.

Schimmer, Russell. "Dili on Fire." Jones, *Evoking*, 238–241.

Scroggins, Mary J., and Jane M. Gangi. "Paul Laurence *Who?* Invisibility and Misrepresentation in Children's Literature and Reading and Language Arts Textbooks." *MultiCultural Review* 13.3 (2004): 34–43.

Sémelin, Jacques. "On Visiting the Auschwitz Museum." Jones, *Evoking*, 133–136.

Simon, David J. "'Never Again,' Again." Jones, *Evoking*, 235–237.

Skloot, Robert. "The Look of Terror." Jones, *Evoking*, 94–96.

———. "Re: question." Message to Jane M. Gangi. 27 July 2012. E-mail.

Springer, Jane. *Genocide.* Toronto: Groundwood, 2006. Groundwood Guide Ser.

Swanwick, Keith. *Musical Knowledge: Intuition, Analysis and Music Education.* London: Routledge, 1994.

———. *Music, Mind, and Education.* London: Routledge, 1988.

Taylor, Christopher. "The Death of 'King' Habyarimana." Jones, *Evoking*, 224–229.
Verdeja, Ernesto. "Morality, Indifference, and Evil." Jones, *Evoking*, 177–180.
White, Joseph Robert. "Documenting Torture in the Early Nazi Death Camps." Jones, *Evoking*, 58–64.
Whitmer, Benjamin. "Re: question." Message to Jane M. Gangi. 29 July 2012. E-mail.
———. "The Westering Holocaust." Jones, *Evoking*, 23–26.
Zimmerman, John C. "Journey through Denial." Jones, *Evoking*, 181–184.
Zylberman, Lior. "The Question of the Act." Trans. Margaret Schroeder. Jones, *Evoking*, 200–203.

Works Cited: American Indians

Archambault, John, Bill Martin, Jr., and Ted Rand (Illus.). *Knots on a Counting Rope*. New York: Holt, 1987.
Banks, Lynne Reid. *The Indian in the Cupboard*. Garden City, NY: Doubleday, 1980.
Bruchac, Joseph. *Lasting Echoes: An Oral History of Native American People*. New York: Avon, 1997.
———. *The Winter People*. New York: Dial, 2002.
Bruchac, Joseph, and Shonto Begay (Illus.). *Navajo Long Walk: The Tragic Story of a Proud People's Forced March from Their Homeland*. Washington, DC: National Geographic, 2002.
Bruchac, Joseph, and S. D. Nelson (Illus.). *Crazy Horse's Vision*. New York: Lee & Low, 2000.
Fire Crow, Chief Joseph. *Cheyenne Nation*. Makoche, 208 N. 4th St., Bismarck, ND 58501. 2000. CD.
Freedman, Russell, and Karl Bodmer (Painter, 1833–1834). *An Indian Winter*. New York: Holiday, 1992.
Jeffers, Susan. *Brother Eagle, Sister Sky*. New York: Penguin, 1991.
Keohane, Sonja. "The Reservation Boarding School System in the United States, 1870–1928." 3 June 2008. Web. 2 Apr. 2013. <http://www.twofrog.com/rezsch.html>
The Mission. Dir. Roland Joffé. Perf. Jeremy Irons and Robert DeNiro. Burbank, CA: Warner. 1986. Film.
Oyate. "Resources: Oyate's Additional Criteria." 2013. Web. 2 Apr. 2013. <http://oyate.org/index.php/resources/42-resources/oyate-s-additional-criteria>
Plain, Nancy. *The Man Who Painted Indians: George Catlin*. New York: Benchmark, 1997.
Rinaldi, Ann. *My Heart Is on the Ground: The Diary of Nannie Little Rose, a Sioux Girl*. New York: Scholastic, 1999.

Works Cited: Armenia

Akçam, Taner. *A Shameful Act: The Armenian Genocide and the Question of Turkish Responsibility*. New York: Holt, 2006.
Bagdasarian, Adam. *Forgotten Fire*. New York: Random, 2000.
Bedoukian, Kerop. *Some of Us Survived: The Story of an Armenian Boy*. New York: Farrar, 1978.
Gilman, Charlotte Perkins. 1903, Oct. "International Duties." *Armenia*, 1.1 (1903): 10–14.
Kherdian, David. *The Road from Home: The Story of an Armenian Girl*. New York: Greenwillow, 1979.

Works Cited: Bosnia

No Man's Land. Dir. Danis Tanović. United Artists. 2001. Film.

Works Cited: Cambodia

The Killing Fields. Dir. Roland Joffé. Perf. Haing S. Ngor, John Malkovich, and Julian Sands. Warner Brothers. 1984. Film.
Short, Philip. *Pol Pot: Anatomy of a Nightmare*. New York: Holt, 2004.

Tuol Sleng Museum. "The S-21 Photographs." n. d. Web. 2 Apr. 2013. <http://www.tuolsleng.com/photographs.php>

Works Cited: Darfur

Bloom, Julia, perf. "Darfur Moon." By Julia Bloom. Web. 2004. <https://soundcloud.com/julia-tindall-bloom/darfur-moon>
SUNY Digital Repository. "Drawings from the Children of Darfur." 26 Mar. 2008. Web. 2 Apr. 2013. <http://dspace.sunyconnect.suny.edu/handle/1951/43011>

Works Cited: The Holocaust

Dahl, Roald. "Genesis and Catastrophe." In *Kiss Kiss*. New York: Knopf, 1959.
Giblin, James Cross. *The Life and Death of Adolf Hitler*. New York: Clarion, 2002.
Górecki, Henryk. "Lento e largo—tranquillissimo." Symphony No. 3 (Symphony of Sorrowful Songs). New York: Elektra Entertainment/Time Warner. 1976. CD.
Innocenti, Roberto. *Rose Blanche*. Mankato, MN: Creative Education, 1985.
United States Holocaust Memorial Museum. "For Teachers: Teaching about the Holocaust." n.d. Web. 2 Apr. 2013. <http://www.ushmm.org/education/foreducators/>
Vander Zee, Ruth, and Roberto Innocenti (Illus.). *Erika's Story*. Mankato, MN: Creative Editions, 2003.

Works Cited: The Middle Passage

Bradley, David. *The Chaneysville Incident*. New York: Harper, 1981.
Feelings, Tom. *The Middle Passage: White Ships/Black Cargo*. New York: Dial, 1995.
Lester, Julius, and Rod Brown (Illus.). *From Slave Ship to Freedom Road*. New York: Dial, 1998.
Lester, Julius, and Jerry Pinkney (Illus.). *The Old African*. New York: Penguin, 2005.
Martin, Michelle H. *Brown Gold: Milestones of African-American Children's Picture Books, 1845–2002*. New York: Routledge, 2004.
McGill, Alice. "Moon Time Child." *Don't Cramp My Style: Stories about That Time of the Month*. Ed. Lisa Rowe Fraustino. New York: Simon & Schuster, 2004. 45–67.
National Association for the Advancement of Colored People. "Criminal Justice Fact Sheet." 2013. Web. 2 Apr. 2013. <http://www.naacp.org/pages/criminal-justice-fact-sheet>
Tambay. *Ten Little Nigger Boys*. 29 Apr. 2010. Web. 7 Mar. 2013. <http://www.shadowandact.com/?p=22425>
Wilson, Jackie Napoleon. *Hidden Witness: African-American Images from the Dawn of Photography to the Civil War*. New York: St. Martin's, 1999.

Works Cited: Rwanda

Lyons, Robert, and Scot Straus. *Intimate Enemy: Images and Voices of the Rwandan Genocide*. New York: Zone, 2006.
Munyurangabo. Dir. Lee Isaac Chung. New York: Film Movement. 2009. Film.
Salem, Richard A., ed. *Witness to Genocide, the Children of Rwanda: Drawings by Child Survivors of the Rwandan Genocide of 1994*. New York: Friendship, 2000.

Chapter Eight
Conclusion
Resisting the Lie

The size of the lie is a definite factor in causing it to be believed, for the vast masses of a nation are in the depths of their hearts more easily deceived than they are consciously and intentionally bad. The primitive simplicity of their minds renders them more easily prey to a big lie than a small one, for they themselves often tell little lies but would be ashamed to tell a big one.

—Adolf Hitler

A dilemma in children's and young adult literature of genocide is how to protect children from trauma while acquainting them with the size of the lies that come into the world: the lie that dominated Cambodia—that Year Zero would bring prosperity to Cambodians; the lie that dominated Guatemala—that all Maya were guerrillas; the lie that dominated Iraq—that all Kurds were allies of Iran; the lie that dominated Bosnia—that the war was the result of ancient ethnic conflicts and all were at fault; the lie that dominated Rwanda—that the genocide was a tribal outburst; and the lie that dominated Darfur—that there was no conflict going on.

And as we have seen, the lie sometimes dominates texts on genocide written for children and young adults. As I came to the end of writing this book, I was reading graduate student Sara Cavaliere's response to an article we read in our "Reading and Literature, Birth to Six" course. In their "Fiction Posing as Truth: A Critical Review of Ann Rinaldi's *My Heart Is on the Ground: The Diary of Nannie Little Rose, a Sioux Girl*" (2001), Debbie Reese (Nambé), Marlene Atleo (Nuu-chah-nulth), Naomi Caldwell (Ramapough Mountain), Barbara Landis, Jean Mendoza, Deborah Miranda (Ohlone-Coasstanoan

Esselen/Chumash), LaVera Rose (Lakota), Beverly Slapin, and Cynthia Smith (Creek) critique Rinaldi's misrepresentation, inaccuracies, and sanitization of the Indian Boarding School experience in her book. Sara's response to this article resonated with my experience in studying representations of genocide in some books for children and young adults. She wrote, "This article was crucial in my realization that an author does not have to be correct in any way, shape or form in order to write a work of art, and that others could enjoy that writing, regardless of its accuracy or lack of respect for the real life group it portrays" (Cavaliere, "Permission"). Some of the authors who write about the genocides in Cambodia, Guatemala, Iraq, Bosnia, Kosovo, Rwanda, and Darfur are not "correct in any way, shape or form." Young readers can read such a work on genocide "regardless of its accuracy or lack of respect for the real life group it portrays." Like the fifth graders described in Chapter Seven, who, when asked about the intentions of authors of problematic books, exclaimed that they did not believe the authors intended to hurt anyone, I want to be kind. But the damage these books cause is inestimable. Ellen Handler Spitz writes: "'Even when they are not intended to do so, picture books provide children with some of their earliest takes on morality, taste, and basic cultural knowledge, including messages about gender, race, and class'" (qtd. in Yenika-Agbaw, 17–18). As fifth grader Mayra said in Chapter Seven, "Maybe the authors don't mean it but they should get their facts straight." Without serious efforts to introduce critical literacy into our schools' curriculum and to demand authenticity, accuracy, and respectfulness, a generation of children will grow up believing, among other things, that:

- Cambodians caused their own problems; it is all right to exoticize them and Buddhism and Christianity are virtually the same.
- The Maya are a simple, happy people who lead uncomplicated lives.
- All Iraqi Kurds were all allies of Iran during the Iran-Iraq war and the Kurdish genocide is not worth much attention.
- Bosniaks were as much the aggressors as the Serbs, and Bosnia has less possibility for peace than the rest of the world.
- Tutsis and moderate Hutus were as much to blame as radical Hutus who carried out the genocide, and that Belgian colonization and European racist beliefs had no effect on the genocide.
- The people of Darfur are as much to blame as the government in Khartoum, and British colonization had no effect.

They will also learn from these books on genocide that people of color are more expendable than White people. Pia Christensen and Alan Prout write:

what may be challenged are those traditional perspectives that neglect the fact that children have little or no influence over their own social representation. The importance of this is highlighted by Dyer's statement that "how we are seen determines in part how we are treated, how we treat others is based on how we see them; such seeing comes from representation." (42–43)

Authors of children's and young adult literature of genocide who misrepresent the genocides about which they write, intentionally or not, teach children how to treat others disrespectfully.

The poet Rumi wrote, "'Sit down and be quiet. You are drunk. And this is the edge of the roof'" (qtd. in Wheatley, 104), which is what I would like to say to publishers, librarians, teachers, professors, and policy makers. We must stop. Publishers must make sure that the books they publish on genocide for children and young adults are accurate, authentic, and responsible. Teachers and librarians must recognize, before they unknowingly share problematic books with students, that—as my fifth-grade friend Samantha said in Chapter Seven— "not everything from a book is true." Professors and teachers should add critical literacy components to their courses; propaganda in some children's and young adult literature on the genocides from Cambodia to Darfur has reached Orwellian proportions. If we don't sit down and be quiet, we will continue to publish and consume books that perpetuate stereotypes and myths and dishonor the victims of genocide, a form of genocide denial.

On March 21, 2013, Chinua Achebe died; he spent much of his life pushing against the lies that have come into the world about Africa. He was quoted in the *New York Times*: "'In the end, I began to understand. . . . There is such a thing as absolute power over narrative. Those who secure this privilege for themselves can arrange stories about others pretty much where, and as, they like'" (qtd. in Kandell, C8). Whether authors are conscious of it or not, it is clear that some, in writing about genocide for young people, have arranged "stories about others pretty much . . . as they like."

Explanations of Genocide

In working with children and young adults, how can we explain genocide? Is there such a thing as "evil"? Is there a malevolent force at work in the universe? Where are the cultures that have not experienced genocide? What could they teach us?

There are genocide scholars who accept the concept of evil. Totten and Bartrop write, "The history of genocide in the modern world would appear to show that evil people are much more dedicated to evil than good people are toward good" (xiv). In this book, we have met evil people dedicated to evil: Pol Pot, Efrain Ríos Montt, Saddam Hussein, Slobodan Milošević, Ratko Mladic, Radovan Karadzic, Théoneste Bagasora, and Omar Hassan al-Bashir, most of them heads of state. I have little doubt that had this ugly crew never had access to ultimate power, the genocides in Cambodia, Guatemala, Iraq, Bosnia, Rwanda, and Darfur would not have occurred.

As I noted in Chapter Six, Jane Springer argues that the "evil man" theory is not enough to capture the complexity of genocide. Although there were pro-testors of the genocides, it cannot be denied that many people either went along or turned a blind eye. "The greatest evil perpetrated," Hannah Arendt wrote, "is the evil committed by nobodies, that is, by human beings who refuse to be persons." The literature we share with students must help them become "persons"—persons who have voice, and who think. In *King Leopold's Ghost: A Story of Greed, Terror, and Heroism* (1998), Adam Hochschild describes the horrific practice of the *chicotte* used by Belgians against the Congolese:

> a whip of raw, sun-dried hippopotamus hide, cut into a long sharp-edged cork-screw strip. Usually the *chicotte* was applied to the victim's bare buttocks. Its blows would leave permanent scars; more than twenty-five strokes could mean unconsciousness; and a hundred or more—not an uncommon punishment—were often fatal. (120)

In his exhaustive research, Hochschild read countless records and diaries of the ghastly practices of the Belgians; however, writes Hochschild, "few Euro-peans working for the regime left records of their shock at the sight of offi-cially sanctioned terror" (121). Primo Levi wrote, "'Monsters exist. . . . But they are too few in number to be truly dangerous. More dangerous . . . are the functionaries ready to believe and to act without asking questions'" (qtd. in Hochschild, 121). Adolf Hitler once said, "What good fortune for those in power that people do not think." Educational models of pouring facts into students' heads will not help them become persons, or to think.

In *Life Laid Bare: The Survivors in Rwanda Speak* (2000), Innocent Rwilizia told Jean Hatzfeld:

> Genocide is not really a matter of poverty or lack of education, and I will tell you why. I am a teacher, so I think that education is necessary to en-lighten the world. But education does not make someone better; it makes that person more efficient. Anyone who wishes to foment evil will find an advantage in knowing about man's obsessions, learning about his nature, studying sociology. The educated man—if his heart is flawed, if he seethes with hatred—will do more harm. . . . The intellectuals are the ones who emancipated the Hutus . . . by planting the idea of genocide in their heads and seeping away their hesitations. . . . since the French were advising our army, some of them knew that the genocide was in the works. Supposedly they didn't believe in it, yet many Whites were familiar with the plan and with Habyarimana's character. (109–110)

If their hearts are flawed, education will only make *génocidaires* more "effi-cient." Journalist Fergal Keane wrote of Rwanda, "Perhaps the most sinister people I met were the educated political elite, men and women of charm and sophistication who spoke flawless French and who could engage in long philo-sophical debates about the nature of war and democracy" (29). As we saw, Pol Pot and Slobodan Milošević could be very charming people. Part of the adult's role must be to help children discern trickery and lies; sharing folkloric stories is one way to help children detect cunning and deception. Charles Dickens once said, "I have known a vast quantity of nonsense talked about bad men not look-ing you in the face. Don't trust that idea. Dishonesty will stare honesty out of countenance any day of the week, if there is anything to be got by it." To fail to help children discern that truth as they grow into adults seems neglectful.

There are also matters of culture and cultural practices. In *The Burning Tigris: The Armenian Genocide and America's Response* (2003), Peter Balakian introduces Irvin Staub's work on the Armenian genocide. In the late 1800s and again in 1909, Turks carried out acts of violence against Armenians, thus laying the groundwork for the 1915–1918 genocide, which Staub calls a "'con-tinuum of destruction'" (qtd. in Balakian, 156). Balakian observes that a "his-tory and cultural orientation . . . can lead to conditions for genocide" (156). Staub posits it as "'a progression of changes in a culture and individuals is usually required'" (qtd. in Balakian, 156). Balakian quotes Staub again: "'Peo-ple learn . . . by doing, by participation,'" and Balakian comments, "People are changed by their participation in destructive and harmful behavior, and the victims are further devalued through this process" (156).

From an education perspective, Staub's analysis makes infinite sense: Learn-ing by doing is thought to be the way children learn best (Darling-Hammond 2010; Dewey 1938). A culture that initiates children into violent practices, as we are now seeing in the Congo with the recruitment of child soldiers, pro-duces children who may grow up to become perpetrators of violence. The pos-sibility of the opposite is raised too: The prevention of genocide could include engaging children and adults in positive forms of experience. An example of this is Estonia, where Estonians used song to gain their independence from the U.S.S.R. A wonderful film, *The Singing Revolution* (2004), shows thou-sands of Estonian children and adults raising their voices in song—song that became a form of activism.

Can Genocide Be Prevented?

In his book *How to Prevent Genocide: A Guide for Policymakers, Scholars, and the Concerned Citizen* (2001), John Heidenrich tells of the Senoi people of Malaysia, who live a hand-to-mouth existence and who have been surrounded by and often victimized by violence, yet who, despite their hardships, have impressed outsiders with their peaceful, nonviolent culture. Heidenrich writes:

> They have few material possessions, their homes little more than grass huts. They subsist on fish, fruit, and animal game, in a jungle whose

numerous dangers include wild tigers. Tropical diseases have long been so deadly that a custom has developed wherein infants are not named until, and unless, they survive to two years of age. Vicious raids by slave traders killed Senoi adults and abducted Senoi children well into the twentieth century. They have also experienced British colonial administrators, brutal Japanese invaders, ethnic Chinese Communist guerillas, and condescending Malaysian bureaucrats.

The Senoi have known violence. "Yet the Senoi are remarkably peaceful. As tribes and as individuals, they abhor violence. Many report that they never feel anger. Family quarrels are rare. Virtually nonexistent are any instances of murder, maiming, or hitting" (21–22).

Children are raised without physical punishment, and their elders embrace their dream life. Heidenrich explains:

> One intriguing Jungian theory holds that the Senoi developed their profound psychological maturity by practicing a form of dream therapy. In Senoi families almost every day, especially at mealtime, children and adults are encouraged to describe their dreams, which are then interpreted. Since dreams can reveal a person's innermost feelings, desires, anxieties, and embarrassments, at least in symbolic terms, the Senoi address these human concerns openly and lovingly, from childhood and throughout adulthood. Simply the mere discussion of these concerns in a lovingly supportive environment can be of immense psychological benefit. (44–45)

Although not everyone accepts dreams and dream therapy as meaningful, what is meaningful is the love and support Senoi adults give their children. To simply listen is of enormous value and is in contrast to old edicts of "Children should be seen and not heard," and "Spare the rod, spoil the child." Part of genocide prevention, it seems, might include creating a culture in which adults take time to listen to children's fears and concerns, which is a strong expression of love and care. If we neglect to affirm children by listening to them and taking them seriously, they may grow up, in Rabbi Harold Kushner's words, with something missing inside of them, which leads to grandiosity. A man in a halfway house told Rabbi Kushner, "'When something is missing inside you, there is something exhilarating about deciding that you're above the law, that the rules don't apply to you'" (125).

Heidenrich records that Saddam Hussein was abused as a child, and Alice Miller, in *For Your Own Good* (1983), observes that Hitler, also, was abused as a child. In fact, many Nazis were abused as children; they grew up in a "spare the rod, spoil the child" culture. In his book *On Evil*, literary critic Terry Eagleton cites the philosopher John Rawls: "'What moves the evil man is the love of injustice: he delights in the impotence and humiliation of those subject to him and relishes being recognized by them as the author of their degradation'" (qtd. in Eagleton, 94). The sad nature of those sociopaths or psychopaths who take pleasure in the suffering of others is beyond understanding, but it is real. The Nazi Heinrich Himmler said, "'We had the moral right, we had the duty to our own people, to kill this people that wanted to kill us. . . . And we have suffered no harm from it in our inner self, in our soul, in our character'" (qtd. in Miller, 8).

It is a mistake to not protect children by helping them learn through the literature of genocide of such people; there is, as my grandmother repeatedly told me when I was a child, "a lot of meanness in the world." But there are also partial answers to meanness in the literature of genocide. Like the Senoi, the Armenians attended to their dream life. In David Kherdian's *The Road from Home: The Story of an Armenian Girl*, a book mentioned in Chapter Seven, it was a dream that prompted Veron's Aunt Lousapere to find Veron in a hospital in Smyrna. Aunt Lousapere dreamt:

> Thursday night your mother came to me in my sleep, and she said, "Lousapere, the apple I was carrying in my pocket fell into the stream—quick, run and grab it before it floats away." I ran at once and caught it and held it up for your mother to see, and when she saw me holding it, she smiled. . . . I went to my neighbor, who understands such things better than I do, and she said, "Apple means soul in dreams," so then I knew it was you. (171)

Like the Senoi and the Armenians, we must attend to children's inner lives. Other partial answers—I say partial because I doubt we will have full answers—are play and the arts: in Armenia, Armenian children created Armenian lace out of their gauze bandages. In Cambodia, Arn Chorn-Pond played the *khim*; a Cambodian child created a marble for Minfong Ho; and Cambodian dancers danced, like Teeda in *The Stone Goddess*. In Bosnia, Vedran Smailovic played the cello; Nadja Halilbegovich kept a diary, wrote poetry, performed on the radio, made toys, sang, drew, played guitar, and helped her peers do the same. Zlata Filipović kept a diary and drew. As an Albanian refugee living in a camp in Macedonia, Edi drew and kept a diary and encouraged other children to do so as well. In Germany, Jeanne told and retold her story of Rwanda to her adoptive mother, Hanna Jansen; Rwandan children shared their stories and art with Wiljo Woodi Oosterom. Darfuri children gave their drawings and writings to Dr. Jerry Ehrlich. In the making of art, children can push back the darkness that surrounds them, creating affirmations of life in the face of those who would destroy them.

For some, spirituality and religion hold an answer: Many Armenians retain their Christian faith despite the awful destruction of their ancestors in 1915–1918. In spite of the Holocaust, Rabbi Steven Jacobs echoes Job, "Though He slay me, yet will I trust in Him; but I will argue my ways before Him" (103). Reverend Peter Pond was motivated by his religious beliefs to go to Thailand, where he rescued Arn Chorn-Pond. Many Maya combine Christian beliefs with their ancestral beliefs and were deeply appreciative of the liberation theologians of the Roman Catholic church, some of whom lost their lives for the Maya. When I traveled to Bosnia, I was grateful for the kindness of the Muslims I met there and admired their disciplined daily prayer life. Immaculée Ilibagiza and Eric Irivuzumugabe have written of their religious renewal in postgenocide Rwanda in *Left to Tell: Discovering God amidst the Rwandan Holocaust* and *My Father, Maker of the Trees: How I Survived the Rwandan Genocide.*

The arts, spirituality, and, as Selma Leydesdorff recommends, attention to the local may be helpful in preventing genocide. Leydesdorff points to Omer Bartov, who argues that genocide prevention lies in "a microlevel historical approach." Leydesdorff writes that Bartov:

> suggested examining limited areas and territories where the origins of hatred can be observed, as well as its growth into violence and, ultimately, genocide. In his eyes, the devil is to be found "in the local." The research should look at how the social equilibrium—the mortar that holds a society together both materially and spiritually—becomes disturbed. (11)

In the early 1990s there were many signs that Rwanda would soon be in serious trouble. Those signs could have been attended to. Observing Slobodan Milošević's ruthless responses to Slovenia and Croatia's declarations of independence, the international community could have inferred what his response to Bosnia's declaration of independence would be.

What strikes me as I study genocide is the pattern of the genocides erupting in April: the Armenian genocide began on April 24, 1915; the Cambodian genocide began on April 17, 1975; the Kurdish Iraq genocide began on April 15, 1987; the Bosnian genocide began on April 6, 1992; and the Rwandan genocide began on April 6, 1994. Perhaps the international community needs to be especially aware of "social equilibrium" during the month of April, which seems to be, as T. S. Eliot said, "the cruelest month."

I began this book with Donna-Lee Frieze's summation of Emmanuel Levinas:

> Always capitalized, the Other is not an alien other who disturbs my freedom, or who is an extension of me. Rather, the Other is the one who is treated ethically, who commands my highest respect, and is apprehended in all their Otherness. . . . to face the Other is to humanize the Other, and to regard the person as a unique being. (222)

Frieze observes that Levinas's conception of "the Other" is "the antithesis of the genocidal perpetrators' assessment of faceless others" (223). During the seven years of writing this book, I have asked others about evil, and "Why genocide?" My son, Peter, said it is "easier to hate than to love. Love is hard work." Perhaps with that understanding—the hard work of love, of treating others ethically, of letting others command our highest respect—there may be hope that genocide will subside. Until then, those of us who focus on children's and young adult literature, especially of genocide, must work to make sure the lie does not come into the world through us and that our work honors, remembers, and bears witness to those who have suffered immeasurably.

Works Cited

Balakian, Peter. *The Burning Tigris: The Armenian Genocide and America's Response*. New York: HarperCollins, 2003.

Cavaliere, Sara. "Permission." Message to Jane M. Gangi. 3 Mar. 2013. E-mail.

Christensen, Pia, and Alan Prout. "Anthropological and Sociological Perspectives on the Study of Children." *Researching Children's Experiences: Approaches and Methods*. Eds. Sheila Greene and Diane Hogan. London: Sage, 2005. 42–60.

Darling-Hammond, Linda. *The Flat World and Education*. New York: Teachers College, 2010.

Dewey, John. *Experience and Education*. New York: Macmillan, 1938.

Eagleton, Terry. *Literary Theory: An Introduction*. Minneapolis: U of Minnesota P, 1983.

Frieze, Donna-Lee. "The Face of Genocide." Jones, *Evoking*, 222–223.

Hatzfeld, Jean. *Life Laid Bare: The Survivors in Rwanda Speak*. Trans. Linda Coverdale. New York: Other, 2000.

Heidenrich, John G. *How to Prevent Genocide: A Guide for Policymakers, Scholars, and the Concerned Citizen*. Westport, CT: Praeger, 2001.

Hochschild, Adam. *King Leopold's Ghost: A Story of Greed, Terror, and Heroism in Colonial Africa*. Boston: Houghton, 1998.

Kandell, Jonathan. "Chinua Achebe, Writer Who Reclaimed a Continent, Dies at 82." *New York Times* 23 Mar. 2013. C8.

Keane, Fergal. *Season of Blood: A Rwandan Journey*. New York: Viking, 1995.

Kherdian, David. *The Road from Home: The Story of an Armenian Girl*. New York: Greenwillow, 1979.

Kushner, Harold. *Overcoming Life's Disappointments*. New York: Knopf, 2006.

Leydesdorff, Selma. *Surviving the Bosnian Genocide: The Women of Srebrenica Speak*. Trans. Kay Richardson. Bloomington: Indiana UP, 2011.

Miller, Alice. *For Your Own Good: Hidden Cruelty in Child-Rearing and the Roots of Violence*. New York: Farrar, 1983.

Reese (Nambé), Debbie, Marlene Atleo (Nuu-chah-nulth), Naomi Caldwell (Ramapough Mountain), Barbara Landis, Jean Mendoza, Deborah Miranda (Ohlone-Coasstanoan Esselen/Chumash), LaVera Rose (Lakota), Beverly Slapin, and Cynthia Smith (Creek). "Fiction Posing as Truth: A Critical Review of Ann Rinaldi's *My Heart Is on the Ground: The Diary of Nannie Little Rose, a Sioux Girl*." *Rethinking Our Classrooms*, vol. 2. Ed. Bill Bigelow. Milwaukee, WI: Rethinking Schools, 2001. 57–62.

The Singing Revolution. Dirs. Maureen and James Tusty. Sky Films. 2004. Film.

Totten, Samuel, and Paul Bartrop, eds. *The Genocide Studies Reader*. New York: Routledge, 2009.

Wheatley, Meg. *Perseverance*. Provo, UT: Berkana, 2010.

Yenika-Agbaw, Vivian. *Representing Africa in Children's Literature: Old and New Ways of Seeing*. New York: Routledge, 2008.

Comprehensive Works Cited

Acevedo, Atenea. "The Multiple Meanings of Lidice." Trans. Margaret Schroeder. Jones, *Evoking*, 70–72.

Achebe, Chinua. *Hopes and Impediments.* New York: Doubleday, 1988.

Adhikari, Mohamed. "*Hotel Rwanda*—The Challenges of Historicizing and Commercializing Genocide." *Development Dialogue* 50 (2008): 173–195.

Affonço, Denise. *To the End of Hell: One Woman's Struggle to Survive Cambodia's Khmer Rouge.* London: Reportage, 2005.

Afoumado, Diane F. "A Tale of Two Children." Jones, *Evoking*, 77–79.

African Rights/Working for Justice. *A Wounded Generation: The Children Who Survived Rwanda's Genocide.* Kigali, Rwanda: Author, 2006.

Akçam, Taner. *A Shameful Act: The Armenian Genocide and the Question of Turkish Responsibility.* New York: Holt, 2006.

Alcoff, Linda. "The Problem of Speaking for Others." *Cultural Critique* 20 (1991–1992, Winter): 5–32.

Altman, Linda. *Genocide: The Systematic Killing of a People.* Berkeley Heights, NJ: Enslow, 2009.

Andrews, Tom. "Breaking: Bashir to Travel to Chad. Demand His Arrest." Message to Jane M. Gangi. 15 Mar. 2013. E-mail.

Andryszewski, Tricia. *Kosovo: The Splintering of Yugoslavia.* Brookfield, CT: Millbrook, 2000.

Apple, Michael. Foreword. *White Reign: Deploying Whiteness in America.* Eds. Joe L. Kincheloe, Shirley R. Steinberg, Nelson M. Rodriguez, and Ronald E. Chennault. New York: St. Martin's, 1998.

Archambault, John, Bill Martin, Jr., and Ted Rand (Illus.). *Knots on a Counting Rope.* New York: Holt, 1987.

Aristotle. *Poetics.* Ann Arbor, MI: U of Michigan P, 1967.

Armenian Relief Cross of Lebanon. *Armenian Embroidery.* Beirut: Author, 1999.

Ashabranner, Brent, and Paul Conklin (Photographer). *Children of the Maya: A Guatemalan Indian Odyssey.* New York: Dodd, 1986.

Aspel, Joyce. "The Processes of Destruction." Jones, *Evoking*, 91–93.

Bagdasarian, Adam. *Forgotten Fire.* New York: Random, 2000.

Baillie, Allan. "Allan Baillie Homepage." n. d. Web. 5 July 2012. <http://www.allanbaillie.com.au/faq.htm>

———. *Little Brother.* New York: Viking, 1985.

Balakian, Peter. *The Burning Tigris: The Armenian Genocide and America's Response.* New York: HarperCollins, 2003.

Banks, Lynne Reid. *The Indian in the Cupboard.* New York: Doubleday, 1980.

Barber, Nicola. *Central Africa.* London: Smart Apple, 2005.

Barnett, Michael. *Eyewitness to a Genocide: The United Nations and Rwanda.* Ithaca, NY: Cornell UP, 2002.

Barthes, Roland. *Mythologies.* 1957. New York: Hill and Wang, 1972.

Bartrop, Paul R. "Where It All Began." Jones, *Evoking*, 55–57.

Bashir, Halima, with Damien Lewis. *Tears of the Desert: A Memoir of Survival in Darfur.* New York: Ballantine, 2008.

Beckett, Sandra L. "Crossover Literature." Nel and Paul, 58–61.

Bedoukian, Kerop. *Some of Us Survived: The Story of an Armenian Boy.* New York: Farrar, 1978.

Bergin, Sean. *The Khmer Rouge and the Cambodian Genocide.* New York: Rosen, 2009.

Bernard-Donals, Michael. "Forgetful Memory and Images of the Holocaust." *College English* 66.4 (2004): 380–402.

Bernstein, Robin. *Racial Innocence: Performing American Childhood from Slavery to Civil Rights.* New York: New York UP, 2011.

Bishop, Rudine Sims. "Mirrors, Windows, and Sliding Glass Doors." 1990. Web. 31 Mar. 2013. <http://www.rif.org/us/literacy-resources/multicultural/mirrors-windows-and-sliding-glass-doors.htm>

Black, Eric. *Bosnia: Fractured Region.* Minneapolis, MN: Lerner Publications, 1999. World in Conflict Ser.

Bloom, Julia, perf. "Darfur Moon." By Julia Bloom. Web. 2004. <https://soundcloud.com/julia-tindall-bloom/darfur-moon>

Bodnarchuk, Kari. *Rwanda: A Country Torn Apart.* Minneapolis, MN: Lerner, 2000. World in Conflict Ser.

Bond, Helen. "'You and I, We Must Change the World.'" Jones, *Evoking,* 156–160.

Book Wish Foundation. *What You Wish For: Stories and Poems for Darfur.* Reston, VA: Author, 2011.

Bosmajian, Hamida. *Sparing the Child: Grief and the Unspeakable in Youth Literature about Nazism and the Holocaust.* New York: Routledge, 2002.

Bradford, Clare. "Fwd: Re: Hello and Question." Message to Jane M. Gangi. 7 July 2008. E-mail.

———. "Postcolonial." Nel and Paul, 177–180.

———. *Unsettling Narratives: Postcolonial Readings of Children's Literature.* Waterloo, Ontario: Wilfrid Laurier UP, 2007.

Bradley, David. *The Chaneysville Incident.* New York: Harper, 1981.

Briggs, John. Introduction. *Creativity and Compassion: How They Come Together.* Eds. John Briggs and Paul Hackett. Wayne, NJ: Karuna, 2012. xvii–xx.

Brill, Marlene Targ, and Harry R. Targ. *Guatemala.* Chicago: Children's, 1993. Enchantment of the World Ser.

Bruchac, Joseph. *Hidden Roots.* New York: Scholastic, 2004.

———. *Lasting Echoes: An Oral History of Native American People.* New York: Avon, 1997.

———. *The Winter People.* New York: Dial, 2002.

Bruchac, Joseph, and Shonto Begay (Illus.). *Navajo Long Walk: The Tragic Story of a Proud People's Forced March from Their Homeland.* Washington, DC: National Geographic, 2002.

Bruchac, Joseph, and S. D. Nelson (Illus.). *Crazy Horse's Vision.* New York: Lee & Low, 2000.

Burr, J. Millard, and Robert O. Collins. *Darfur: The Long Road to Disaster.* Princeton, NJ: Markus Wiener, 2008.

Caplan, Gerald. "From Rwanda to Darfur: Lessons Learned?" Totten and Markusen, 171–179.

Carpenter, R. Charli. "'The Enemy We Seek to Destroy.'" Jones, *Evoking,* 247–251.

Carr, Rosamond Halsey, with Ann Howard Halsey. *Land of a Thousand Hills: My Life in Rwanda.* New York: Viking, 1999.

Cavaliere, Sara. "Permission." Message to Jane M. Gangi. 3 Mar. 2013. E-mail.

Čekić, Smail. *The Aggression against the Republic of Bosnia and Herzegovina: Planning, Preparation, Execution.* Trans. Branka Ramadanović. Sarajevo, Bosnia: Institute for the Research of Crimes against Humanity and International Law, U of Sarajevo, 2005.

———. *Research of Genocide Victims, with a Special Emphasis on Bosnia and Herzegovina: Problems and Issues in Scientific Theory, Methods and Methodology.* Trans. Branka Ramadanović and Samir Kulaglić. Sarajevo, Bosnia: Institute for the Research of Crimes against Humanity and International Law, U of Sarajevo, 2009.

Čekić, Smail, Muhamed Šestanović, Merisa Karović, and Zilha Mastalić-Košuta. *Zločini nad djecom Sarajeva u opsadi (Crimes against Children in the Siege of Sarajevo).* Sarajevo, Bosnia: Institute for the Research of Crimes against Humanity and International Law, U of Sarajevo, 2010.

Chandler, David P. *The Land and People of Cambodia.* New York: HarperCollins, 1991.

———. *The Tragedy of Cambodian History: Politics, War, and Revolution since 1945.* New Haven: Yale UP, 1991.

Cheadle, Don, and John Prendergast. *Not on Our Watch: The Mission to End Genocide in Darfur and Beyond.* New York: Hyperion, 2007.

Child of Hope: Darfur Dreams of Peace. Dir. Tim Salem and Danbury High School Students. 2006. Web. 17 July 2013. <http://www.youtube.com/watch?v=Sjnv_i80Mb8>

Ching, Jacqueline. *Genocide and the Bosnian War*. New York: Rosen, 2009.

Christensen, Pia, and Alan Prout. "Anthropological and Sociological Perspectives on the Study of Children." *Researching Children's Experiences: Approaches and Methods*. Eds. Sheila Greene and Diane Hogan. London: Sage, 2005. 42–60.

Churchill, Ward. "'A Bargain Indeed.'" Jones, *Evoking*, 18–22.

Cochran-Smith, Marilyn. *Walking the Road: Race, Diversity, and Social Justice*. New York: Teachers College, 2004.

Cohan, Sara. "My Grandfather's Testimony." Jones, *Evoking*, 27–31.

———. "Re: question." Message to Jane M. Gangi. 2 Aug. 2012. E-mail.

Colijn, G. Jan. "Eichmann, Mulisch, and Me." Jones, *Evoking*, 161–163.

Collins, Robert O. "Disaster in Darfur: Historical Overview." Totten and Markusen, 2–24.

Combres, Élisabeth. *Broken Memory. A Novel of Rwanda*. Toronto: Groundwood, 2010.

Connolly, Sean. *Sudan*. Vero Beach, FL: Rourke, 2008. Countries in Crisis Ser.

Cornwell, Nicki, and Karin Littlewood (Illus.). *Christophe's Story*. London: Francis Lincoln, 2006.

Cox, John M. "Lost Worlds." Jones, *Evoking*, 8–10.

Crew, Linda. *Children of the River*. New York: Doubleday, 1991.

———. "Linda Crew Website." n. d. Web. 21 Jan. 2013. <http://www.lindacrew.com/children_of_the_river_55440.htm>

Croy, Anita. *Guatemala*. Washington, DC: National Geographic, 2009. Countries of the World Ser.

Cutler, Jane, and Greg Couch (Illus.). *The Cello of Mr. O*. New York: Dutton, 1999.

Dahl, Michael. *Guatemala*. Mankato, MN: Bridgestone, 1998. Countries of the World Ser.

Dahl, Roald. "Genesis and Catastrophe." In *Kiss Kiss*. New York: Knopf, 1959.

Dalal, Anita. *Guatemala*. Danbury, CT: Grolier, 1999. Fiesta Ser.

Dallaire, Romeo. *Shake Hands with the Devil: The Failure of Humanity in Rwanda*. New York: Carroll & Graf, 2005.

Darling-Hammond, Linda. *The Flat World and Education*. New York: Teachers College, 2010.

De Groen, Els. *No Roof in Bosnia*. Trans. Patricia Compton. Barnstaple, Devon, UK: Spindlewood, 1997.

de Londras, Fiona. "Confronting the *Porrajmos*." Jones, *Evoking*, 142–144.

Deady, Kathleen W. *Rwanda: A Question and Answer Book*. Mankato, MN: Capstone, 2005.

Debelo. Hawi. "Re: Darfur." Message to Jane M. Gangi. 11 Mar. 2013. E-mail.

Dendiger, Roger E. *Guatemala*. Philadelphia: Chelsea, 2004. Modern World Nations Ser.

Des Forges, Alison. *Leave None to Tell the Story: Genocide in Rwanda*. New York: Human Rights Watch, 1999.

Destexhe, Alain. *Rwanda and Genocide in the Twentieth Century*. New York: New York UP, 1995.

Dewey, John. *Experience and Education*. New York: Macmillan, 1938.

DiPiazza, Francesca. *Sudan in Pictures*. Minneapolis, MN: Twenty-First Century, 2006. Visual Geography Ser.

Dorros, Arthur. *Under the Sun: A Novel Based on True Stories of Survival during War*. New York: Amulet, 2006.

Downing, David. *Africa: Postcolonial Conflict*. Chicago: Raintree, 2004.

Doyle, Clar. *Raising Curtains of Education: Drama as a Site for Critical Pedagogy*. Westport, CT: Bergin & Garvey, 1993.

Durenmatt, Friedrich. *Writings on Theatre and Drama*. London: Jonathan Cape, 1976.

Eagleton, Terry. *Literary Theory: An Introduction*. Minneapolis: U of Minnesota P, 1983.

el-Kareem, Nadia. "Life, Death, There's No Big Difference." Walzer, 135–147.

Ellis, Deborah. *The Breadwinner*. Toronto: Groundwood Books, 2000.

———. *Children of War*. Toronto: Groundwood, 2010.

———. "Kids Are Tough Enough for the Truth." *Toronto Star* 22 Mar. 2006: A18.

———. *Mud City*. Toronto: Groundwood, 2003.

———. *Off to War: Voices of Soldiers' Children*. Toronto: Groundwood, 2008.

———. *Parvana's Journey*. Toronto: Groundwood, 2002.

———. *Three Wishes: Palestinian and Israeli Children Speak*. Toronto: Groundwood, 2004.

———. *Women of the Afghan War*. Westport, CT: Praeger, 2000.

Eltringham, Nigel. *Accounting for Horror: Post-Genocide Debates in Rwanda*. London: Pluto, 2004.

Englar, Mary. *Bosnia-Herzegovina in Pictures*. Minneapolis, MN: Twenty-First Century, 2007. Visual Geography Ser.

Esparza, Marcia. "Photography, Memory, and Denial." Jones, *Evoking*, 204–209.

Facing History and Ourselves. "Educator Resources." 2013. Web. 2 Apr. 2013. <http://www.facing.org/educator-resources-0>

Falla, Ricardo. *Massacres in the Jungle: Ixcán, Guatemala, 1975–1982.* Boulder, CO: Westview, 1994.

Feelings, Tom. *The Middle Passage: White Ships/Black Cargo.* New York: Dial, 1995.

Feinstein, Stephen C. "Genocide and the Shock Process in Conceptual Art." Jones, *Evoking*, 148–151.

Felman, Shoshana, and Dori Laub. *Testimony: Crises of Witnessing in Literature, Psychoanalysis, and History.* New York: Routledge, 1992.

Filipović, Zlata. *Zlata's Diary: A Child's Life in Sarajevo.* New York: Scholastic, 1994.

Filipović, Zlata, and Melanie Challenger. *Stolen Voices: Young People's Diaries, from World War I to Iraq.* New York: Penguin, 2006.

Fire Crow, Chief Joseph. *Cheyenne Nation.* Makoche, 208 N. 4th St., Bismarck, ND 58501. 2000. CD.

Flint, David. *Bosnia: Can There Ever Be Peace?* Austin, TX: Raintree Steck-Vaughn, 1996.

Flint, Julie, and Alex de Waal. *Darfur: A Short History of a Long War.* London: Zed, 2005.

Freedman, Russell, and Karl Bodmer (Painter, 1833–1834). *An Indian Winter.* New York: Holiday, 1992.

Friedman, Jonathan C. "The Holocaust as the Holocaust." Jones, *Evoking*, 108–113.

Frieze, Donna-Lee. "The Face of Genocide." Jones, *Evoking*, 222–223.

———. "'The Wealth of All Humanity.'" Jones, *Evoking*, 139–141.

Fujii, Lee Ann. "At Seventeen." Jones, *Evoking*, 185–187.

Galaijatović, Sabina Subašić. "Sexual Abuse of Women in Bosnia and Herzegovina—An Instrument of the Crime of Genocide." International Network of Genocide Scholars. University of Sussex, Brighton, UK. 29 June 2010. Reading.

Ganeri, Anita. *Why We Left: I Remember Bosnia.* Austin, TX: Raintree Steck-Vaughn, 1995.

Gangi, Jane M. Letter. *Reading Today* Oct.–Nov. 2005: 22.

———. "Inclusive Aesthetics: The Vanguard of Small, Multicultural Presses." *Children's Literature Association Quarterly* 30.3 (2005): 243–264.

———. "The Unbearable Whiteness of Literacy Instruction: Realizing the Implications of the Proficient Reader Research." *Multicultural Review* 17.2 (2008): 30–35.

Gangi, Jane M., and Ellis Barowsky. "Listening to Children's Voices: Literature and the Arts as Means of Responding to the Effects of War, Terrorism, and Disaster." *Childhood Education* 85.6 (2009): 357–363.

Gangi, Jane M., and Aimee Ferguson. "African American Literature: Books to Stoke Dreams." *The Tennessee Reading Teacher* 34.2 (2006): 29–38.

George, Alexander. "At the Wall." Jones, *Evoking*, 137–138.

Giblin, James Cross. *The Life and Death of Adolf Hitler.* New York: Clarion, 2002.

Gigliotti, Simone. "There's No Place Like Home." Jones, *Evoking*, 145–147.

Gilman, Charlotte Perkins. Oct. "International Duties." *Armenia*, 1.1 (1903): 10–14.

Goldman, Francisco. "Footprints in History: A Documentary of Remembrance." Moller, 93–95.

Gordy, Eric. "Ugliness and Distance." Jones, *Evoking*, 164–168.

Górecki, Henryk. "Lento e largo—tranquillissimo." Symphony No. 3 (Symphony of Sorrowful Songs). New York: Elektra Entertainment/Time Warner. 1976. CD.

Gourevitch, Philip. *We Wish to Inform You That We Will Be Killed with Our Families: Stories from Rwanda.* New York: Farrar, 1998.

Graff, Nancy, and Richard Howard (Photographs). *Where the River Runs: A Portrait of a Refugee Family.* Boston: Little, Brown, 1993.

Greene, Maxine. "In Search of a Critical Pedagogy." *Harvard Educational Review* 56.4 (1986): 427–441.

Grodsky, Brian. "When Two Ambiguities Collide: The Use of Genocide in Self-Determination Drives." *Journal of Genocide Research* 14.1 (2012): 1–27.

Grünfeld, Fred. "Re: question." Message to Jane M. Gangi. 30 Aug. 2012. E-mail.

———. "The Role of the Bystander." Jones, *Evoking*, 97–100.

Halilbegovich, Nadja. *My Childhood under Fire: A Sarajevo Diary.* Tonawanda, NY: Kids Can, 2006.

Hallam, Elizabeth, and Brian V. Street, eds. Introduction. *Cultural Encounters: Representing 'Otherness.'* London: Routledge, 2000.

Hamblet, Wendy C. "Different Kinds of People." Jones, *Evoking*, 242–246.

Hankins, Elizabeth. *I Learned a New Word Today.* Toronto: Key, 2009.

Harff, Barbara. "The Etiology of Genocides." Totten and Bartrop, 108–120.

Harrison, Nicholas. *Postcolonial Criticism: History, Theory and the Work of Fiction.* Cambridge, UK: Polity, 2003.

Hart, Kate. "Uncovering YA Covers." 16 May 2012. Web. 31 Mar. 2013. <http://www.katehart. net/2012/05/uncovering-ya-covers-2011.html>

Hassig, Susan M and Laith Muhmood Al Adely. *Iraq.* New York: Cavendish, 2004. Cultures of the World Ser.

Hatzfeld, Jean. *The Antelope's Strategy: Living in Rwanda after the Genocide.* Trans. Linda Coverdale. New York: Farrar, 2009.

———. *Life Laid Bare: The Survivors in Rwanda Speak.* Trans. Linda Coverdale. New York: Other, 2000.

Hawk, Beverly G., ed. "Introduction." *Africa's Media Image.* Westport, CT: Praeger, 1992. 3–14.

Hayse, Michael. "A Boy Who Refused to Grow Up, and One Who Did." Jones, *Evoking*, 73–76.

Heidenrich, John G. *How to Prevent Genocide: A Guide for Policymakers, Scholars, and the Concerned Citizen.* Westport, CT: Praeger, 2001.

Heleta, Savo. *Not My Turn to Die: Memoirs of a Broken Childhood in Bosnia.* New York: Amacom, 2008.

Hertling, Viktoria. "Lessing's Wisdom." Jones, *Evoking*, 84–86.

Hewitt, William. "Trauma and Transcendence." Jones, *Evoking*, 129–132.

Heywood, Denise. *Cambodian Dance: Celebration of the Gods.* Bangkok, Thailand: River Books, 2009.

———. "Re: Cambodian Paper." Message to Jane M. Gangi. 19 June 2011. E-mail.

Hiçyilmaz, Gaye. *Smiling for Strangers.* New York: Farrar, 1998.

Higgins, Winton. "The Moral Capital of the World." Jones, *Evoking*, 152–155.

Hill Collins, Patricia. *Black Feminist Thought: Knowledge, Consciousness, and the Politics of Empowerment.* New York: Routledge, 2000.

Hinton, Alex. "Brotherhood." Jones, *Evoking*, 252–253.

Ho, Minfong. *The Clay Marble.* New York: Farrar, 1991.

———. *The Stone Goddess.* New York: Orchard, 2003.

Hochschild, Adam. *King Leopold's Ghost: A Story of Greed, Terror, and Heroism in Colonial Africa.* Boston: Houghton, 1998.

Hotel Rwanda. Dir. Greg Carson. Perf. Don Cheadle. MGM. 2004. Film.

Houston, Deryk. "Vedran Smailović—The Cellist of Sarajevo." *The Economic Voice.* 7 Feb. 2013. Web. 10 Feb. 2013.

Hughes-Hassell, Sandra, and Ernie J. Cox. "Inside Board Books: Representations of People of Color." *Library Quarterly* 80.3 (2010): 211–230.

Hughes-Hassell, Sandra, Heather A. Barkley, and Elizabeth Koehler. "Promoting Equity in Children's Literacy Instruction: Using a Critical Race Theory Framework to Examine Transitional Books." *American Association of School Librarians.* 2010. Web. 17 July 2013. <http. www.ala.org/aaslpubsandjournals/slmrl>

Huizinga, Johan. *Homo Ludens: A Study of the Play-Element in Culture.* Boston: Beacon, 1955.

Human Rights Watch/Middle East. *Iraq's Crime of Genocide: The Anfal Campaign against the Kurds.* New Haven: Yale UP, 1995.

Huy, Peauladd. "Ways of the Khmer Rouge." Powers, 103–120.

Ilibagiza, Immaculée, with Steve Erwin. *Led by Faith: Rising from the Ashes of the Rwandan Genocide.* Carlsbad, CA: Hay, 2008.

———. *Left to Tell: Discovering God amidst the Rwandan Holocaust.* Carlsbad, CA: Hay, 2006.

Innocenti, Roberto. *Rose Blanche.* Mankato, MN: Creative Education, 1985.

Irivuzumugabe, Eric, with Tracey D. Lawrence. *My Father, Maker of the Trees: How I Survived the Rwandan Genocide.* Grand Rapids, MI: Baker, 2009.

Isaac, John (Photographs), Keith Greenberg. *Bosnia: Civil War in Europe.* Woodbridge, CT: Blackbirch, 1997. Children in Crisis Ser.

———. *Rwanda: Fierce Clashes in Central Africa.* Woodbridge, CT: Blackbirch, 1997. Children in Crisis Ser.

Ishag, Ahmed. "We Wanted Israel's Protection. That Was All." Walzer, 199–236.

Jacobs, Steven Leonard. "Re: question." Message to Jane M. Gangi. 27 July 2012. E-mail.

———. "'Revisiting Again and Again the Kingdom of Night.'" Jones, *Evoking*, 101–103.

Jansen, Hanna. *Over a Thousand Hills I Walk with You.* Trans. Elizabeth D. Crawford. Minneapolis, MN: Carolrhoda, 2002.

January, Brendan. *Genocide: Modern Crimes against Humanity.* Minneapolis, MN: Twenty-First Century, 2007.

Jeffers, Susan. *Brother Eagle, Sister Sky*. New York: Penguin, 1991.

Jensen, Steven L. B., ed. *Genocide: Cases, Comparisons and Contemporary Debates*. Trans. Gwynneth Llewellyn. Njalsgade, Denmark: The Danish Center for Holocaust and Genocide Studies, 2003.

Jones, Adam. "Apocalypse Soon." Jones, *Evoking*, 195–199.

———. *Genocide: A Comprehensive Introduction*. 2nd ed. New York: Routledge, 2010.

Jones, Adam, ed. *Evoking Genocide: Scholars and Activists Describe the Works That Shaped Their Lives*. Toronto: Key, 2009.

———. "Re: question." Message to Jane M. Gangi. 30 July 2012. E-mail.

Kalayjian, Ani. "Conspiracy of Silence." Jones, *Evoking*, 45–48.

Kandell, Jonathan. "Chinua Achebe, Writer Who Reclaimed a Continent, Dies at 82." *New York Times* 23 Mar. 2013: C8.

Karahasan, Dzevad. *Sarajevo, Exodus of a City*. Trans. Slobodan Drakulić. New York: Kodansha International, 1993.

Keane, Fergal. *Season of Blood: A Rwandan Journey*. New York: Viking, 1995.

Keat, Nawuth, with Martha E. Kendall. *Alive in the Killing Fields: Surviving the Khmer Rouge Genocide*. Washington, DC: National Geographic, 2009.

Keohane, Sonja. "The Reservation Boarding School System in the United States, 1870–1928." 3 June 2008. Web. 2 Apr. 2013. <http://www.twofrog.com/rezsch.html>

Kertzer, Adrienne. *My Mother's Voice: Children, Literature, and the Holocaust*. Peterborough, Ontario: Broadview, 2002.

Kherdian, David. *The Road from Home: The Story of an Armenian Girl*. New York: Greenwillow, 1979.

Kidd, Kenneth B. "A" is for Auschwitz: Psychoanalysis, Trauma Theory, and the "Children's Literature of Atrocity." *Children's Literature*, 33 (2005): 120–149.

———. "Re: Introduction." Message to Jane M. Gangi. 31 Mar. 2013. E-mail.

Kidder, Tracy. *Strength in What Remains*. New York: Random, 2009.

Kiernan, Ben. *The Pol Pot Regime: Race, Power, and Genocide in Cambodia under the Khmer Rouge, 1975–1979*. New Haven: Yale UP, 1996.

The Killing Fields. Dir. Roland Joffé. Perf. Haing S. Ngor, John Malkovich, Julian Sands. Warner Brothers. 1984. Film.

King, David C. *Rwanda*. Tarrytown, NY: Cavendish, 2006.

King, John. *Iraq: Then and Now*. Chicago: Raintree, 2006. The Middle East Ser.

Kinzer, Stephen. *A Thousand Hills: Rwanda's Rebirth and the Man Who Dreamed It*. Hoboken, NJ: Wiley, 2008.

Koff, Clea. *The Bone Woman: A Forensic Anthropologist's Search for Truth in the Mass Graves of Rwanda, Bosnia, Croatia, and Kosovo*. New York: Random, 2004.

Kokkola, Lydia. *Representing the Holocaust in Children's Literature*. New York: Routledge, 2003.

Koopmans, Andy. *Pol Pot*. New York: Thomson Gale, 2005.

———. *Rwanda*. Philadelphia: Mason Crest, 2005.

Krieger, Nina. "'The Desire to Communicate Something of My Torment.'" Jones, *Evoking*, 35–42.

Kulidžan, Nikolina. "Across the River." Powers, 65–74.

Laderman, Scott. "Beyond Good and Evil." Jones, *Evoking*, 188–190.

Ladson-Billings, Gloria, and William Tate, eds. *Education Research in the Public Interest: Social Justice, Action, and Policy*. New York: Teachers College, 2006.

Leembruggen, Melissa. *The Sudan Project: Rebuilding with the People of Darfur, A Young Person's Guide*. Nashville, TN: Abingdon, 2007.

Lemarchand, René. "Comparing the Killing Fields: Rwanda, Cambodia and Bosnia." Jensen, 141–173.

Lemkin, Raphael. "Genocide: A Modern Crime." Totten and Bartrop, 6–11.

Lester, Julius, and Rod Brown (Illus.). *From Slave Ship to Freedom Road*. New York: Dial, 1998.

Lester, Julius, and Jerry Pinkney (Illus.). *The Old African*. New York: Penguin, 2005.

Levey, Jane. *Genocide in Darfur*. New York: Rosen, 2009. Genocide in Modern Times Ser.

Levy, Patricia, and Zawiah Abdul Latif. *Sudan*. New York: Cavendish, 2008. Cultures of the World Ser.

Leydesdorff, Selma. *Surviving the Bosnian Genocide: The Women of Srebrenica Speak*. Trans. Kay Richardson. Bloomington: Indiana UP, 2011.

Lieberman, Benjamin. "Warning: Here There Be Experts." Jones, *Evoking*, 43–44.

Loewen, James W. *Lies My Teacher Told Me: Everything Your American History Textbook Got Wrong*. New York: New, 1995.

Lord, Michelle, and Shino Arihara (Illus.). *A Song for Cambodia*. New York: Lee & Low, 2008.

Lowry, Lois. *Number the Stars*. Boston: Houghton, 1989.

Luke, Allan, and Peter Freebody. "Further Notes on the 4 Resource Model." *Reading Online*, 1999–2000. Web. 31 Mar. 2013. <http://www.readingonline.org/research/lukefreebody.html>

Lynn, Steven. *Texts and Contexts: Writing about Literature with Critical Theory*. 2nd ed. Boston: Longman, 2011.

Lyons, Robert, and Scot Straus. *Intimate Enemy: Images and Voices of the Rwandan Genocide*. New York: Zone, 2006.

Maass, Peter. *Love Thy Neighbor: A Story of War*. New York: Knopf, 1996.

Maclean, Pam. "Not the Holocaust Memorial." Jones, *Evoking*, 87–90.

Maddy, Yulisa Amadu, and Donnarae MacCann. *Neo-Imperialism in Children's Literature about Africa: A Study of Contemporary Fiction*. New York: Routledge, 2009.

Magilow, Daniel. "Children's Photos." Jones, *Evoking*, 219–221.

Magno, Catherine, and Jackie Kirk. "Imaging Girls: Visual Methodologies and Messages for Girls' Education." *Compare* 38.1 (2008): 349–362.

Maitles, Henry. "Keeping Memory Alive." Jones, *Evoking*, 114–117.

Malcolm, Noel. *Bosnia: A Short History*. New York: New York UP, 1994.

Mandani, Mahmood. *When Victims Become Killers: Colonialism, Nativism, and the Genocide in Rwanda*. Princeton, NJ: Princeton UP, 2001.

Martin, Michelle H. *Brown Gold: Milestones of African-American Children's Picture Books, 1845–2002*. New York: Routledge, 2004.

Marx, Trish, and Cindy Karp (Photographer). *One Boy from Kosovo*. New York: HarperCollins, 2000.

McGill, Alice. "Moon Time Child." *Don't Cramp My Style: Stories about That Time of the Month*. Ed. Lisa Rowe Fraustino. New York: Simon & Schuster, 2004. 45–67.

McNair, Jonda C. "Innocent Though They May Seem: A Critical Race Theory Analysis of Firefly and Seesaw Scholastic Book Club Order Forms." *MultiCultural Review* 17.1 (2008): 24–29.

———. "The Representation of Authors and Illustrators of Color in School-Based Book Clubs." *Language Arts* 85.3 (2008): 193–201.

Mead, Alice. *Adem's Cross*. New York: Farrar, 1996.

———. *Girl of Kosovo*. New York: Farrar, 2001.

Meierhenrich, Jens. "The Language of Klemperer." Jones, *Evoking*, 122–128.

Melvern, Linda. *A People Betrayed: The Role of the West in Rwanda's Genocide*. London: Zed, 2000.

Menchú, Rigoberta, with Dante Liano, and Domi (Illus.). *The Girl from Chimel*. Trans. David Unger. Toronto: Groundwood, 2005.

Mikaelsen, Ben. *Tree Girl*. New York: HarperCollins, 2004.

Milivojevic, JoAnn. *Bosnia and Herzegovina*. New York: Children's, 2004. Enchantment of the World Ser.

Miller, Alice. *For Your Own Good: Hidden Cruelty in Child-Rearing and the Roots of Violence*. New York: Farrar, 1983.

The Mission. Dir. Roland Joffé. Perf. Jeremy Irons and Robert DeNiro. Burbank, CA: Warner. 1986. Film.

Moller, Jonathan. *Our Culture Is Our Resistance: Repression, Refuge, and Healing in Guatemala*. New York: powerHouse, 2004.

Montejo, Victor. *Voices from Exile: Violence and Survival in Modern Maya History*. Norman: U of Oklahoma P, 1999.

Moore, Jina. "The Attic and the Imagination." Jones, *Evoking*, 80–83.

Morrison, Marion. *Guatemala*. New York, Scholastic, 2005. Enchantment of the World Ser.

Moses, A. Dirk. *Genocide*. New York: Routledge, 2010.

Munyurangabo. Dir. Lee Isaac Chung. New York: Film Movement. 2009. Film.

Nagy, Thomas J. "A Reluctant Genocide Activist." Jones, *Evoking*, 215–218.

National Association for the Advancement of Colored People. "Criminal Justice Fact Sheet." 2013. Web. 2 Apr. 2013. <http://www.naacp.org/pages/criminal-justice-fact-sheet>

National Governors Association Center for Best Practices, Council of Chief State School Officers. *Common Core State Standards*. Washington DC: Author, 2010.

Nel, Philip, and Lissa Paul, eds. *Keywords for Children's Literature*. New York: New York UP, 2011.

No Man's Land. Dir. Danis Tanović. United Artists. 2001. Film.

Oosterom, Wiljo Woodi. *Stars of Rwanda: Children Write and Draw about Their Experiences during the Genocide of 1994.* Kigali, Rwanda: Silent Work Foundation, 2004.

Oppong, Joseph R. *Rwanda.* New York: Chelsea, 2008.

———. *Sudan.* New York: Chelsea, 2010. Modern World Nations Ser.

Organization of African Unity. "Rwanda: The Preventable Genocide." 2000. Web. 1 Apr. 2013. <http://www.africa-union.org/official_documents/reports/report_rowanda_genocide.pdf>

Orr, Tamara. *George Clooney and the Crisis in Darfur.* New York: Rosen, 2009. Celebrity Activists Ser.

Oyate. "Resources: Oyate's Additional Criteria." 2013. Web. 2 Apr. 2013. <http://oyate.org/index.php/resources/42-resources/oyate-s-additional-criteria>

Parekh, Shayna. "A Simple Task." Jones, *Evoking,* 230–234.

Pastore, Clare. *A Voyage from Cambodia in 1975.* New York: Berkley Jam, 2001. Journey to America Ser.

Paterson, Katherine. *The Day of the Pelican.* Boston: Houghton, 2009.

Paulino, Edward. "Discovering the Haitian Massacre." Jones, *Evoking,* 49–54.

The Pawnbroker. Dir. Sidney Lumet. Perf. Rod Steiger. Landau Company. 1964. Film.

Perl, Lila. *Four Perfect Pebbles: A Holocaust Story.* New York: Avon, 1999.

———. *Genocide: Stand By or Intervene?* New York: Cavendish, 2011.

Phillips, Douglas A. *Bosnia and Herzegovina.* Philadelphia: Chelsea, 2004. Modern World Nation Ser.

Pipe, James. *Hoping for Peace in Sudan: Divided by Conflict, Wishing for Peace.* New York: Gareth Stevens, 2013.

Plain, Nancy. *The Man Who Painted Indians: George Catlin.* New York: Benchmark, 1997.

Pomeray, J. K. *Rwanda.* Philadelphia: Chelsea, 2000. Major World Nation Ser.

Ponsford, Simon. *Iraq.* North Mankato, MN: Smart Apple, 2008. Countries in the News Ser.

Porter, Jack Nusan. "Sexuality and Genocide." Jones, *Evoking,* 65–69.

Powell, Christopher. "The Wound at the Heart of the World." Jones, *Evoking,* 11–17.

Power, Samantha. *"A Problem from Hell": America and the Age of Genocide.* New York: Basic, 2002.

Powers, J. L., ed. *The Mad Game: Growing Up in a Warzone: An Anthology of Essays from around the Globe.* El Paso, TX: Cinco Puntos, 2012.

Pran, Dith, comp., and Kim DePaul, ed. *Children of Cambodia's Killing Fields: Memoirs by Survivors.* New Haven: Yale UP, 1997.

The Promise. Dir. Tim Salem and Danbury High School Students. 2006. 17 July 2013. Danbury High School. Web. <http://www.youtube.com/watch?v=o67BmBEAGmM>

Ramet, Sabrina Petra. *Balkan Babel: The Disintegration of Yugoslavia from the Death of Tito to Ethnic War.* 2nd ed. New York: Westview, 1996.

Randolph, Brenda. "Picture Books Sweep the 2007 Children's African Book Awards." *Sankofa* 6 (2007): 74–84.

Reese (Nambé), Debbie, Marlene Atleo (Nuu-chah-nulth), Naomi Caldwell (Ramapough Mountain), Barbara Landis, Jean Mendoza, Deborah Miranda (Ohlone-Coasstanoan Esselen/Chumash), LaVera Rose (Lakota), Beverly Slapin, and Cynthia Smith (Creek). "Fiction Posing as Truth: A Critical Review of Ann Rinaldi's *My Heart Is on the Ground: The Diary of Nannie Little Rose, a Sioux Girl." Rethinking Our Classrooms,* vol. 2. Ed. Bill Bigelow. Milwaukee, WI: Rethinking Schools, 2001. 57–62.

Reeves, Eric. "Re: question." Message to Jane M. Gangi. 13 Aug. 2012. E-mail.

———. "'A Single Child.'" Jones, *Evoking,* 254–256.

Reger, James P. *The Rebuilding of Bosnia.* San Diego, CA: Lucent, 1997. World in Conflict Ser.

Reilly, Mary Ann, and Rob Cohen. "Sowing the Seeds of Social Justice through Performative Pedagogy: Middle School Students Explore Genocide." *Growing a Soul for Social Change: Building the Knowledge Base for Social Justice.* Charlotte, NC: Information Age, 2008. 383–398.

Reilly, Mary Ann, Jane M. Gangi, and Rob Cohen. *Deepening Literacy Learning: Art and Literature Engagements in K–8 Classrooms.* Charlotte, NC: Information, 2010.

Report of the Commission for Historical Clarification. "Guatemala: Memory of Silence." 5 Feb. 1997. Web. 30 Mar. 2013. <http://shr.aaas.org/guatemala/ceh/report/english/toc.html>

Republic of Rwanda. "French judges release report on the plane crash used to start genocide in Rwanda." 2012. Web. 1 Apr. 2013. <http://www.gov.rw/French-Judges-release-report-on-the-plane-crash-used-as-a-pretext-to-start-genocide-in-Rwanda>

Ricciuti, Edward R. *War in Yugoslavia: The Breakup of a Nation.* Brookfield, CT: Millbrook, 1993.

Rieff, David. "Youth and Consequences." *The New Republic* (1994, Mar. 28): 31–34.

Rinaldi, Ann. *My Heart Is on the Ground: The Diary of Nannie Little Rose, a Sioux Girl*. New York: Scholastic, 1999.

Rixecker, Stefanie. "The Horror." Jones, *Evoking*, 191–194.

Romano, Tom. "A Place to Start." *Blending Genre, Altering Style: Writing Multigenre Papers*. Portsmouth, NH: Heinemann, 2000. 7–14.

Roth, John K. "Will Only the Darkness Remain?" Jones, *Evoking*, 104–107.

Rugasaguhunga, Yvette. Message to Jane M. Gangi. 24 Mar. 2008. E-mail.

———. "RE: question." Message to Jane M. Gangi. 26 Feb. 2008. E-mail.

Ryan, Tammy. *The Music Lesson*. Woodstock, IL: Dramatic, 2002.

Sabbah, Ann Carey. *Kurds*. Mankato, MN: Smart Apple, 2000.

Said, Edward. *Orientalism*. New York: Vintage, 1978.

Salem, Richard A., ed. *Witness to Genocide, the Children of Rwanda: Drawings by Child Survivors of the Rwandan Genocide of 1994*. New York: Friendship, 2000.

Sanford, Victoria. *Buried Secrets: Truth and Human Rights in Guatemala*. New York: Macmillan, 2003.

———. "Images of Impunity." Jones, *Evoking*, 210–214.

Schabas, William. "Werfel, *Musa Dagh* and the Armenian Genocide." Jones, *Evoking*, 32–34.

Schaller, Dominick J. "Identity and Contested Authenticity." Jones, *Evoking*, 118–121.

Schaller, Dominick, and Jürgen Zimmerer. *The Origins of Genocide—Raphael Lemkin as a Historian of Mass Violence*. New York: Routledge, 2009.

Schimmer, Russell. "Dili on Fire." Jones, *Evoking*, 238–241.

Schindler's List. Dir. Steve Spielberg. Perf. Ben Kingsley and Ralph Fiennes. Universal City. 2004. Film.

Schuman, Michael. *Angelina Jolie: Celebrity with Heart*. Berkeley Heights, NJ: Enslow, 2011.

———. *Bosnia and Herzegovina*. New York: Facts on File, 2004.

Scroggins, Mary J., and Jane M. Gangi. "Paul Laurence *Who*? Invisibility and Misrepresentation in Children's Literature and Reading and Language Arts Textbooks." *MultiCultural Review* 13.3 (2004): 34–43.

Sell, Louis. *Slobodan Milosevic and the Destruction of Yugoslavia*. Durham, NC: Duke UP, 2002.

Sémelin, Jacques. "On Visiting the Auschwitz Museum." Jones, *Evoking*, 133–136.

Sheehan, Sean, and Magdalene Koh. *Guatemala*. New York: Cavendish, 1998. Cultures of the World Ser.

Shields, Charles J. *Guatemala*. Philadelphia: Mason Crest, 2003. Discovering Central America Ser.

Short, Philip. *Pol Pot: Anatomy of a Nightmare*. New York: Holt, 2004.

Simon, David J. "'Never Again,' Again." Jones, *Evoking*, 235–237.

The Singing Revolution. Dirs. Maureen and James Tusty. Sky Films. 2004. Film.

Skloot, Robert. "The Look of Terror." Jones, *Evoking*, 94–96.

———. "Re: question." Message to Jane M. Gangi. 27 July 2012. E-mail.

Slovic, Paul. "The More Who Die, the Less We Care: Psychic Numbing and Genocide." International Network of Genocide Scholars. San Francisco State University, San Francisco. 29 June 2012. Reading.

Smith, Alexander McCall. "The Strange Story of Bobby Box." Book Wish Foundation, 1–11.

Smith, Icy, and Sopaul Nhem (Illus.). *Half Spoon of Rice: A Survival Story of the Cambodian Genocide*. Manhattan Beach, CA: East West Discovery, 2010.

Sokoloff, Naomi B. "The Holocaust and Literature for Children." *Prooftexts* 25.1–2 (2005): 174–194.

Spalding, Frank. *Genocide in Rwanda*. New York: Rosen, 2009. Genocide in Modern Times Ser.

Springer, Jane. *Genocide*. Toronto: Groundwood, 2006. Groundwood Guide Ser.

Stahl, Steven A., and Cynthia Shanahan. "Learning to Think Like a Historian: Disciplinary Knowledge through Critical Analysis of Multiple Documents." *Adolescent Literacy Research and Practice*. Eds. Tamara L. Jetton and Janice A. Dole. New York: Guilford, 2004. 94–118.

Stassen, Jean-Philippe. *Deogratias: A Tale of Rwanda*. New York: First Second, 2006.

Steele, Philip. *Sudan, Darfur and the Nomadic Conflicts*. New York: Rosen, 2013.

Stoll, David. *Rigoberta Menchú and the Story of All Poor Guatemalans*. Boulder, CO: Westview, 1999.

Streissguth, Tom. *Rwanda in Pictures*. Minneapolis, MN: Twenty-First Century, 2008. Visual Geography Ser.

Summerfield, Derek. "The Social Experience of War and Some Issues for the Humanitarian Field." *Rethinking the Trauma of War*. Eds. Patrick J. Bracken and Celia Petty. London: Free Association/Save the Children, 1998.

SUNY Digital Repository. "Drawings from the Children of Darfur." 26 Mar. 2008. Web. 2 Apr. 2013. <http://dspace.sunyconnect.suny.edu/handle/1951/43011>

Swanwick, Keith. *Music, Mind, and Education*. London: Routledge, 1988.

————. *Musical Knowledge: Intuition, Analysis and Music Education*. London: Routledge, 1994.

Tambay. *Ten Little Nigger Boys*. 29 Apr. 2010. Web. 7 Mar. 2013. <http://www.shadowandact.com/?p=22425>

Taylor, Christopher. "The Death of 'King' Habyarimana." Jones, *Evoking*, 224–229.

Tekavec, Valerie. *Teenage Refugees from Bosnia-Herzegovina Speak Out*. New York: Rosen, 1997.

Testa, Maria. *Something about America*. Cambridge, MA: Candlewick, 2005.

Thomas, Joseph T. "Aesthetics." Nel and Paul, 5–9.

Totten, Samuel, and Erick Markusen, eds. *Genocide in Darfur: Investigating the Atrocities in the Sudan*. New York: Routledge, 2006.

Totten, Samuel, and Paul Bartrop, eds. *The Genocide Studies Reader*. New York: Routledge, 2009.

Tuol Sleng Museum. "The S-21 Photographs." n. d. Web. 2 Apr. 2013. <http://www.tuolsleng.com/photographs.php>

Twagilimana, Aimable. *Hutu and Tutsi*. New York: Rosen, 1998.

Ung, Loung. *First They Killed My Father: A Daughter of Cambodia Remembers*. New York: HarperPerennial, 2000.

United States Holocaust Memorial Museum. "For Teachers: Teaching about the Holocaust." n. d. Web. 2 Apr. 2013. <http://www.ushmm.org/education/foreducators/>

Vander Zee, Ruth, and Roberto Innocenti (Illus.). *Erika's Story*. Mankato, MN: Creative Editions, 2003.

Verdeja, Ernesto. "Morality, Indifference, and Evil." Jones, *Evoking*, 177–180.

Wagner, Heather Lehr. *The Kurds*. Philadelphia: Chelsea, 2003. Creation of the Modern Middle East Ser.

Waldorf, Lars. "Revisiting *Hotel Rwanda*: Genocide Ideology, Reconciliation, and Rescuers." *Journal of Genocide Research* 11.1 (2009): 101–125.

Walters, Eric. *Shattered*. Toronto: Puffin Canada, 2007.

Walzer, Craig, comp. and ed. *Out of Exile: Narratives from the Abducted and Displaced People of Sudan*. San Francisco: McSweeny's, 2009.

Waterlow, Julia. *A Family from Bosnia*. East Sussex, UK: Wayland, 1997.

Wellburn, Elizabeth, and Deryk Houston (Illus.). *Echoes from the Square*. Oakville, Ontario: Rubicon, 1998.

Wheatley, Meg. *Perseverance*. Provo, UT: Berkana, 2010.

————. *Turning to One Another: Simple Conversations to Restore Hope in the Future*. 2nd ed. San Francisco: Berrett-Koehler, 2009.

When the Mountains Tremble. Dir. Thomas Sigel Newton and Pamela Yates. Perf. Rigoberta Menchú. Skylight Pictures. 1983. Film.

White, Joseph Robert. "Documenting Torture in the Early Nazi Death Camps." Jones, *Evoking*, 58–64.

Whitmer, Benjamin. "Re: question." Message to Jane M. Gangi. 29 July 2012. E-mail.

————. "The Westering Holocaust." Jones, *Evoking*, 23–26.

Wiesel, Elie. *Dawn*. New York: Bantam, 1982.

————. *Night*. 1982. New York: Hill and Wang, 2006.

Wilkes, Sybella. *One Day We Had to Run! Refugee Children Tell Their Stories in Words and Paintings*. Brookfield, CT: Millbrook, 1994.

Wilson, Jackie Napoleon. *Hidden Witness: African-American Images from the Dawn of Photography to the Civil War*. New York: St. Martin's, 1999.

Winckelmann, Thom. *Genocide: Man's Inhumanities*. Yankton, SD: Erickson, 2009.

Xavier, John. *Darfur: African Genocide*. New York: Rosen, 2008. In the News Ser.

Yale University. "Cambodian Genocide Program." 2010. Web. 6 Feb. 2013.

Yenika-Agbaw, Vivian. *Representing Africa in Children's Literature: Old and New Ways of Seeing*. New York: Routledge, 2008.

Zentella, Yoly. "Review Essay: Speaking from the I: Testimonio, Credibility and Indigena Rights." *Journal of Third World Studies* 28.1 (2011): 321–328.

Zimmerman, John C. "Journey through Denial." Jones, *Evoking*, 181–184.

Zylberman, Lior. "The Question of the Act." Trans. Margaret Schroeder. Jones, *Evoking*, 200–203.

Index